THE BAMBOO WORKSHOP

THE BAMBOO WORKSHOP

R.S. SANSOME

MERLIN BOOKS

First published in Great Britain 1995

Published by Merlin Books Ltd.
Braunton, Devon, England

British Library Cataloguing in Publication Data.
A catalogue record for this book is available from the British Library.

ISBN 0 86303 699–6

Printed in England by
Advance Laser Press Limited, St Ives, Cambridge, England

Foreword

It was known as The Forgotten Army; the British 14th Army in Burma during the Second World War. Equally forgotten at least during the early years of that campaign, were the Royal Air Force squadrons operating in the theatre. And even further from the public gaze, both at the time and in the years that have followed, were the numerous support units that kept the aircraft flying. Using a mixture of official records and personal reminiscences, this book tells the story of just one such organization, the Repair and Salvage Units.

The dauntless men on these units had the task of retrieving any of our aircraft that crashed or made forced landings away from base; and very many of them there were too, as the book makes clear! It was work that had to be carried out in often appalling conditions.

The terrain was a mix of dense jungle, leech-infested marsh, mosquito-ridden swamp, switchback ranges of hills, swiftly running rivers, and generally few if any roads. Very often the local natives were unhelpful; maps were inaccurate or non-existent; there was usually no precise indication of where a missing aircraft had come down; and of course there were the Japanese to contend with. As the book shows, the R and S units very often had to break off their rescue efforts to avoid Japanese patrols, or even occasionally to keep clear of a full-scale military operation.

The author is the late Reg Sansome, himself a member of Repair and Salvage Units, a survivor of the fall of Singapore and an airman who then spent the rest of the war in India and Burma. I first met Reg through the local Royal Air Forces Association in Glastonbury, and even at first acquaintance it was obvious that here was a remarkably versatile man, brimming over with ideas, with energy and with many talents including beautiful model making and the gift of a fluent pen when it came to committing his memoirs to paper.

He very sadly died just before this book was ready for the printers, but I had enjoyed many interesting sessions with him discussing the book and some of the events that it describes, events that made a most important contribution to the success of the RAF in the Burma campaign. The book is thus both a contribution to the history of that campaign, and it is a fitting epitaph to Reg, who devoted endless research effort into devilling out all the facts and into producing so detailed and accurate an account of a little known aspect of the Second World War.

Air Chief Marshal Sir Michael Armitage,
KCB, CBE, RAF (Retired)

Acknowledgements

I am grateful to all the ex-Repair and Salvage men from all over the world, especially Len Kebbell in Australia who sent me reams of information from his own diaries and Eric King from South Africa for his memories of No. 1 Airborne Salvage. Many have patiently borne my incessant questioning, both verbal and written, and have dug deep into memories of almost half a century ago to provide some of the narratives. Without their collaboration and interest this book could never have been considered.

I am particularly indebted to Stan Charman who has spent a great deal of his time, energy and money in locating ex-RSU members. In 1979 he introduced the Annual Reunion, an event which in the past two or three years has given me the opportunity to collect many of the reminiscences whilst at the same time enjoying the hospitality of RAF Scampton.

Invaluable help was given by Squadron Leader D. W. Warne (Joe) who continually extolled the virtue of checking basic facts before committing them to paper. In spite of his own research he always found time to point me in the right direction as well as providing me with information and photographs.

My sincere thanks go to the Office of Air Force History, USAAF, Washington and in particular Top Sergeant Barry Spink, the NCO i/c Records, for providing evidence to show that at the time official accounts regarding the events surrounding General Wingate's tragic accident were totally inaccurate and misleading; also to Colonel Commissariat at Shillong who was with the Assam Rifles and is now Editor of their official journal, the *Custodian*, for supplying information regarding the discovery of the aircraft and the photographs of the recovered engine and cannon.

I am extremely obliged to the staff at the Public Records Office at Kew for their help in finding the relevant references when I had almost given up hope. I owe a debt of gratitude to countless others who have encouraged me to continue when I began to despair of ever completing the book. I am also obliged to Tim Purchase for his patience and interest in bringing back to life many of the 45-year-old, almost unrecognizable photographs.

My greatest debt is to my wife Greta who has provided endless cups of tea, emptied countless ashtrays and borne with tolerance her own company whenever I have been engrossed in trying to make sense of my own notes.

Finally, I hope that Warrant Officer John Sansome and Squadron Leader Alexa Sansome are now convinced when I say, 'In our day, things were different and RSU men were a special breed.'

Introduction

A great deal of material, both factual and fictional, has been written about the campaign in Burma during World War II. The exploits of the 14th Army as they pushed the Japanese back is very well documented and they are no longer the 'Forgotten Army'. There is also a profusion of stories and histories of the RAF squadrons and the ground crews who serviced the aircraft during that same period.

But not one single word has ever been written about the men or the units whose specific task was to salvage aircraft which had crashed 'out in the blue', except perhaps in a passing reference to a particular aircraft accident. Even then, no identifying number or credit is given to the unit concerned.

This account is not intended to be a war story as such, though plainly the circumstances and incidents which occurred are part of the backcloth of the struggle for victory against the Japanese.

In order to fully appreciate the contribution that Repair and Salvage Units made in this theatre of war, it is necessary to understand the vastness of the area which had to be covered and the circumstances under which many had to operate: tracts that stretched north and north-east as far as the foothills of the Himalayas; southwards to Ceylon and the long coastline of the Bay of Bengal and the Sunderbans as far as Chittagong; west across the great plains of India and eastwards to the inhospitable, hostile environment of the mountainous and jungle regions of Assam and Burma, in which many of the salvage operations took place under conditions which cannot be imagined from viewing a flat map of the area.

By December 1943, there were officially over thirty units to cover this vast expanse, plus Forward Repair Depots, an Airborne Salvage Unit and, although not dealing specifically with aircraft, various Mobile Transport Salvage Units. Many of these units were only 'paper' units and were short-lived as far as their identity numbers and salvage policies were concerned, being absorbed into other units almost as soon as they were formed. On more than one occasion, however, some re-emerged under other guises. The records of these ghost units are very sparse and only very brief accounts can be given about their activities.

Many of the personnel were away from their main units for months on end in order to be nearer the areas where most accidents were expected, in particular hastily constructed airfields used by squadrons engaged in sorties against the Japanese or dropping equipment to troops in forward areas.

In common with all Services, the men of these units came from diverse backgrounds, had different personalities and varied hopes for the future. Personal opinions had to be shelved in the alien surroundings. Things which in normal Service life could never have been envisaged let alone accepted, had to be learned and endured.

Most of the salvage operations in these out of the way places usually required, at the most, no more than a dozen men of assorted trades and versatility. On site, it was never a question of 'it's not my job'; all had to contribute in one way or another to coexist. Apart from minor disagreements, which were inevitable when a bunch of men are thrown together, differences of opinion were usually quickly resolved.

Almost fifty years later, it is strange to reflect on the unlikely compatibility of these assorted characters. Today's psychologists would have had a field day trying to analyse the interpersonal relationships of the time. In those far-off days there must have been an unknown catalyst which kept men together. Perhaps it was the endless soya and bully beef or the char whose formula and taste never seemed to vary no matter the circumstances which were the common denominators. Maybe it was the interminable exposure to the bugs, leeches, jungle ticks, sweat and prickly heat, to name but a few of the discomforts, that did not differentiate between either the Supremo or the lowliest erk, which formed the common bond between men.

Back at Blighty, no one would have believed the conditions under which some salvage units had to work. Not for them the luxury of hangars to shelter from the weather, or fitted workshops and specialist tools. The main tools in the vast majority of cases had to be initiative and enterprise, plus a great deal of motivation in order to get the job done.

To have spares to hand was a luxury; in many instances repairs would be carried out by the simple expedient of cannibalizing other aircraft waiting for a specialist part from a maintenance unit. It was a vicious circle, swapping and borrowing bits. It all depended on the priority. A crashed aircraft which was Cat. ES, a write-off, would more often than not yield a badly needed spare for an aircraft which was almost airworthy.

Apart from the constant shortages, there was always Mother Nature to contend with. If it wasn't the heat that blistered hands on mainplanes exposed to the sun, it was the humidity as the seasons changed, giving way to pouring sweat and the dreaded side-effects of prickly heat which at times went septic and necessitated having to suffer the indignity of being painted with 'gentian violet'. It not only stained clothes but gave everyone who suffered this malady a ghastly and embarrassing appearance.

There was the inevitable monsoon rains which turned dust into mud, making roads almost impassable and turned dry weather *khacha* strips into something resembling paddy fields, grounding the aircraft as the oozing mud clung to their wheels like glue. Fox holes and slit trenches would fill to the brim, making them almost impossible to locate on waterlogged ground and unusable in the event of an air raid. The chances of drowning were often greater than becoming a casualty in an air raid.

Bashas and tents leaked incessantly, clothes and boots turned green with mould while precious photographs delaminated and faded beyond recognition. The only saving grace was that the rain cured prickly heat almost overnight.

There were flies and mosquitoes to cause dysentery and malaria; poisonous snakes hid in boots; ants invaded charpoys or made a meal of kit, in spite of the so-called insect proof tin boxes; kite hawks circled patiently, waiting to swoop down and snatch food from the plates of unwary airmen. The list of irritations was endless.

In many cases the discomforts on a domestic site had to be added to other hazards of 'going out into the blue' to salvage aircraft. More often than not the accidents which occurred away from an airfield were in the most out of the way locations and extremely difficult to get at. When eventually located, they often revealed gory and gruesome evidence made even less acceptable when the occupants had been in the aircraft for some time prior to discovery.

Salvage crews were expected to reach their objective whatever the cost, sometimes with the minimum of information other than a general location of somewhere with an unpronounceable name and sometimes aided only by a quarter-inch Ordnance Survey map or a compass which were valueless in terrain covered by almost impenetrable jungle. More often than not, salvage crews would have to rely solely on local information, information that might well be withheld until a suitable reward was negotiated.

Travel to these sites was by air, gharry, train, water, bullock cart or any combination of these with the final leg of the journey inevitably completed on foot. It was very seldom a straightforward exercise but in any event it was rare for a search to be abandoned.

It would be impossible in one book to describe every detail and give a blow by blow account of each Repair and Salvage Unit involved in the Burma campaign. However, the incidents portrayed give a true picture of the circumstances and events as they occurred, based on the Operational Record Book and memories of men who experienced those 'hairy' days in Burma. Their deeds have always been anonymous and without plaudit but their performance can be judged by the number of aircraft salvaged and serviced, amounting to the equivalent of many squadrons.

For any memories left out which may have been deemed worthy of description I can only apologize and hope that some of the chapters will invoke similar memories of those almost forgotten distant days.

It is hoped that this book will go some way to putting the record straight and allow the exploits of those Repair and Salvage Units of the Royal Air Force who served throughout the Burma campaign to take their rightful place in historical records alongside their contemporaries.

What follows is the story of these other 'Forgotten Men'.

R. S. Sansome
Westbury-sub-Mendip
1992

To all Repair and Salvage Unit men of the
Royal Air Force, past, present and future
and in memory of all the aircrew who failed
to make it back to a safe landing.

Your deeds are not forgotten, in that unfriendly sky,
Nor are the mountains and the jungle in which your bones now lie
A monument of glory and everything sublime
As a symbol of your sacrifice until the end of time.

Chapter 1

No. 3 Repair and Salvage Unit

No. 3 RSU was originally formed in October 1942 at Wadi Natrun in North Africa under the command of Sqn/Ldr R. Riley. With the campaign in the Western Desert drawing to a close, the unit was sent to India and re-formed with effect from 5 November 1943 under the control of 186 Maintenance Wing, 226 Group. They were based at Barrackpore, the advance party arriving on 21 November with the final party arriving a week later accompanied by Flt/Lt H. J. Moon, the unit Technical Engineer.

At that time the area was pretty well covered by four other RSUs, and until a salvage policy for the unit could be devised, it was obvious that the powers that be were not going to allow somewhere in the region of 200 men to kick their heels in idleness. A detachment of 120 tradesmen was sent to assist 123 RSU with its commitments in Calcutta and Dum-Dum, plus a similar batch to help clear the commitments of 122 RSU at Asansol prior to that unit's intended move to Bishnupur. The remainder would be available to help out with any servicing requirements at Barrackpore.

At the beginning of January 1944, the unit was informed that it would soon be moving to Chittagong, though as yet no date for the move had been fixed, and that the site they now occupied would be taken over by No. 13 School of Technical Training.

It was to be four months before they were finally ensconced at Chittagong.

On 20 January 1944 an advance party left Calcutta for Dechuapalong and by 3 February all members of the unit were under canvas on the site. Three days later, without any prior warning, they were told that the site had to be vacated by 0400 hours the following day. No explanation was given by the Army who had issued the instructions, except to say, 'Reasons at present cannot be committed to writing.' They were to move to a new site, three miles south at Dhoapalong where they stayed for almost three months, sending out detachments to service and salvage aircraft at Ramu, Bawli and Hove.

Most of the accidents involved aircraft returning from sorties into Burma. One write-off, however, was the unit's Tiger Moth which had been flown by Flt/Lt Moon to Kaladan village where he was to inspect a Hurricane that had force landed. He managed to land close to the crash but couldn't have foreseen that had he landed a few minutes later, he would not have witnessed his own aircraft being written off and having to recategorize two aircraft instead of one.

While he was inspecting the Hurricane, a flight of RAF supply Dakotas arrived and began dropping their loads to the Army. To his horror, a crate of bully beef hurtled down and struck the starboard mainplane, sheering the spar before embedding itself in the lower wing. It looked as if it was going to be a long walk home. Fortunately for him, he managed to hitch a ride back with an Army convoy. Having to report that his aircraft 'had been bombed by a case of bully' must have caused some ribald remarks.

On 1 May the unit was informed of an impending move back to Chittagong for the monsoon season. An advance party with Flt/Lt G. S. Ainsworth left Dhoapalong on the 10th but owing to the barricades in operation on the Arakan Road, the 100 miles journey was to take sixteen frustrating hours.

On arrival, the unit was accommodated as a lodger unit with 126 RSU on Patanga airfield and immediately had to send out detachments to service the Hurricanes of No. 6 Royal Indian Air Force and 20 Squadron at Ratnap and Hove.

Following a visit by Air/Cdre, the Earl of Bandon, AOC 224 Group at Chittagong, the unit was again informed that it would soon be on the move once more, this time into Burma. Again the date had yet to be fixed.

Sadly, the unit's test pilot P/O B. Christianson was killed while testing a Spitfire for 126 RSU and was buried with full military honours at Sholashamar.

In the middle of October came the long awaited signal for the unit to move to Tulihul on the Imphal Plain, in preparation for a final move into Burma. Sqn/Ldr Riley, who had been with the unit since it was originally formed in North Africa, was posted to 230 Group, his place being taken by the former Technical Engineer, Flt/Lt H. J. Moon, now promoted to Sqn/Ldr.

The unit was to move *en masse* in two parties; all the transport and ground equipment would go by road via Feni and the personnel by rail. A simple enough exercise on the face of it, except that the ever growing demands for supplies to the Eastern Front, placed on the already congested railways, precluded the use of rail flats to transport the forty vehicles of the unit. But as there was no way that transport could get through the Chin Hills to their destination, there was no alternative but a long circuitous route on roads which in places were more suitable for bullock carts.

After a somewhat gruelling five-day journey via Sylhet to Shillong, where they stayed a couple of days at No. 3 Hill Station to service the vehicles, the convoy set off for the two-day trip to Nowgong where they rested for a further day on the banks of the Kalang River before forging ahead for the final leg of the journey to Dimapur and their destination at Tulihul.

In the meantime, the rear party had set off from Chittagong by rail a week later, hoping to arrive almost simultaneously as the road party at Tulihul. However, they were to suffer a set-back, for on arriving at Akhaura they were informed that owing to a line blockage in one of the tunnels approaching Lumding, they were to be diverted to the northern rail system via Mymensingh and pick up the steamer ferry from Tistamukh to Pandu before entraining again at Nowgong for the journey to Lumding and thence to Dimapur. What was envisaged as no more than a forty-eight hour trip for the four hundred odd miles was to turn out to be almost twice the distance taking more than a week to complete.

Arriving finally at Tulihul, the unit was accommodated on the same site as 132 RSU. While waiting for final instructions for the move into Burma, some of the personnel were lent to 132 RSU to help with their extensive commitments. Others had the more mundane tasks of scrimming camouflage nets and dying tents with cutch dye and ferrous sulphide.

Everyone was issued with Sten guns and olive green battledress and the whole unit given TAB, ATT and anti-cholera injections.

Vehicles which were suspected of being unlikely to survive the journey were exchanged for new at No. 363 Maintenance Unit at Palel. The unit was divided into four sections to be known as No. 1 Mobile Repair Section, No. 2 Mobile Repair Section and so on, and wherever No. 1 MRS pitched its tent, that would be the HQ of the unit.

Each section was allotted the number of vehicles it required to transport its own equipment and personnel, so that the airmen who were to escort the equipment were the tradesmen specializing in the care and maintenance of that particular gear. The idea being that should they be required to use it at a moment's notice, it would be readily available with the minimum of delay. The atmosphere was one of preparing for full-scale invasion.

The establishment at that time comprised the Commanding Officer, Sqn/Ldr H. J. Moon; the Adjutant, P/O A. Campbell; the Medical Officer, Flt/Lt W. A. Porter; the CTO, Flt/Lt R. W. Hill; two test pilots, Flt/Lt G. A. Hanson, who was also officer i/c MT, and P/O N. E. Holliday, an Australian, plus three warrant officers and 173 airmen.

At midday on 9 December 1944 the whole unit moved out with forty-five vehicles *en route* to their new location at Kalemyo.

Arriving at Yazagio two days later, everyone was glad to take advantage of the nearby river Neyinzaya to wash off the thick layers of dust which had accumulated on the journey through Tamu and the Kabaw Valley. Unlike subsequent convoys that had to travel down this notorious road, the unit suffered no serious hold-ups or breakdowns with the vehicles.

Here they had their first sight of the Japanese, not on the offensive but as prisoners of war and guarded by the Army.

Leaving behind No. 3 MRS under WO Morley at Yazagio, the convoy finally arrived at Kalemyo and, after spending a day hacking a clearing in the dense undergrowth of the jungle, the remainder of the unit set up their tents alongside the airstrip, in company with an advance party of HQ 909 Group.

Two further parties were detached, No. 2 with WO Linfield at Taukkyan, about eight miles south in the Kale Valley, while No. 1 with WO King and No. 4 remained at Kalemyo. The latter section, being without a senior NCO was to be used to supplement other sections when and if circumstances demanded.

Although Jap patrols were still reported to be very active in the area, a request from the Army for assistance in salvaging a bulldozer which had broken down near Fort White could not be ignored so the unit's wrecker and two MT fitters were dispatched immediately. What amazed the two drivers more than the sight of the bulldozer tipped on its side in a *chuang*, was that the following morning they found everything covered in a white frost. When they arrived back at base five days later, they had difficulty in convincing their mates that they had actually witnessed frost and had not been befogged by an overindulgence of 'Zu'.

A signal had also been received. A Liberator had crashed somewhere south of Kalemyo. Rather than send a crew out on spec, the CO and F/O Cutting, the recently arrived Chief Test Pilot replacing Flt/Lt Hanson who had been posted to 308 MU at Allahabad, set off in the unit's Tiger Moth in an attempt to locate the aircraft. They eventually sighted it in the marshes about twenty miles south of Kalemyo.

A salvage party was immediately organized under F/O E. Leedale, a crash inspector recently arrived from 230 Group, and, accompanied by Flt/Lt Morris, the Medical Officer of 221 Group, set out to find the aircraft. Not having appreciated the nature of the area, they couldn't get anywhere near it and had to return to base. Unwilling to abandon the attempt, the CO, the Adjutant and F/O Leedale, again accompanied by the Group MO, set off by road with extra equipment to try again.

Again the ten feet high elephant grass, the lack of vantage points and the swampy nature of the ground frustrated their attempts to reach it by road and the vehicles had to be abandoned and the search resumed on foot. Although being conscious of the fact that the aircraft might only be a few hundred yards away, after some hours of hacking through the dense undergrowth and getting no nearer the crash site, with the coming of nightfall the party had to admit defeat.

In the meantime Flt/Lt Morris had detached himself from the main party and was searching in another direction, with the result that he was still in the jungle after the rest had got out. Despite waiting for him for some time and firing signal shots, there was no sign of him. There was no alternative but to return to base and resume their search for him the following day, hoping that he had not suffered any mishap.

Early the following morning, F/O Cutting and the CO flew over the area and locating Flt/Lt Morris, dropped blankets and food for him. Although the supplies appeared to have landed within fifty yards of him, it turned out that the denseness of the jungle intervened and he was unable to locate the rations.

A road crew had also set out at first light, this time with Burmese guides, but even after spending eight hours searching, neither he nor the aircraft could be located and it seemed that Flt/Lt Morris might well have become another casualty of the jungle and the search was reluctantly abandoned.

Unbeknown to the ground party at the time, however, Flt/Lt Morris was safely ensconced back at 909 Wing having been found by some natives who had guided him out. They had also informed him that the aircraft had crashed during the time that the Japanese had occupied the area and that all eight members of the crew had been taken prisoner.

Unperturbed at his lone sojourn and near miss in the jungle, Flt/Lt Morris, after giving an assurance that he would not leave the main party, again accompanied a salvage crew, with Cpl Ecclestone, an F2A, to try to locate another Liberator, KZ4277, reported crash landed at Nimzawl.

Again, the almost impenetrable jungle forced the salvage crew to abandon their vehicles and a dawn to dusk trek along narrow jungle trails had to be undertaken. With little in the way of recognizable features to guide them and reliant only on compasses for a general direction, it very soon became apparent that the search might have to be aborted. Suddenly, much to their relief, they stumbled on a small village. Although the inhabitants were outwardly friendly and helpful, they could speak no English, nor for that matter, could the crew speak any Burmese!

After much sign language mixed with Urdu and pidgin English, it became apparent that they knew of the crash and having negotiated a suitable fee, they agreed to supply guides to the scene of the crash. After spending the night in the headman's hut, along with the usual domestic animals, they set off the following morning through the thick jungle. Six hours later they came across the aircraft. It was a complete write-off but there was no trace of the crew nor any human remains. After collecting a few personal items for subsequent identification, the remaining cargo, which strangely enough had not been looted and comprised small arms, ammunition, detonators, fuses and gelignite, mostly damaged, being too heavy to carry back, was blown up along with the remains of the aircraft.

The unit was now servicing the eight strips at Yazagio, Indianggye, Mawlaik, Kalewa, Kalemyo, Thazi, Taukkyan and Kani but there had been no increase in the number of personnel. Because of the shortage of tradesmen, many of the damaged aircraft which otherwise might have been repaired and put back into service eventually, were categorized as Cat. E.

Occasionally there were bonuses in crash recovery, as was the case when Cpl Shepherd and a party went by road to salvage a Spitfire which had force landed south of Pyingaung at Maukkadaw Chaung. When they arrived at the scene, they found not one but two Spitfires, one was a complete write-off, the other Cat. B. The latter aircraft was dismantled without any trouble and towed across the dried up river bed by the winch vehicles and loaded on to the 'artic'. The Merlin 66 and other useful spares were removed from the Cat. E aircraft and loaded into the Chevrolet winch.

On the return journey to the banks of the Chindwin River, they spotted a crashed Tiger Moth. There was no sign of the occupants but the aircraft had broken its back and one of the mainplanes had been torn off. It was obviously a write-off and would be allocated eventually to the unit, being the only RSU in the area. In order to save the time in making another trip, the Gypsy Major was removed without further ado and joined the rest of the salvage. The whole operation had taken ten days but in this instance the 'prizes' had made it worth while.

The only snag encountered was a shortage of petrol for the vehicles. Fortuitously, the crew who had plenty of rations, met an Army patrol with petrol to spare but very little food. With typical Service negotiations an adjustment was made, to everyone's satisfaction.

The Cat. B Spitfire and Merlin engine were flown back from Kalemyo to No. 4 Civil Maintenance Unit at Barrackpore in one of the special cradles in a Dakota of 85 RSU. The help given by this unit to 3 RSU was invaluable. Not only did it save precious time by flying crews to various locations but could also fly out Cat. B Spitfires. In one instance, a Spitfire, JG500, which had crashed at Pinlebu was back at Barrackpore within four days.

In February 1945, HQ 221 Group ordered 3 RSU to move from Kalemyo to the airstrip at Monywa, but to leave detachments at various locations to deal with any aircraft until they were firmly ensconced at their new location.

Although Monywa had been taken a month previously by the 32nd and 100th Brigade and supplies were being sent down the Chindwin, the unit convoy had to travel a circuitous route, first due east to Ye-U then south to Monywa, a distance of some 140 miles.

During one of the many halts on the journey, it was found that the continuous low gear had burned up fuel at an alarming rate. Nearly all the vehicles had used up their spare fuel and the tanks were almost empty. It was decided that a party must go to collect petrol from the petrol, oils and lubricants (POL) depot at Ye-U, in accordance with instructions received by Movement Control.

Accompanied by the CO, a Jeep and a 15-cwt. truck with all the available petrol drums, the foraging party arrived at the POL depot only to find that it had moved forward some three weeks previously and that the nearest bulk stock was at a POL depot at Schwebo, some thirty miles in the opposite direction to Monywa. They had no alternative but to carry on. They were to receive a further shock when they were informed on arrival that petrol in that area was rationed to two gallons per vehicle per day. Anything above that would need a special 'chitty'. It was a ludicrous situation; two gallons per vehicle would have moved the convoy about ten miles nearer its destination.

The CO demanded to see the OC of the Royal Indian Army Service Corps and explained the situation. Finally, with some reluctance because of the absence of official authorization, he allowed 300 gallons to be issued. It had taken some fourteen hours to obtain sufficient fuel for the convoy to move on.

Arriving finally at Monywa and setting up camp, they found themselves beset by another local problem. When they went to collect the rations from the local RIASC depot, in addition to being offered only half rations, several of the commodities they were entitled to were not even available. Again the CO had to intervene but was informed that they had not expected such a large influx of men. In spite of pointing out that the 'large influx' was only about seventy officers and men, it fell on deaf ears, though he was informed rather cynically that they had passed another ration depot at Schwebo. By this time it was too late to take further action.

The following day, fed up with excuses, Sqn/Ldr Moon visited 909 Wing and brought the inadequacies of the rations to the attention of Gp/Capt Finlay, as he felt, quite rightly, that the issues were insufficient for airmen expected to do heavy work on aircraft and that to send men into unknown territory searching for aircraft with short rations was courting trouble.

As if to add insult to injury, Lady Mountbatten flew in to Group to enquire about welfare facilities. No record exists as to the thoughts or comments of any of the airmen at the time.

In the two months since it moved to Tulihul, the unit had handled at the various detachments' locations, over ninety aircraft, servicing the Spitfires of 17, 28, 152 and 607 Squadrons, the Thunderbolts of 20 Squadron, the Hurricanes of 11, 60 and 1 (Royal Indian Air Force) Squadrons, not to mention various other aircraft.

Following a visit to the unit site by Gp/Capt D. O. Finlay, DFC, AFC, the OC of 909 Wing, and Sqn/Ldr Barber, 230 Group Liaison Officer at HQ 221 Group, the unit was allocated a Harvard 2B, FS988, to replace the rather battered Tiger Moth, NL708, which had served the unit faithfully for some time.

A change of unit policy was arranged so that the salvage of miscellaneous crashed aircraft would now be of a secondary nature, it being infinitely better to keep highly trained tradesmen in complete mobile repair sections, returning aircraft with the least delay, than to 'lose' a party of up to ten men in dealing with an aircraft which might not even be worth salvaging when found.

There were occasions when discretion was the better part of valour when it came to trying to locate crash sites, as on the occasion when Sqn/Ldr Moon and the unit Adjutant, P/O Campbell set off by road from Monywa to do a recce for a Thunderbolt of 20 Squadron which had crashed while on operations in the Kanlan area, east of the Irrawaddy River. Crossing the river without much difficulty on one of the country boat ferries, they had got to within about three-quarters of a mile from Kanlan when they were confronted by an Army patrol who wanted to know who they were and where they were going.

Explaining the purpose, they were informed with some amusement that troops were about to make an attack from Kanlan and that the area in which the aircraft had crashed was at that very moment coming under heavy artillery fire. It was further suggested that if the aircraft was not a write-off when it landed, it most certainly would be by the time the barrage had ceased. Accepting that as a distinct possibility and not wishing to argue, the CO and the Adjutant beat a hasty retreat back to base.

By this time, 132 RSU had also moved out from Tulihul and were now occupying strips parallel to 3 RSU at Tabingaung, Onbauk and Sadaung. Their salvage policies, however, were not the same. As it was inevitable that their paths would cross while salvaging aircraft in the fifty miles separating the units between the Chindwin and Irrawaddy Rivers, some mutual policy would have to be worked out to avoid a waste of valuable resources.

After a meeting with Gp/Capt Rutherford, the Senior Engineering Officer of 230 Group, Sqn/Ldr Barber, the liaison officer, Sqn/Ldr Meredith of HQ BAFSEA and the COs of 132 and 3 RSUs at Sadaung, it was agreed that 132 would provide assistance to deal with the greater commitments of 3 RSU who at that time were not only servicing eight fighter squadrons but Dakota transports bringing supplies in to Indainggale and Alon. Even a plea for help from the USAAF when one of their Curtiss Commandos pranged on landing was not ignored and a party under Cpl Castleman was sent to help raise the aircraft with inflation bags and stayed to assist the American crew to change one of the engines which had been shock loaded with the impact.

On 16 March 1945, Sqn/Ldr Moon, who had been the CO since April 1944, was repatriated to the UK. His place was taken by Flt/Lt L. Kendrick, a Tech E from 326 MU based at Agartala.

Occasionally incidents would occur that were beyond belief. Following a report that a Sentinel L5 had crashed near Myaung, F/O Cutting and F/O Leedale set off in another L5 borrowed from Group Communications Flight to locate the site and establish the aircraft's damage category. Without much difficulty they located it in a clearing in the bush but their aircraft developed engine problems and they went back to Monywa. Two days later they returned in another aircraft. To their amazement the Sentinel had vanished and the only evidence of a crash landing was the torn up earth.

After searching around and finding bits of the aircraft, it was discovered that it had been skilfully dismantled by the local Burmese and spirited away, presumably being hidden until the Service interest had waned. The RSUs were beginning to discover that this was an increasingly common occurrence. What value the bits were or who they hoped to flog them to in these remote areas of jungle will always remain a mystery.

The size of the aircraft seemed to make little difference, as in the case of a Mosquito of 82 Squadron which crashed in the Maungdaung area. Because of inaccurate pinpointing and the denseness of the jungle, previous air and road recces had proved unsuccessful.

After a very trying journey by road, the salvage convoy eventually located the crash site by using a system of air to ground signals. On arrival they found that the entire aircraft had been vandalized by the locals, having discovered that the aircraft was made of wood. No doubt the panels and frames would be put to another use.

Although there were language difficulties, they were able to establish that one of the crew had been buried near the site and the survivor had tried to make it on foot to the Chindwin River in the hope of contacting British troops. However, on the pretext of helping him, it seemed that the pro-Jap headman had handed him over to a Japanese patrol in the area. Some of the salvage crew were so incensed by this act of treachery that they were prepared to shoot the headman on the spot and had to be restrained by F/O Campbell. Instead, he was forcibly made to return with the salvage party and handed over to the Army authorities for them to deal with.

With the retaking of airfields as the Army moved down into Burma and the need for clearing the commitments at what were now rearward airfields, the unit was being hard pressed to keep up with the additional work. Only forty extra personnel had been posted in during the previous months and the Mechanical Transport section, already sixty per cent below strength with only one corporal fitter and two aircraftsman mechanics, was unable to cope with the servicing of vehicles subjected to constant battering on the rough roads of Burma.

Appeals for more articulators and MT personnel for the loading, unloading and transportation of spares brought in by the airborne 85 RSU to the various detachments fell on deaf ears; squadron requirements were a number one priority. It didn't seem to occur to anyone at the time that whilst squadrons usually managed to remain as an entity in their moves and requirements, 3 RSU's commitments were increasing almost daily across the area and with the increase, there was a reduction in personnel and vehicles available for salvage sorties.

The unit was still servicing the squadrons of two separate wings, 907 at Sinthe and 909 at Monywa. To ease the situation, a decision was taken by the AOC, Air/Cdre Blockey to curtail the salvaging of Hurricanes and to give maximum priority to Spitfires. These aircraft were beginning to suffer from some serious defects. One was a failure of the drive coupling to the IAE hydraulic pump. This resulted in the emergency undercarriage lowering system failing to operate the tail wheel, consequently emergency landings caused severe damage to the stern posts and rudder. Far more serious were petrol leaks from the fuel transfer valves when operating the wing tanks, caused by frequent breaking of the stack pipes in the tanks.

The pilots were also finding boost flickering at high altitudes which, after a process of elimination and innumerable test flights, was finally attributed to the aircraft taking off from dirt strips with the air intake shutter open, the dust blocking the altitude correction aneroid in the carburettor.

All these problems merely added to the workload of the already overburdened unit. A certain amount of help was given by 132 RSU who had moved to Sinthe and its detachmant was assisting with clearing the commitments of 907 Wing.

On 9 March, the CO was informed that 909 Wing would be moving from Monywa to Meiktila and that 3 RSU would accompany them. This seemed an ill-considered order when on the one hand they were being pressed to clear their holdings and at the same time being given instructions to move. Sqn/Ldr Moon suggested that rather than disrupt the work on at least forty aircraft, a concentration of manpower should be used to clear the backlog and that since 132 RSU was also in Meiktila, it could hold the fort for a while.

Although this argument was reluctantly accepted, Gp/Capt Finlay's only concession was to give the unit ten days to clear its commitments before moving. It was an almost impossible undertaking, not helped by the start of the rainy season and only possessing two test pilots for the two airfields. If that wasn't bad enough, it was reported from Sinthe that 152 Squadron, who had been having problems with propeller cracks and boost regulators on their Spitfire VIIIs, had been robbing the Cat. AC Spitfires held on charge by 3 RSU. Although Group remedied the position by sending a Dakota of 85 RSU immediately for the necessary spares, it had created additional unnecessary delay in air testing.

On 24 April, the main body of the unit left Monywa at 0800 hours *en route* for Thedaw, a satellite strip just north-west of Meiktila. Once established, communications with outlying detachments so far back up the line began to create problems. Spares which had been indented for were being delivered to airfields long since vacated by the unit. Worse still, the all important morale booster of mail was taking anything up to a fortnight to reach the hands of the recipient.

The start of the monsoons created its own particular dilemmas in moving aircraft, particularly at Sinthe when the unit was informed that the Irrawaddy was rising rapidly and that the Army proposed closing the Myitche to Nyaung ferry by 17 May. This closure would mean that the detachment of nearly fifty airmen and twenty-one aircraft undergoing repairs would be cut off from any road communication. Immediate plans were made for all available transport and men to remove all salvage and repairable engines from Sinthe to a dump across the river.

It was also decided that half the existing detachment should pull out of Sinthe and join 907 Wing at Magwe on the east bank of the Irrawaddy. The remainder were to continue at Sinthe until all the aircraft had been cleared and flown out or the worsening weather conditions prohibited any further flying or use of transport. In the latter instance, they would walk out and make their way across the river by raft.

On 6 May, a violent storm broke out and the airfield took on the appearance of a flooded paddy field, making any attempts at servicing impossible, though the unit transport still managed to run a steady shuttle service carrying salvageable engines across on the ferry. It was to be a further ten days until the strip was serviceable enough to recommence flying activities.

The announcement by Winston Churchill that the war in Europe was over did not help the morale of the unit as much as one would have expected. Their usual good spirits had been undermined by poor and inadequate food, equally poor water supplies, long working hours, constantly floundering about in mud and the endless detachments. Worst of all, as far as the men were concerned, a beer ration which had been promised week after week had still not arrived, though other units and Army personnel in the area had received theirs.

By 24 May the airfield had been cleared. Twenty-seven aircraft had been flown out and a Dakota of 85 RSU had been sent in to clear all the personnel and ground equipment, except for five airmen and F/O Leedale left behind to complete the work on a Mosquito of 82 Squadron which had been well and truly bogged down for days. With the weather worsening it looked as if this aircraft would have to remain. In the event, however, with a helping hand from the local population, the aircraft was released from its bed of mud and flown out by F/O Walbank, AFC. It was not a moment too soon, for the following day a violent storm hit the area and the airstrip soon resembled a vast sea of mud.

It looked as if the remains of the detachment would have to literally walk out after all. By a stroke of good fortune, the Dakota of 85 RSU returned to pick them up. Considering the state of the runway, it looked debatable whether he would come in, but after a couple of dummy runs, decided to risk it and landed safely if somewhat erratically, throwing up great sprays of mud and water in the process. The salvage crew wasted very little time in getting aboard, and within minutes the Dakota was again floundering through the mud, taking the whole length of the runway to get airborne as the oozing mud clung to its wheels like glue.

Although the detachments had now been withdrawn from Sinthe and Monywa, the unit was still hard pressed to keep up with the demands and personnel were dispersed to Tennant and Toungoo, following in the wake of 909 Wing and the Spitfires of 152 and 155 Squadrons.

Added to this, they not only had to deal with clearing a number of Hurricanes of 20 Squadron at the satellites at Magwe (Maida Vale) but to take over the commitments of 124 RSU, servicing the Thunderbolts of 34, 42, 79 and 113 Squadrons at Meiktila, as this unit had been ordered forward and airlifted to Hwambi for servicing the Mosquitoes of 47 and 110 Squadrons of 908 Wing.

With only two small attachments of 132 RSU at Prome (Park Lane) and Pegu (Pilsener) to help out, 3 RSU was becoming the general dogsbody in the area and at the beck and call of three different wings, in a line of communication stretching for some 250 miles from Meiktila to Mingladon. They were even having to provide refuelling facilities from borrowed bowsers for visiting aircraft at many of the airstrips down the line.

Crash and salvage recoveries were still an essential part of the unit's function, though more often than not the priority of aircraft servicing took precedence and some reported crashed aircraft simply had to be written off and struck off charge.

One search, however, was called off for reasons other than functional priority, when the detachment at Toungoo was detailed to carry out an urgent ground search and determine the fate of the crew of a twin radial engined aircraft reported to have crashed north-east of Yadashe in the Karen Hills. Having got as near as they could to the map reference by road, the party had to proceed on foot.

After wading waist deep across the Sittang River and floundering through waterlogged paddy fields for hours, they finally came across a small isolated Burmese village. Explaining to the bewildered natives why they were there and the sort of aircraft they were seeking, the crew were informed that Japanese troops were also approaching from the opposite direction. Without wishing to verify the accuracy of the statement and anxious to avoid a confrontation, the salvage crew made a dignified retreat and abandoned the search.

Although the reason for aborting the salvage was accepted, a week later a signal from 221 Group requested that a more extensive search should be mounted to find the aircraft. This time, just in case Intelligence had been wrong in their assurances that there were no longer Japs in the area, the party would be accompanied by a detachment of RAF Regiment.

No details had been given about the aircraft but the need for a second search suggested that it must have been a very important Dakota, probably carrying VIPs and long overdue. Having survived cloudbursts, paddy fields, rivers and thick undergrowth, the shattered remains of the aircraft were finally discovered. To the amazement of the salvage crew, it wasn't a Dakota after all but a Japanese Mitsubishi version of the same aircraft. There was no sign of any of the aircrew and it was assumed that had the warning by the villagers a week previously been correct, any survivors would have been picked up by their own men. Ever mindful of the warnings of booby traps, no attempt was made to discover the cause of the crash or collect souvenirs.

Instructions had now been received from Group that the whole unit would be moving to Mingladon as soon as all the detachments had cleared the commitments at the various sites, but no suitable accommodation was yet available.

Anxious to be out of Thedaw before the full onset of the monsoons, the CO and the unit MO flew to Rangoon to see the situation for themselves and were disappointed to find that not only were Group right for once but that it had been decided the unit's interests would best be served by staying at Thedaw for the monsoon season. This came as a real blow to the airmen who had been looking forward to being near a large town with 'modern' facilities after eight months under canvas with few amenities.

VJ Day saw the unit HQ still at Thedaw and although morale soared with thoughts of an early demob, being given a day off and a bottle of beer to celebrate, underneath it all the unit still felt it was the orphan of the storm, for in spite of frequent signals to all RAF Postal Units that 3 RSU was still at Thedaw, no mail had been received for almost a fortnight.

The unit still had detachments at six airfields, some no longer of any strategic value now that the Burma campaign was drawing to a close, and had become neglected with few remaining facilities and useful only as emergency landing grounds, though such aircraft that did land were sometimes stranded for weeks until a servicing detachment could be spared.

Due to acute shortages in manpower, the unit now found it necessary to impose increased working hours in order to cope with a further instruction from Group. At least forty qualified tradesmen and a senior NCO were to be sent to Zayatkwin to assist 132 RSU in the preparation of Thunderbolt squadrons for Operation Zipper, the invasion of Malaya. Considering the unit's own workload and that it was already assisting 101, 124 and 132 RSUs, the CO pointed out that the request was a little unjust and would severely hamper the clearing of strips already demanded by Group. Group was adamant. Operation Zipper was number one priority.

By mid-October the civil administration was handed back to Burma and with it came further problems for the unit. Aircraft were often found to be looted or mindlessly vandalized, ground equipment disappeared, batteries, fuel tanks, spare wheels and tyres just vanished overnight without trace, or aircraft were drained of petrol.

One incident at Magwe could have cost an airman his life. A patrol of the 4th Jammu and Kashmir Regiment ambushed a party of dacoits who were stealing drums of petrol. Hearing a scuffle outside their tent, LAC Davison and Alf Frappell went outside to investigate. They were approached by two Indians holding a struggling Burmese prisoner who managed to break free. One of the Indian patrol fired but the bullet missed the prisoner, narrowly missed Alf Frappell and hit Davison in the thigh, luckily only causing a nasty flesh wound. He was flown to 62 Military Field Hospital in Rangoon and returned to work two weeks later none the worse for his ordeal.

On 28 October 1945 a signal was received stating that the unit was shortly to proceed to Japan.

By 1 February 1946, for the first time in its history, the unit had no aircraft on its books requiring servicing. All ground equipment had been serviced or replaced and was packed ready for the move. Until the final Movement Order came through men took breaks at the Army rest camp on the Burma Road at Maymyo or were entertained at the Garrison Theatre. They were also given lectures on Japanese customs and the need for vigilance against a race who saw the surrender as a loss of face and had a smouldering hatred for their conquerors.

The unit was also advised that soap was a very scarce commodity in Japan. Foraging parties, armed with impress money, found little locally. It seemed that other units had had the same idea. What could be found was only obtainable at an exorbitant price, the locals obviously seizing on the opportunity of making a fast profit. Needless to say, they were soon told what to do with their soap.

Undaunted, WO Major flew to Chittagong and came back with the unit Harvard bursting at the seams. The news of the Service soap requirements had obviously not filtered through to the Indian bazaar merchants so the unit's other test pilot, F/O Smith, also flew down and purchased every scrap of soap available. Its collection required two further trips. The unit now had soap coming out of its ears.

All the unit's MT, the packed ground equipment and the airmen's kit were loaded aboard the coastal vessel SS *Santroy*; none of it was to be escorted which, in the event, was to prove to be a fatal mistake.

On Sunday 28 March, the unit embarked on the SS *Tao's Victory*, *en route* for Hong Kong. Except for some bad weather, the trip was uneventful and the boat docked at Kowloon mid-afternoon on 2 April. All the officers were allowed ashore straight away but the shore authorities refused to allow a large influx of British other ranks (BORs) the same privilege. Naturally they were somewhat put out at not being allowed to stretch their legs. Although the CO tried to get permission for the men to go ashore the following day, he was informed that the ship would be sailing on the early tide. However, for once Mother Nature intervened when a typhoon warning was given and the sailing cancelled, allowing the personnel ashore for eight hours.

The following day the ship sailed through the Kowloon Roads but after one day out another typhoon warning was received and the ship immediately changed course for Shanghai. Though it followed the outer edge of the storm for a day and night, the ship was tossed about like a cork, nearly everyone was violently seasick and given the choice at that moment, would have preferred to be back in Burma which seemed friendly by comparison.

By 7 April the ship was able to turn back on course for Japan. Two days later it entered the Iyo Sea and berthed at the naval base at Kure on the island of Honshu. After disembarking, all RAF personnel were entrained for the air station at Iwakuni where they were met by Air Marshal Bouchier who gave them a short talk on the policy and role of the British Commonwealth Occupation Force in Japan (BCOFJ).

Until the equipment and MT arrived, the unit had time to look around the countryside which showed a marked contrast to the jungles and mountains of Burma. A visit to the awesome ruins of Hiroshima, only about twenty miles away, made many realize just why the Japanese had surrendered at the dropping of the atomic bomb. However, it is doubtful if many would have been keen to go sightseeing had they known at the time the effects of radiation.

With the arrival at Iwakuni of the aircraft carrier HMS *Vengeance* with the personnel and aircraft of 17, 11 and 4 (RIAF) Squadrons, a detachment of the unit was detailed to help with the unloading and servicing of the aircraft, ready for them to fly to Miho.

The SS *Santroy* finally arrived at Kure with the unit's vehicles and ground equipment, along with the airmen's personal kit. When it was unloaded it was found that a great deal of it had been stolen, including much of the soap which was no doubt being resold by enterprising merchants to other units, whilst the airmen's kit was probably adorning someone back at Rangoon. Although an investigation was set up by the Special Investigation Branch, as expected, nothing was ever found.

Following the arrival of the aircraft carrier HMS *Vindex* with thirteen Spitfire XIVs, all ex 132 Squadron, it was found that the majority of the aircraft were in very poor condition and required considerable servicing. Some had received structural damage by inadequate slinging and were Cat. BC.

Although it had been the intention to drive to Miho from Iwakuni to familiarize the drivers with the lie of the land, a road survey conducted by the Brindiv had shown that the route was impassable with heavy vehicles and arrangements had to be made to convey everything by rail. After an all-night journey by special train, the bulk of 3 RSU arrived finally at Miho, leaving two mobile sections at Iwakuni.

The airfield at Miho had been extensively bombed by the USAAF and many of the hangars had been badly damaged, but after some temporary repairs they were made usable for aircraft servicing, while temporary offices and technical sections were set up in tents alongside the buildings.

With the unit firmly ensconced, with 4, 11 and 17 Squadrons also based on the airfield, the station began to take on a more Service-like routine. Gradually, with the help of Japanese POWs along with civilians, who by decree had been ordered to work on the camp for at least one day per month, the hangars and buildings were repaired and made serviceable.

Not unnaturally with aerial activity resuming, accidents began to occur as aircraft started daily recces, not seeking the enemy but mainly on security patrols as part of the Occupation Forces. It was, after all, still a very hostile land and feelings towards the Allies could hardly be described as friendly.

British and Commonwealth Air Communication squadrons seemed to be having more than their fair share of their Austers force landing in remote places. One Auster, TJ315, had force landed on a hillside north of Su Sa. A crew went out immediately only to find that the aircrew had escaped unhurt and had got back to base but the Comm Squadron had already been to the aircraft, removed the engine and serviceable spares then burned the remains. This cannibalization and lack of communication began to create problems, as it had in Burma. Spares had only just begun to trickle in and squadrons and the RSU vied with one another to get their hands on any available items.

As befitted an RAF station, there were various off-duty facilities available. Inter-unit soccer matches were organized by Flt/Lt W. H. Dainty, the CTO and unit's Sports Officer, and eventually there was a well stocked canteen and library with a recreation room. Cpls Mitchell and Dodd built their own glider from bits salvaged from crashed aircraft and set up a gliding club. Additional to this, liberty runs were organized to Yanago, a few miles south of the camp.

As in Burma, crews always went out on receipt of casualty signals in the hope that the aircrew had survived. Sadly, the pilots of two Spitfires of 4 RIAF (TX979 and SM925) which had collided in mid-air and crashed at Nimmi and Kam-i-wami were killed. Only the body of F/O Sekhon was recovered. Both aircraft were completely destroyed with nothing worth salvaging.

Similarly, although the pilot survived, a Spitfire of 17 Squadron (RM967) had crash landed 400 yards from the shore off Mikurya and was submerged in twenty-five feet of water. With the help of a Japanese salvage vessel and a diver, it was successfully raised and brought to shore.

Towards the end of December, the weather was a stark contrast to Burma. Men more accustomed to working in shorts and shirts and pouring with sweat, found their teeth chattering with cold, having to wear pullovers, Balaclavas and gloves as icy rain and snow, coming in off the China Seas, swept the area. Typhoon warnings continually interrupted work while exposed aircraft were lashed down. Even worse was to follow when just prior to Christmas 1946, an earthquake rocked Japan, followed by giant tidal waves. Hangars and buildings swayed alarmingly and it looked as if all the hard work put into repairing the previous bomb damage would have been wasted.

Even the AOC, Air Marshal Bouchier had to vacate his Japanese-style residence pretty sharply when the walls cracked and the ceilings fell in. In spite of being mortal enemies only weeks before, British forces in Japan rendered what assistance they could with food and medical aid, 3 RSU being no exception.

By 1947, the unit was well established as a 3rd Line servicing unit with an engine section dealing with Griffon engines and modifications, a propeller unit, two mobile salvage units at Miho and Iwakuni and were working in collaboration with No. 481 Australian Maintenance Squadron.

One of the unit's duties under the roster arranged by the HQ BCAIR was to detail a party of men to take part in the Tokyo guard duties at the Imperial Palace, rather like the changing of the guard at Buckingham Palace. To some it seemed a perverse arrangement that there they were having to do what amounted to an honour guard for the Son of Heaven who had previously been ultimately responsible for all the traumas in the Far East.

On 1 March 1948, the unit was disbanded at the Air Station at Miho. Its last CO was Flt/Lt H. C. Brown.

It had one unique distinction, it had travelled further than any other unit, had lasted longer than all of its contemporaries and had survived for five and a half years without a change of unit prefix.

Chapter 2

No. 4 Repair and Salvage Section

No. 4 RSS was formed at Dacca in March 1943 from personnel drawn from other units. It was commanded by Flt/Lt Barber. Many of the men had been recruited by him originally at Asansol to form No. 2 Forward Repair Depot at Jessore. The unit was ideally suited for its purpose as a central collecting and dispatching point for aircraft that needed extensive repairs beyond the capability of the resources available, or for those aircraft that were only suitable for spares, all of which were destined for the MU at Kanchrapara near Calcutta.

The unit was billeted about a mile from town in the requisitioned Eden School for girls which though only partly built, made a change from straw huts. Its outbuildings were admirable workshops.

The site was unique in having convenient access to a rail link and a small grass airfield north of the town at Kurmitola. Far more importantly, it had a direct approach to the Brahmaputra River which was navigable for almost 700 miles from Dibrugarh in the north to where it merges with the Ganges in the south before entering the Sunderbans and the Bay of Bengal. It also had the added advantage of access to the Surma River and the ferries at Kulaura and Badapur in Central Assam.

Although shipping salvaged aircraft by water sounds a relatively easy task, it was by no means a 'Carter Patterson' operation. In order to appreciate the problems in moving aircraft over long distances, it must be understood that first of all the railway system in Assam was only single line and what few roads there were were only intended to meet the needs of the local tea plantations and little more than Jeep tracks, often impassable during the wet season.

East of Calcutta, travel to the North-East Frontier and Central Assam, other than by air, was via the somewhat archaic rail system and the Brahmaputra River which separated Assam from India. The water levels could rise thirty feet above normal during the monsoon so no bridges spanned the river anywhere along its length. Steamer ferries and barges were the only means of getting from one rail system to the other.

The rail networks basically formed two loops. The outer loop to the north, commencing at Sealdah Station in Calcutta, comprised a broad gauge double line until it reached Abdulpur then single track to Santahar. Here passengers and freight would change to the single metre gauge which skirted the north bank of the Brahmaputra. Airmen going on leave would carry on to Siliguri to pick up the 'toy train' to the hill station at Darjeeling.

Access to the central network and the junction at Lumding meant a change at Rangia for the Amingaon–Pandu ferry. The advantage of this ferry as opposed to others was that the coaches or trucks were shunted directly on to barges equipped with sections of line, obviously removing the need for unloading and reloading. These barges were about 120 feet long and would carry about twenty-eight trucks at a time. A large mixed convoy would sometimes require one or more trips before it was finally marshalled on the other side. Motor transport ferries were simply large flat wooden barges towed across by steamers.

The second loop from Chittagong in the south ran through the centre of Assam, terminating at Sooteratang and involved crossing the River Surma at the Badapur–Chandranathpur ferry. This line did, however, have a very steep hill section and a great many tunnels as it climbed to about 6,000 feet via a long loop round a spur in the mountains at Haflong. This section slowed the journey considerably and was something of a bottleneck as it restricted the tonnage of rolling-stock until it finally reached Lumding where additional trucks could be attached.

Although it was an extremely important junction and one of the main means of access across country to the Brahmaputra, it was a nightmare tangle of lines and sidings giving the impression that when the lines had been offloaded they had been joined together where they fell. It was always jam-packed with rolling-stock of every description and through trains to Dimapur and beyond were frequently held up as wagons overspilled on to the main line. On more than one occasion, it was only Providence that prevented a collision when someone forgot to change the signals. How goods were ever marshalled into any semblance of order from this maze of tracks was a miracle.

Access to the river network could also be obtained by way of three broad gauge spurs leading to the steamer ghats at Khulna, Goalundo and Siraganj. These additional waterborne facilities became even more important, for with the increase in traffic of troops and supplies for the Burma front through the only road link at Dimapur, rail journeys became a major problem. There was often a shortage of rolling-stock and engines. Loaded flat cars were often shunted into sidings and forgotten. Occasionally a convoy of wagons would get separated and turn up at Chittagong weeks later.

With the formation of the unit at Dacca, some of these problems disappeared although the volume of salvaged aircraft increased. Aircraft could now be shipped by rail from Dimapur direct to Akhaura only about forty miles away from Dacca (at least that was the theory). The advantage was that not only could the aircraft be collected by the unit's own transport from the steamer ghat, but the short link between Dacca and Akhaura could be controlled more easily by personal contact.

Alternatively, the salvage could be shipped directly by barge from Akhaura, down the Surma River to where it converged with the Ganges, then direct to Khulna to be offloaded on to the broad gauge line direct to Kanchrapara.

The one flaw in an otherwise perfect solution to transporting aircraft by water was that the unit was solely reliant on the whims of the Army Water Transport Units. Any delay in their co-operation meant that huge piles of aircraft were left waiting for the arrival of barges.

The CO, Flt/Lt Barber, could see the distinct advantage in the unit having its own fleet of barges to overcome any delay caused by the non-arrival of the official barges. Whether or not he had an ear in high places is not certain, but one day he went off to Narayanganj, further down the river, to inspect a sailing barge fitted with an auxiliary engine with a view to the possibility of using it for salvage work. Sure enough, it arrived back a few days later at the Dacca Steamer Ghat with him at the helm. Whether or not it was purchased or commandeered is not recorded.

Up to this point, barges were loaded with salvaged aircraft by manhandling at the steamer ghat. It was not only very labour intensive and slow but coolie labour was not very reliable in terms of availability or safety. Anything that required a bit extra muscle was usually dropped without warning. Not only that, the barges could only be loaded whenever the landing stage was not in use by the steamer ferries.

As it was pointless in having a barge unless it could be loaded at will, and refusing to be frustrated by waiting on the convenience of the steamers, the CO decided that the only way round it was to have a private jetty built for the exclusive use of the unit. It was not to be constructed of bamboo as most of the jetties were at that time, but properly engineered so that vehicles could get close to the water's edge and be offloaded directly on to the barges, or the steamer ferry.

To compensate for the high tides, the ramp was adjustable by means of hydraulic jacks and had a derrick fitted for the loading, reducing the need for a great deal of manpower and, just as importantly, would afford greater safety. Most of the materials including the girders were 'borrowed' from a derelict warehouse in Dacca. Everyone who could be spared set to with a will and within a few weeks the jetty was operational. It was a good example of the enterprise and skill of the RAF tradesmen who were not a bit perturbed at being given this unusual task, and it would be no great surprise to find out that it was still in use after all these years.

This added facility was to be a boon. 'Bent' aircraft of all descriptions began to pour in for onward transmission to Kanchrapara.

Somehow another four barges were allocated to the unit on a permanent basis. They were named the *Naroda*, *Rangellah*, *Aberdeen* and the *Oxus*. Whether there was any significance in the names of the last two is not clear. They were in use within days of arrival and 'Barber's Private Navy' was now fully operational.

Escort duties by rail were not the most popular, being uncomfortable, dirty and, in the main, boring. Travelling on a forty-foot flat with only an aircraft for company and forced to sleep under a tarpaulin sheet or the cab of a vehicle

with the distinct prospect of being shunted into sidings at the whim of the stationmaster was not the ideal way to travel.

Depending on the weather, occasional escort duties by barge made a welcome change. The cooling breezes coming off the river, though laden with pungent and unidentifiable smells, were a welcome respite from the heat and dust of Dacca. The accommodation and toilet facilities were by no means to cruising standards but they did offer the opportunity for a little peace and quiet, with little to do but sleep or watch the activities of the passing floating warehouses and perhaps envy those who were travelling in relative comfort on the ferry steamers with names like *Emu*, *Ostrich*, *Kite* and *Sherpa*. However, the sight of the hospital steamers, *Mallard* and *Mikir*, as they carried sick and wounded to base hospitals, made one realize that war in Burma had its price.

One of the main problems of salvage, and the most time consuming, was getting to the site of the crash in order to categorize the damage and make a decision as to the viability of salvage. In some cases a crash inspector could make a decision on the spot and either burn the aircraft there and then or return to the unit and make the necessary arrangements for men, rations, transport and equipment to effect a full salvage or a fly-out repair. In the latter case, on completion of the repair it would entail a test pilot doing the same journey and with probably the same hassle.

Helicopters were still in their infancy and VTOL (vertical take-off and landing) only a vision of things to come but the Austers and Taylorcraft could take off and land on a handkerchief.

One such aircraft, a Taylorcraft MA924 belonging to the Comm Flight of 170 Wing was reported crash landed near Rayjeswarpur, not far from Hailakandi, and a party was sent out to recover it. Because of the lightness of its construction, it was relatively easy to salvage and was brought back to Dacca.

As mentioned earlier, the CO always had an eye for the main chance in improving the efficiency of the unit. This was no exception, for he could see the advantage of such an aircraft for visiting sites or inspecting detachments. True to form, he managed to get the aircraft struck off strength then promptly had it repaired for his own use.

He was in his element, hopping from place to place, but there is no doubt that apart from keeping him happy, it was a valuable asset to the unit. Unfortunately, even he was vulnerable and it pranged some months later while trying to land in a somewhat inaccessible place. He was unhurt but the aircraft was really beyond repair this time.

The area of activity of 4 RSS was vast; locations varied from airfield to jungle or river. There were very few occasions though when a crash was abandoned. Always at the back of the mind was the thought that a pilot or crew had survived. Sadly it was sometimes to the contrary and required a strong stomach to deal with the discovery.

One such occasion was when two Wellingtons of 99 Squadron, BE112 and HE131, had a mid-air collision near Dacca on 15 March 1943. An eyewitness recounted how he saw the two aircraft flying one above the other when one of them suddenly seemed to drop on to the other, chopping off the tail of the lower aircraft which immediately went out of control and burst into flames.

This aircraft, subsequently identified as BE112 and piloted by F/Sgt L. G. Dobson and Sgt D. R. McDougle, crashed in the River Ganga at Fatulla, not far from Narayanganj. None of the eleven passengers and crew survived. Those who could be identified were named as 635886 Sgt C. S. Westcott, 1189895 AC1 J. Sweeny, 1031351 AC1 Nottingham, D. P. H. McDougal, 553775 Franklin and 1177069 S. A. Morris. The body of 748808 LAC Jopson was never recovered although his pay book was found on the river bank three days later. All the bodies were taken to the Mitford Hospital Mortuary in Dacca before being interred in the Government Cemetery.

The other aircraft (HE131), piloted by F/Sgt D. S. Rowlands and Sgt R. Shakeshaft, managed a wheels-up forced landing in a paddy field at Pubdihi, four miles from the west bank of the River Burhiganga, injuring five airmen who were taken to the hospital at Dacca by the locals. The aircraft was guarded by the local authorities to prevent looting.

This aircraft had lost a propeller in the collision and it was subsequently recovered from the middle of a nearby village. By a miracle no one had been hurt as it scythed its way through some of the huts.

The salvage party was split into two groups to deal with both the crashes simultaneously. Of the two, the aircraft which crashed in the river proved the most difficult in terms of salvage. It was partially submerged and required the use of barges as a platform to work from. Airmen had to strip off and dive under the wreck to attach cables to allow it to be winched close to the bank to facilitate its dismantling.

Only one Pegasus engine was recovered from the river; the other had been torn from its mountings and was lying somewhere deep in the water. The bulk of the fuselage was eventually salvaged and loaded on to a barge.

Access to the second aircraft presented one or two problems. There were no bridges across the river and it would entail two ferry crossings to get to the site so it was decided to float the Chevrolet winch and a trailer across on some large native rowing boats. Unfortunately, these boats were shorter than the wheelbase of both the winch vehicle and the trailer. The only alternative was to lash the boats together with the front wheels of the vehicle on one boat and the rear wheels on the other.

These precarious cargoes were eventually negotiated safely across the river with the winch going first. A tow-line from the winch was attached to the trailer to assist it up the long steep slope of the bank. Half-way up the slope, to everyone's horror, the winch vehicle slid backwards, stopping just short of the water's edge. The trailer disappeared beneath the surface as did two of the accompanying men who reappeared down river, their heads bobbing like a couple of walruses. Luckily both Bill Kelly and 'Red' Skelton were very good swimmers.

This second aircraft (HE131) had crashed on relatively firm ground and there were no real difficulties in dismantling it. It was obviously a write-off so no finesse was required; bolt croppers and axes were the order of the day. The real problem was to get it to the river and loaded on to a barge.

It took eight days of hard graft for the dismantled aircraft to be manhandled and winched yard by yard to the river bank, on to an improvised staging constructed from bamboo, before it could be loaded on to one of the Higgin's barges which had been towed up from Dacca.

Though describing the events on paper makes it seem relatively simple, it needs imagination to conjure up the conditions and hazards of working in the murky waters of the river, constantly plagued by persistent mosquitoes and flies that seemed to take a delight in attacking bare flesh softened by constant immersion in water, as well as hordes of leeches taking the opportunity of a meal. By contrast, the other team inland had to work in the open in blistering heat.

It was almost a month before the two tasks were successfully completed and the shattered remains of the dual tragedy sent by barge to Kanchrapara.

On another occasion when the unit's adaptability was put to the test was when a Hurricane of 136 Squadron (HV635), based at Alipore, force landed with an engine malfunction near to the village of Nagarpur, about 150 miles north of Dacca. It had sustained little structural damage and the crash inspector's opinion was that it could be flown out after suitable repairs.

As the site was nearer to the river than the rail junction, a salvage crew, complete with Chev winch, was sent by steamer to Aricha Ghat, the closest point to the site. The repairs were soon effected and the salvage crew with some local labour began to level the ground into some semblance of an airstrip.

The NCO i/c, satisfied that everything was in order and leaving a party behind to help guard the aircraft, reported back to Dacca that everything was now in order for the 'fly out'. A signal was sent to No. 2 RAP and within a few days F/O Gauthier, a test pilot, arrived at the unit before setting off by steamer to Aricha Ghat.

Although satisfied that the aircraft was airworthy, he expressed some reservations as to the state of the 'airstrip' and requested that the guns and ammo be removed to lighten the aircraft. This meant getting a message through to Dacca to dispatch an armourer urgently to dismantle the guns. In the meantime, the crew and pilot put some finishing touches to the take-off area.

Two days later the armourer arrived and duly removed the weaponry and ammo. Early next day, under the eyes of crowds of Indians who had gathered to watch what to them must have been a momentous event in their otherwise humdrum lives, the Hurricane took off in a cloud of dust, much to the relief of the salvage crew.

It landed safely at Kurmitola strip, about twenty miles from Dacca, an hour or so later. It was serviced again before returning to its base. The whole operation, though a comparatively simple one, had taken exactly a month to complete.

To say that the salvage of aircraft in the jungle and mountains of Burma was fraught with all sorts of difficulties would be an understatement, to say the least. In comparison, the recovery of aircraft from the Sunderbans in the Ganges Delta presented an equally, if somewhat different, form of hazard.

This vast mangrove swamp of 1,500 square miles, formed by centuries of silt swept down by the Brahmaputra and the Ganges into the Bay of Bengal, was literally a gigantic mud bank. Dozens of tributaries formed countless small islands, some inhabited, others, liable to flooding during the monsoons, were deserted. The two largest 'islands' were Dakhin Sharbazpur and Haita Island. Three of the main channels from the Ganges, which were navigable and served by steamer ferries, were the Meghna, Tetulia and the Sharbazpur rivers.

Though these flat mud banks covered in Kewa grass afforded a somewhat softer landing than that of the jungle for aircraft forced to crash land after sorties over the Akyab area, they did not in any way lessen the hazards of survival and recovery. Because of their immediate access to the river and the availability of the barges at their disposal, 4 RSS at Dacca were the obvious choice for the recovery of aircraft from this region.

After getting as near as possible to the crash site by recognized steamer routes, salvage crews were expected to reach their objective by relying on native boats of dubious seaworthiness in unknown creeks, with only native fishermen as guides and navigators. Until then their only experience in small boats was probably a trip round the bay at Weymouth or a couple of hours on the Serpentine.

One such waterborne recovery began on 30 March 1943, when a Hurricane of 258 Squadron (BG814) was reported to have force landed at Char Lalmohan at the southern tip of Dakhin Sharbazpur Island. It was the largest island in the delta, about forty miles long by ten miles wide and 150 miles by river from Dacca. It was criss-crossed by countless small waterways with the tall standing roots of the mangrove trees through which boats could weave their way, reminiscent of the Everglades in Florida. There were no roads as such and what paths there were, were only suitable for bullock carts in dry weather.

The nearest point by steamer was at Barisal, some thirty miles from the actual site. Two country boats were hired for the final leg of the journey downstream, the intention being that these same boats could be loaded with the stripped aircraft for the return journey. Little did they know as they were rowed down the river, that what seemed to be a pleasant interlude then would develop into a frustrating and extremely difficult salvage experience lasting many weeks.

The crew were beset from the start by all sorts of problems. The aircraft's undercarriage had collapsed in the soft ground; they had no lifting gear and no materials were available locally to construct any. The ground was waterlogged and as fast as they cleared the ground to begin dismantling the aircraft, it filled again with water overnight. Snakes were found everywhere and although being assured by the natives who accompanied them that they were harmless, and proving it by catching them, it took strong nerves to ignore their presence. Giant crabs which seemed unafraid of man and capable of giving a nasty nip were a constant nuisance. The offer of catching some and cooking them was also diplomatically refused.

The area was also the home of tigers whose natural prey were the deer and wild boar which inhabited the islands. The crew, to their relief, never caught sight of any although, on a number of occasions, they did observe crocodiles basking in the sun on the banks of the water channels.

Armed with a large stick, everyone took it in turn to fend off the unwelcome attention of any snakes and crabs. A Sten gun was used for anything more ferocious.

After almost three weeks under these conditions, moving the aircraft yard by yard to a suitable site to load it on to boats and seemingly getting nowhere, it was decided to send a signal back to Dacca requesting reinforcements. This entailed an airman being rowed back up river to Barisal to send it. (Why they never equipped salvage crews with radio or an amphibious vehicle will always remain a mystery.)

Reinforcements arrived five days later with extra rations and equipment but even this proved to be inadequate. Almost a month had passed and the crew were no nearer completing the job. They were becoming frustrated by the circumstances and the conditions they were facing and it seemed, on the face of it, that the salvage should be abandoned.

Again an airman was sent to Barisal to signal Dacca for permission to abort the salvage. The CO would not accept the failure. Having been allotted the salvage, it would be completed whatever the circumstances. The reputation of the unit was to be maintained, whatever the cost.

A further party was sent to assist. Again the aid was of little value. Nothing short of a herd of elephants could have made any lasting impression. It was now becoming farcical. However, such was the CO's determination that the salvage would succeed having spent well over a month on the operation, that another party was sent in an all-out attempt to complete the task. This additional support turned the tide and the aircraft was finally manoeuvred to a position where it could be loaded on to two country boats lashed together and taken to Barisal where it was reloaded on to a Higgin's barge for its final journey to Dacca.

It had taken twenty men two months from beginning to end to salvage the Hurricane which, in the event, was only reduced to scrap and became just another statistic on a wall chart.

With a sigh of relief at seeing the end of a difficult and unrewarding job completed, the crew were looking forward to going back to the relative comfort of Dacca, some decent food and a comfortable bed.

Any dreams of a well-earned rest were soon dispelled when they were met by Flt/Lt Richardson, a Tech E recently arrived on detachment at Dacca. With six men and a civilian crash inspector, he had been sent to locate and effect the salvage of a Beaufighter of 27 Squadron (EL356), crewed by Sgt Graham and WO Pondrill, which had crash landed on the neighbouring island of Haita while on its way back to Agartala.

Although a much larger aircraft and still beset by the same natural hazards of the area, the salvage was reasonably straightforward, except that is for loading the aircraft on to a Higgin's barge brought down for the purpose. It was found necessary to request some iron girders from Dacca, which duly arrived escorted by two airmen a few days later.

Unfortunately, the final loading had to be abandoned in rather a hurry when the crew were informed that an epidemic of cholera had broken out on the island. Not until two months later, in the middle of August, was the aircraft finally brought back to Dacca.

The convenience and accessibility of the rail and river network was soon to come to and end when the facilities were taken over by 137 RSU.

Up till March 1943, when 4 RSS was formed at Dacca, it had been the custom to send out salvage crews on detachments to Imphal from 2 FRD at Jessore to deal with repairs on the spot or bring the aircraft back with them.

With the formation of 4 RSS, it was decided that a more practical solution would be to have a permanent detachment at Imphal, with a similar one at Kumbhirgram.

Though responsible ultimately to the base at Dacca, the permanent detachment at Imphal became an almost autonomous unit in its own right with WO Bannister in charge. Its salvage equipment was somewhat limited to begin with. The sole means of towing or lifting fuselages or engines was a Dodge truck fitted with a lifting beam. In the dispersal, that eventually was to become a huge scrapyard, was a steel A frame gantry which had been procured from an Army workshop. This was supplemented by a plentiful supply of bamboo to make any staging required.

Imphal at that time was a comparatively new strip, one of the two all-weather strips in the Imphal Valley. It ran parallel to the main road and was raised some two or three feet to shed water in the rainy season. It was flanked on the airfield side by a deep monsoon ditch. The other side of the field was open ground dotted with slit trenches for use in the event of an air raid but in wet weather they were useless and a hazard as they filled to the brim with water.

The vagaries of the strip had not yet been fully recognized, in particular, the strong crosswinds which funnelled through the gaps in the surrounding hills. Many of the early crashes were caused by aircraft being caught in these winds, veering off the runway and getting bogged down in the soft earth at the edge of the strip.

As the activities in the valley escalated and the number of sorties increased, it was inevitable that the number of malfunctions and crashes would also increase, not only in the valley but in the surrounding hills as aircraft limped back from sorties over Burma.

Most of the squadrons using the strip would fly out in the evening to their bases at Agartala, Kumbhirgram or Comilla in the Surma Valley where they rested and refuelled before coming back at first light. They were to present an ever growing list of aircraft types that the detachment had to deal with. In particular, there were the Hurricanes of 28 Squadron and the Mohawks of 155.

The latter aircraft had been in action from the first day they had arrived in mid-1942. That they had given a good account of themselves is without question, but there is a limit to which any aircraft can be pushed. They were becoming tired, rivets became fatigued, creating loose panels. Zeus fasteners were stretching and cowlings difficult to fit without some brute force. Heat affected the Plexiglass panels of the cockpits causing them to warp and craze which no amount of polishing with Brasso could eliminate though this was not peculiar only to Mohawks.

The unit's first encounter with Mohawks had been whilst on temporary attachment to Imphal. They gave the unit its first taste of salvaging and recovering a Mohawk in the hitherto unknown regions of the Naga Hills and jungle which surrounded Imphal, when, in the middle of February, an aircraft of 5 Squadron (AR650) force landed in the Lushai Hills. The pilot, F/Sgt Morgan, was unhurt and returned to the squadron ten days later having walked out, one of the very few pilots to survive a walk out from hostile territory in the months ahead.

Because of the difficult terrain, it was almost six weeks before the aircraft could be recovered and shipped, via Dacca to the MU at Kanchrapara. This was the start of what was to become a love–hate relationship with Mohawks at Imphal which lasted until the squadron was re-equipped with Spitfires in January 1944.

Many of the accidents were caused by tyres bursting and undercarriages collapsing during take-off or landing. One was AR672 of 155 Squadron, piloted by F/Sgt Ferguson, which crash landed nose down. After extensive repairs, including a new prop, it was again ready for service, the spares as usual coming from written-off aircraft.

A somewhat easier Mohawk salvage occurred at Dimapur when BK850 of 155 Squadron conveniently crash landed on the dirt strip that had been bulldozed out of the Nambur Forest. It was simply dismantled and loaded directly on to rail trucks for dispatch to Dacca as spares. Three months before, this aircraft had also crashed at Dum-Dum when F/O Chancellor overshot the strip. A similar fate awaited AR653, also of 155 Squadron, which had sustained severe damage to its undercarriage when it crashed at Imphal.

Two Mohawks, again of 155 Squadron, which could not be recovered were BK879 and AX889. After an aerial combat, one had crash landed in the Naga Hills, at a location that made it virtually impossible to get at. The other had force landed near Kalemyo and had been burned by the pilot, F/O MacGregor, who had walked back to base.

Apart from salvage operations, Cat. AC prangs which could be repaired on site or shipped to MUs, and Cat. B engine changes, minor repairs and malfunctions became a regular occurrence. The squadron crews were hard pressed to keep all aircraft serviceable and airborne and it would be too much to expect them to deal with crashes as well so 4 RSS was frequently called upon to help out with servicing and repairs.

In many cases it was expedient, for the simple reason that the unit had spares gleaned from Cat. ES (written-off) aircraft, salvage that had been officially allocated to the unit in the first place. These allocations technically struck the aircraft off the strength of the particular squadron and they were jealously guarded by the CO to enhance the salvage and servicing returns of the unit, and of course the unit's own reputation for efficiency.

As far as the ground crews and 4 RSS were concerned, there was never any antagonism or petty jealousies. Keeping the aircraft airborne was a mutual task and both respected each other's duties. It was, after all, the same war. One flaw in this joint venture was that the system did not allow for the exchange of essential parts. Understandably, the squadrons themselves were reluctant to part with any stock in case it was needed urgently so, in the main, RSUs relied on what could be salvaged from crashed aircraft and it was not unknown to adapt from different marques when urgency demanded.

Although crashed aircraft were officially allocated to the RSUs, all too often it was found that the squadron ground crews, in their enthusiasm, had got there first and had stripped the aircraft of useful parts. On one occasion, this eagerness for spares resulted in a Hurricane which had only suffered a damaged undercarriage on landing, having to be recategorized as a write-off.

One particular aircraft, a Mohawk of 155 Squadron (AR649), was given a new lease of life three times. The fourth, however, was to be its final appearance on site but, sadly, only to take its place in the recycling chain as usable scrap.

In the first instance, this aircraft had developed oil problems, to which the Cyclone engine was prone, causing severe overheating. The second occasion was when the propeller pitch control went u/s. The third mishap occurred when the synchro-gear for the nose guns went haywire and some bullets were buried in one of the blades. With no spare prop available, they were simple filed flush and allowed to remain.

Its final connection with 4 RSS, now strangely addressed as 4 FRD, was more dramatic and final. Returning from a sortie into Burma, it crash landed in the Lower Kabaw Valley near Sibong, about fifteen miles from Tamu and some sixty miles south-east of Imphal. A salvage crew set out to recover it with a high loader and a Dodge truck fitted with a lifting beam.

Arriving at the site, known locally for some reason as Dead Mule Gulch, it was only too apparent by its condition that it was a complete write-off. It lay on its belly on the river bank at the fringe of the jungle. One mainplane had sheared off completely, the other lay crumpled alongside the fuselage whilst the engine had torn clean away from its mountings. Judging by the position of the aircraft, it looked very much as if the pilot had attempted to land on the narrow road and missed. The pilot, happily, had survived and had been rescued by an Army patrol and taken to hospital.

Fortunately, the river was reasonably shallow and ran parallel to the road. This was a bonus as far as the salvage operation went as equipment did not have to be carried very far. Because of the narrowness of the road and the continuous troop movements, there was no way in which any gear could be set up to remove the aircraft bodily. Items which could be dismantled easily and potential spares were removed before the remains were reduced to manageable sections with axes and bolt croppers.

Being close to 'civilization', the crew were able to call on the assistance of the Army Road Recovery Company stationed near by. Their quarter-ton Jeeps fitted with winches could drag most of the larger sections and the engine across the river with comparative ease. The trucks which had had to be parked off the road during this operation, were finally manoeuvred into position and with the help of a borrowed mobile crane, the vehicles were loaded. The road had to be reduced to single-line traffic while this was going on.

By five o'clock that evening the crew were back at base and another pile of twisted metal joined the ever increasing mountain of scrapped aircraft. The whole operation had taken just over three days to complete.

By far the most unpleasant side of the task was the continual and persistent attacks by leeches which infested the area. Working on the river bank and sometimes waist deep in water made the crew very vulnerable. As fast as they were burned off with a cigarette, others would invade clothing and boots. It was a losing battle. Eventually, they had to just grit their teeth and ignore the discomfort. The routine was to work for an hour or so then take time out to get rid of them.

No matter where men were working, either in the dispersal pens, or on the airstrip, they always had to be prepared to drop anything they were doing to go to the assistance of aircraft which had come to grief, either on landing or take-off. Some were minor prangs but others were more serious. Geordie Hopper recalls one of the most tragic which he could never forget. One morning he was working on a Hurricane of 28 Squadron and stopped to watch some of the Mohawks of 155 Squadron taking off on ops.

'The last aircraft was hardly airborne when there was a terrific explosion and the kite plunged into the deck, on fire.

'We all tore down the runway, but by the time we got to the scene, the kite was totally enveloped in flame. We couldn't get anywhere near it, ammo was exploding all over the place. We could only stand at a safe distance and watch with horror. It was obvious that the pilot never had a chance and must gave been killed instantly.

'It was a terrible sight, and affected everyone. After the medics had recovered what little remains there were, we dragged the charred wreckage way out of sight to the other side of the airstrip.

'There was very little banter or joking that day as the blokes carried on with their duties.

'We were told later that the aircraft was AR677, piloted by Flt/Lt B. M. Ross-Maginty and that the accident was caused by one of the 20lb. bombs which must have come adrift as he was taking off.'

Sadly, following a busy ten months, the 4 RSS detachment at Imphal and the one at Kumbhirgram were disbanded, at least as far as the unit number was concerned. The base at Dacca was taken over by the newly formed 137 RSU.

A paper transaction had taken place in which the CO, now promoted to Squadron Leader, was to take over the newly formed 124 RSU at Masimpur with effect from 28 December 1943. The airmen left at Dacca were to be absorbed into 137 RSU from the same date. Personnel at Imphal were now given an almost ignominious and meaningless label of 28 Section.

Without doubt, during its existence, 4 RSS was a successful unit with a good reputation. It was the best as far as the men themselves were concerned and they took pride in their achievements. Since its inception it had dealt with seventy-three aircraft which included nineteen Mohawks, sixteen Blenheims, three Wellingtons, twenty-two Hurricanes, two Lysanders, two Beaufighters, six Vultee Vengeances, two Dakotas, a Hudson, plus the CO's private enterprise, the Taylorcraft.

The salvage returns were now reduced to nil, the scoreboard of successful salvages wiped clean. From now on, all the repair and salvage work still on the books would enhance the records of 124 RSU.

Two months later, on 14 February 1944, the detachment was again taken over, this time by 132 RSU based at Tulihul and once again retitled, as No. 1 Section. Of course, the change of numbers did not change the workload by any means, only the status. By September 1944 it had received 150 aircraft for repair and servicing, not counting innumerable salvages.

At the northern end of the Imphal airstrip were the dispersals and workshops of the unit, hacked out of the scrub and hillsides. To move aircraft from the strip to these dispersals entailed crossing the main road each time, causing traffic hold-ups and long tailbacks, much to the consternation of the Military Police who probably saw it as a deliberate attempt to create chaos and sabotage the war effort. As far as they were concerned, the Army was number one priority and were fighting a different war from the 'Brylcreem Boys'.

In spite of concern at these hold-ups, there was no alternative way to get to the site, and to have located the workshops and dispersals on the open ground of the airfield would have been begging for trouble.

On one occasion when an aircraft was being towed across to the dispersal, an Indian Army Service Corps 15-cwt. truck slammed into the tail of the Hurricane, causing more damage than the actual accident. The truck spun off the road, spilling its load and landing upside down in the monsoon ditch. Fortunately there were no casualties. From then on, in spite of the protestations of the Army, either one of the gharries or the Holmes wrecker would be drawn across the road as a barrier until the aircraft had been safely negotiated to the dispersal.

Any help in removing crashed aircraft on the airfield at Imphal in an emergency was always welcomed. Sometimes it would be the Indian Army Service Corps who happened to be picking up supplies from the Dakotas, or airmen from other units who were available and willing to muck in in a panic situation. In one instance, however, the help, unrequested, came from a rather unexpected source and their contribution to clearing the wreck was somewhat unorthodox to say the least.

A Dakota of 31 Squadron, returning from a sortie, came into Imphal for some reason and one of its undercarriage legs collapsed on landing. The aircraft skidded sideways, coming to a sudden stop in the monsoon ditch that flanked the strip and the main Imphal road. Its port mainplane crumpled into a tangle of twisted metal as it tore along the ground, whilst the port engine broke away completely from its mountings.

The salvage crew, who had arrived on the scene almost at once, were contemplating the speediest action to take to clear the road which, of course, was totally blocked, holding up a convoy of vehicles. Suddenly, a rather impatient Army officer appeared on the scene demanding to know how long it was going to be before the aircraft was moved.

'No idea, Sir,' came a rather laconic reply from an airman who refused to be intimidated into a definite commitment.

Without further ado, the Army officer bellowed some sort of command to his Gurkhas waiting near by in their trucks. No one had the slightest idea as to what he said, though the subsequent actions made it very plain when they descended from the vehicle with axes and proceeded to chop the tangle of metal which obstructed the road into small pieces, throwing the bits into the ditch.

The salvage crew could only look on in astonishment and they were certainly not going to argue or intervene as the hordes of grinning Gurkhas made short work of the obstruction. In about twenty minutes a pathway was cleared. They boarded their vehicles and vanished as quickly as they had arrived, leaving the salvage crew to finish the task of dismantling the remainder of the aircraft by more orthodox means.

A day or so later, a Dakota of No. 1 Airborne Salvage Section flew in to collect the one serviceable mainplane and engine along with other sundry spares that had escaped the attention of 'cannibals' from other Dakota squadrons.

The domestic quarters had been established at Ghari village about two miles away at the southern end of the strip and were shared with 28 Squadron and 1 RIAF. These living quarters consisted of thatched bamboo bashas. The walls were plastered with mud (*mutti*) and the windows were just square holes protected by a crude shutter propped open with a bamboo pole to keep out the rain but did little to keep out the flies.

One hut, set apart from the others, was the cookhouse. It had been furnished with trestle tables and bench seats which had been scrounged from somewhere or other.

Personal comfort inside the living quarters was a matter of choice and originality. Lockers were of individual design and quite often unique. They were constructed from anything suitable that came to hand: petrol cans, ammo boxes or bits from scrapped aircraft. The only universal issue was the ubiquitous charpoy with bamboo poles at each corner to hold a mosquito net as securely as possible to keep these pests out at night. The legs of the assembly were immersed in tins of paraffin or oil to keep out the 'crawlies'. Needless to say, they were only partly effective and did nothing to prevent other nasties from dropping from the roof. Even grease bands were not entirely effective; ants and the like would simply crawl over the bodies of those that had got trapped.

Very little could be done to prevent the rat-snakes, kraits and cobras which slithered in through gaps in the walls and had a penchant for discarded boots. Calls of nature at night could be highly dangerous if one failed to check footwear for unwelcome occupants. The more prudent and experienced always kept their boots inside their 'mozzie' nets as a precautionary measure.

Washing facilities comprised a framework from which was suspended a perforated jam tin to act as a spray, water being supplied via a stirrup pump and a four-gallon petrol can heated by a flame thrower. One or more showered while another pumped like mad. It was crude but effective and had the added advantage of saving water. This was a prime consideration as it had to be collected by bowser from Kanglatongbi about ten miles down the road where there was a stand-pipe guarded by an ancient Manipuri armed with an equally ancient shotgun.

The toilet facilities comprised a deep trench over which was laid stout bamboo poles covered by woven rattan matting and supporting four 'thunder boxes'. The whole structure was covered by a thatched roof and surrounded by a privacy screen about three feet high, looking for all the world like a cricket pavilion.

Because of the changing wind conditions, it was quite some way from the domestic site and it was not always prudent to visit after dark, especially so after the Siege commenced. Shadowy figures in the dark were apt to draw the attention of trigger-happy patrols.

One day there was a surprise low level attack by six Army 97s. The alarm sounded simultaneously with the bombs falling. Everyone dived for whatever cover they could find. After the raid a roll-call was taken. All but one were accounted for. Suddenly a plaintive voice (who shall remain anonymous) was heard crying 'Help, help' from the direction of the toilets. The structure had collapsed from the vibration of the bomb blasts. A search revealed the unfortunate occupant up to his waist in the contents of the trench. Showing great relief in being rescued from what could have been an undignified end, his immediate response was to remark in no uncertain terms, 'You can't even have a s...t in peace.' It was some time before anyone would go near him.

The town of Imphal had very little to offer in the way of amenities. There was a bazaar which offered a hotchpotch of goods at inflated prices, a small cinema which showed out-of-date films, usually the long-legged chorus girl type or corny war films. The ribald remarks and cat-calls when the film broke down or reels were shown out of sequence were entertainment in themselves. In spite of the antiquity of some of the programmes, there were always queues to get in.

The only drink available was the native rice-beer which could be bought at some of the bazaar stalls. It was pretty potent and, though the ingredients were somewhat suspect, it did serve to satisfy the need for those who craved alcohol, sometimes with disastrous results.

A Chinese 'restaurant' of dubious hygiene waited to serve those whose digestive systems could cope with the mysterious menus on offer. Meat of uncertain origin, highly spiced to camouflage its true identity, was often suspected to be that of pye-dog which had strayed into the kitchen, though it was deemed by the Nagas to be a delicacy with medicinal powers when roasted.

The cookhouse was utilized as a canteen and an improvised stage had been constructed at one end. A gramophone had been 'won' from somewhere. Goods on offer varied according to what could be scrounged or brought back from Calcutta by someone returning from leave or escort duties. Housey-housey became the main preoccupation with a chance to win a few rupees. Char was always on tap in a large urn on the cookhouse fire. It was topped up at regular intervals with water and another tin of condensed milk. It got stronger and stronger as the evening wore on and was an acquired taste.

Two of the chaps, Bert Brown and Geordie Hopper, were past masters in the art of obtaining the unattainable. One day they decided to go foraging, not locally, but in Calcutta. Somehow or other they wangled a lift in a Dakota flying direct to Dum-Dum on the outskirts of Calcutta. Everyone chipped in to provide funds and just over a week later they returned. Everyone was curious as to what they had brought back.

There were just three crates marked PRIORITY A — URGENT AGS (aircraft ground spares). No goodies were evident and the men were pretty disappointed at the apparent lack of success. Playing them along, Bert said that he couldn't get anything aboard the aircraft as there was only room for these urgent spares which he handed over to the store basher who promptly began to open them. They revealed not aircraft spares but tinned turkey, cake, sweets, tins of fruit, jam, biscuits, decent cigarettes, everything in fact that the blokes hadn't seen in a long time.

There was booze of every kind and even a tin of kippers for one of the chaps aptly named Kipper Kebbell who was always saying he'd give an arm and a leg for this delicacy. No one asked any questions as to how they had fiddled it as an official assignment. The only query that ever arose was when a newly arrived very junior pilot officer, on seeing the empty crates with the priority label, wanted to know what had arrived in them. The storekeeper must have fobbed him off with a plausible story for nothing was said.

Though the daytime activities had in no way lessened, there was something about having a canteen that gave a greater sense of community. It was somewhere to meet rather than having to visit other bashas for conversation. This new facility gave the opportunity for impromptu concerts, especially when the beer ration arrived. Hughie Moore on his harmonica, accompanied by Bert Brown on his accordion along with Kilpatrick and his mandolin were always in demand.

Most of the skits were bluish in origin and almost always knocked authority or highlighted a particular person or incident; all pretty inocuous stuff but always a welcome diversion.

Another ingenious arrangement for bringing in extras was based on the bright idea of converting some long-range fuel tanks into food canisters to supply Army patrols in isolated areas. It was quite a simple conversion; the noses of these jettison tanks were simply unriveted and reassembled with clips to keep them in place.

Up to that time, supplies had always been dropped by Dakotas, but some of the dropping zones were difficult to hit, with the consequence that the supplies fell into Jap hands. With this new idea, the Hurricanes could get in low and fast and literally drop these tanks into the laps of the patrols; bomb them with food, as it were.

The idea was not lost on many squadrons who also saw this as an ideal way to supplement the meagre allowances of their own messes with additional Rosa Rum, Carew's Whisky and Dyer Meakins Beer. No doubt sorties in search of these commodities were listed as essential recces! Before long, orders for this new modification became a regular feature at the 132 dispersal. Even a visiting Spitfire pilot came to enquire as to the possibility of doing the same mod. Unfortunately, the design of their long-range tank made it an impractical proposition.

There was of course a limit to the number of new jettison tanks that could be indented for and had to be backed up with a logical reason. Fortunately, 28 Squadron, with Hurricane 11Bs, who shared the site at Ghari village with 132 RSU, were regular customers and seemed to be able to wangle the necessary authority and documentation.

Their co-operation also extended to lending some of their pilots for air testing. Sadly, one of them, Sgt Chester, was shot down and killed on ops. Another, F/Sgt Nigel Sinclair-Hill whose father was a wing commander, became friendly with the unit instrument basher, who had repaired his watch, when he learned they had the same taste in classical music. One day, however, the friendship nearly came to an end. Sammy, who had borrowed one of his precious records, was returning to his billet when he was asked to help to push start one of the gharries. Unthinking, he put the record on the bonnet of the truck. Within minutes the record had softened with the heat of the metal and had taken on the shape of the bonnet. Although he tried to reverse the process in the same way, the record, though still playable, wobbled badly.

Tragically, the exchange of records was cut short when Sinclair-Hill, taking the place of another, went missing on ops in May 1944 and was last seen diving towards the ground near Kohima and presumably to his death. However, a contemporary account, though difficult to confirm, stated that Sinclair-Hill did in fact survive and was rescued by an Army patrol. Leaving a message on the offchance that his aircraft might be found, he joined them, hoping to walk out to safety. As bad luck would have it, the patrol was ambushed by the Japanese and he was shot. Although his remains were never found, his name does appear on column 433 on the Singapore Memorial.

In January 1945, 1 Section, along with 132 RSU, their parent unit, prepared to move into Burma in the wake of the Army. All their outstanding commitments would be taken over by 124 RSU who had now moved into

Tulihul from Masimpur. Many of the chaps had been at Imphal for the best part of two years, were accustomed to the changing moods of the environment and had witnessed many dramatic facets in the struggle for the Imphal Plain, including the trauma of the Siege.

They had serviced and salvaged hundreds of aircraft which included fighters, twin-engine bombers and transports, and had witnessed the mountain of scrap aircraft grow higher and higher. Now they looked forward to a change of scenery, in spite of the fact that their next move would be an unknown quantity. Subsequent events made many wish they could have stayed in the relative comfort of Ghari village.

Chapter 3

Nos. 60 and 126 Repair and Salvage Units

Prior to the formation of 60 RSU, the only salvage unit in the Far East was No. 81 at Seletar which had been formed in September 1941. There was, of course, little military flying in India at that time and what aircraft there were could be handled quite easily by the squadron ground crews. Audaxes, Harts and Wapitis did not require the specialist equipment which the more modern aircraft of that time required subsequently, nor was there any real need for repair and salvage units. At that time, an aircraft depot at Karachi was responsible for aircraft assembly, engine repairs and supplying equipment to the squadrons in India under AHQ India.

The Japanese threat, at least in India, was not quite so apparent. Europe and the Western Desert were the priorities and it was decided to form another repair and salvage unit to supplement those already in the Middle East. So, in November 1941, 60 RSU came into being at Padgate with Flt/Lt F. N. B. Bennett as OC, P/O H. J. Winfield as Tech E and 167 allied tradesmen.

They sailed on 11 November 1941 via Durban to Basra in Iraq. One airman didn't make it; a Cpl Inglis was taken ashore at Durban and admitted to the military hospital with an ulcerated stomach and returned to England.

The surprise attacks on Malaya, Pearl Harbor, the Philippines and Hong Kong, announcing the Japanese entry into the Second World War, on 7 December 1941 occurred while the convoy was *en route* to Iraq. Arriving at Basra, the unit received orders that it was to be diverted to India and arrived in Bombay on 8 January 1942. After an overnight stay at the transit camp at Worli, the unit travelled by troop train to Asansol in Bengal, arriving there on 13 January.

Accommodation was in hurriedly erected tents, toilet facilities were simply trenches with bamboo perches and the airstrip appeared to be little more than a wide dirt road but work was in progress to improve it. There were no workshops, no aircraft awaiting servicing and the place was almost deserted.

Now, one thing the hierarchy cannot stand is airmen with nothing to do. Time off has to be authorized so, in spite of the heat and the substandard accommodation, the unit spent its time in foot drills, route marches and PT, all organized with a view to maintaining the physical and mental well-being of personnel for the work ahead. After a little over three weeks of this rather pointless and non-productive activity, much to their relief, they were informed that they would now be moving to Burma.

On 15 February 1942, the very day that Singapore fell to the Japanese, they embarked on the SS *Elleng* at Kidderpore Docks in Calcutta, bound for Rangoon some 800 miles away across the Bay of Bengal. It was a leisurely trip and a change from humdrum square-bashing. Having completed about 600 miles of the journey, orders were received for the ship to return immediately to India.

Arriving back at Calcutta not knowing exactly what the next move would be but fully expecting that it would be back to Asansol, they were informed that another RSU was now in residence there and they would be going to Bareilly in the United Provinces, some 600 miles north-west of Calcutta. This entailed another journey by troop train, eventually arriving on 26 February. The unit, except for a brief sojourn at Asansol, had now been on the move for just over three months.

Again with no aircraft to work on, the unit once more had to occupy its time with drill and route marches. Frustration was now at an all-time high, with morale the direct opposite.

However, at the beginning of March 1942, it appeared that at last some definite policy regarding the technical activity of the unit had been resolved with the dispatch of seven small parties of airmen and NCOs for servicing duties to Allahabad, Lahore, Ambala, Kohat, Peshawar, Dum-Dum, Kanchrapara and the Air Landing School at Delhi. The whole unit, except for about forty men left behind at Bareilly, had now been dispersed.

The expectation of some real activity at last was short-lived when two weeks later every detachment was recalled to Bareilly and once again they found themselves on yet another troop train bound for Kanchrapara near Calcutta.

On arrival, they found three Blenheims, V6238, Z9741 and Z9667 of 113 Squadron waiting for repair and servicing, as well as Hurricane V7673 which had crash landed at Dum-Dum and needed to be picked up on behalf of 304 MU who were already on site.

The site at Kanchrapara occupied by No. 1 CMU was a repair depot of the Bengal Assam Railway. Though lacking in Service facilities, it had one advantage in that it had a Railway Workshops facility and a reasonably serviceable grass airfield, until the monsoons arrived and turned it into something resembling a paddy field.

At this stage, to say that the unit's equipment was inadequate would be an understatement. Although ten men had journeyed to 308 MU at Allahabad to collect equipment, it proved to be a very disappointing hotchpotch of spares which bore no resemblance to the needs of a salvage unit and the unit had to content itself with continual improvisation. Nevertheless, it is to the unit's credit that by the end of March it had salvaged one Hurricane and carried out repairs on ten Blenheims and a further six Hurricanes.

The unit was to suffer a severe set-back when two aircraft shelters and an

MT compound, which had been improvised and constructed by the airmen to afford some shelter from the blistering heat, were destroyed by a sudden violent storm. Signals to the recently formed Bengal Command requesting priority for buildings and adequate workshops so that work could carry on unhindered during inclement weather fell on deaf ears.

Of all things, there was no telephone on site. Anything urgent entailed a visit to the Railway Workshops. Even these were inadequate and very ancient, and on more than one occasion it proved to be quicker to get a response by driving to Headquarters in Calcutta.

Ground equipment was still at a premium, MT even scarcer. Although the establishment called for something like seventy-five assorted vehicles, including a mobile crane, artics, workshop lorries and 3-tonners, the total MT was only twenty vehicles. There were, however, following the Japanese example of mobility, twenty bicycles which, although useful for taking messages from one part of the camp to the other, were hardly adequate for towing aircraft.

The number of accidents was rising rapidly, many in the inhospitable region of the Ganges Delta. None was straightforward and, through lack of suitable equipment, required considerable ingenuity and enterprise to deal with successfully. Flotation gear was invariably in the form of empty barrels and well-patched inner tubes.

Inadequacies were fast becoming a major set-back to the efficiency of the unit. Gantries and staging had to be constructed from bamboo. Aircraft were refuelled by hand from four-gallon tins, a slow process considering fuel had to be filtered through chamois leather, and not without an element of danger as it vaporized in the heat.

In spite of desperate messages from Sqn/Ldr Bennett to Headquarters, no action was taken by Maintenance Wing to alleviate the situation. The only response to one such urgent appeal, which bordered on appeasement, was a reply from Gp/Capt Walkington, the Chief Maintenance Officer, which read: 'Your report has been read with some interest, and it is desired to record the appreciation of this HQ for the continued good work being carried out by your unit; this appreciation should be conveyed to all ranks.' Such flannel from the comfort of Calcutta did very little to ease the general predicament of the unit.

Although two other units had now been formed, 122 RSU at Asansol and 101 RSU in Calcutta, most of the salvage work to the east of the river was still carried out by 60 RSU. No clearly defined lines of activity had been laid down and occasions arose when a crew would arrive on site only to find a crew from another unit already there.

This problem of overlap was resolved in September 1942 when an agreement was finally reached with 224 Group that 101 RSU in Calcutta would take over crashes at Dum-Dum, Alipore and Red Road. It also agreed that 101 would reinforce salvage parties from 60 RSU to gain experience of the difficult terrain and problems encountered in the Sunderbans and the eastern area of Assam.

Crashes to the west and south of Asansol would be dealt with by 122 RSU which, on many occasions, did venture into the areas of 60 RSU. Why lines of demarcation were never really adhered to is difficult to understand. There are two possibilities: the desire of the COs of each unit to chalk up a good score and the admin wallahs at Headquarters had their favoured units to whom they allotted the tasks. Whatever the reason, it was a constant source of irritation and a waste of scarce manpower.

Meanwhile, with the Jap threat to India growing, Kanchrapara began to make preparations for defence. Infantry trenches and gun pits were constructed and RAF Regiment personnel were drafted in. To add to manpower problems, details of airmen spent two days a week on defence training courses organized by F/O John, the defence officer of 79 Squadron also based at Kanchrapara, while others were given gas training by Cpl Kyte for one hour on three days a week.

To add to the confusion, orders had been received that the unit would move to Agartala, about 300 miles north-east of Calcutta, and that 130 RSU, recently formed at Agartala, would be attached to 60 RSU. This move was strongly contested by Sqn/Ldr Bennett as being too far from the operational area and possessed inadequate communications. Not only that, but as 130 RSU was a new unit, it would mean thoroughly equipping it, either from 60 RSU's still inadequate resources or encountering the same problems that 60 RSU had had at Kanchrapara in obtaining its own equipment.

His point regarding shortcomings in the system was highlighted when a workshop trailer, which had been desperately awaited, arrived at the same time that the only airman qualified to use it, Cpl Cooper, was posted. A singular case of one hand not being aware of what was needed by the other.

In spite of the lack of personnel and equipment, from the time of their arrival in March until moving to Agartala, the unit had salvaged no fewer than ninety-six aircraft including fifty-seven Hurricanes and nineteen aged Blenheims. With few exceptions, these aircraft were in the most out of the way places causing extremely arduous conditions but only a few were abandoned. Some lived to fly another day, others joined the piles of scrap. On site at Kanchrapara no fewer than fifty-nine were repaired. Again, the main customers were Hurricanes and Blenheims.

They also had the distinction of repairing a Miles Whitney Straight (VT/AKF MA949), one of twenty-two impressed into the RAF in 1936, which was the only one of its kind in India and had force landed at Barapada. After fitting a new oleo leg it was flown back to the Comm Flight at Dum-Dum.

On 16 December 1942, the first party with P/O Connelly departed by rail for Agartala. The following day, Sgt Smith and sixteen airmen travelled by a special train with the unit's MT and equipment, via Santahar to Agartala. The rear party arrived five days later with F/O Winfield only to find on arrival at Agartala that they were met not by their own transport but borrowed vehicles. The unit's own transport and equipment had fallen foul of the Bengal Assam Railways' love of shunting goods into sidings somewhere along the way and had not yet arrived.

The non-arrival of equipment caused something of a set-back, for the unit was expected to start work immediately on two Mohawks of 5 Squadron (BJ446 and BB979) which had crash landed a couple of weeks earlier. Both were write-offs. Although one pilot had survived uninjured, the other pilot, Sgt Smith, was badly injured.

Two Blenheims of 113 Squadron (Z7985 and Z9745) also required the unit's immediate attention and another (Z7345) required an engine change. All this had to be accomplished with borrowed tools and staging or sheer legs constructed from bamboo. The lesson learnt was that in future moves airmen would travel with their own tool kits. The thought of lugging heavy tool kits as well as personal kit was not exactly welcomed by the airmen.

Worse was yet to follow. They had been at Agartala for less than a week when a further instruction came from HQ Bengal, saying that the unit would now move immediately to Chittagong. The fact that it was almost Christmas meant nothing.

Indeed, on Christmas Eve a salvage party went out to pick up a Hurricane of 67 Squadron which had force landed at Cox's Bazar while another party was dispatched on Christmas Day to escort some aircraft spares and engines back to Kanchrapara. For some inexplicable reason, the escort party, instead of being routed the shorter distance to the ferry at Chandpur, had to go north to pick up the steamer service at Kulaura before backtracking south along the Surma River to Khulna, passing Chandpur on the way, before finally transferring to the broad gauge to Kanchrapara. Goodwill to all men, especially to those who had decreed the need for the journey at that time, certainly was not uppermost in the minds of the escort.

As luck would have it, the camaraderie of all servicemen towards anyone who apparently had had a rough deal at the hands of their superiors, was extended by some Army personnel who were having a Christmas celebration on board the steamer. In the event, it proved to be considerably jollier than being back at Agartala.

On 27 December, the vehicles and equipment lost *en route* from Calcutta a week previously, were once again packed up and sent by rail to Chittagong, along with a working party of twenty men from 60 and 130 RSUs. In the meantime, a large quantity of vehicles and equipment arrived at Agartala from 308 MU at Allahabad and had to be redirected to Chittagong, a round trip of some 700 miles. Communication between those at Group responsible for admin and technical affairs must have been sadly lacking for the latter not to have known the unit had moved. The distance could have been halved by a sea voyage across the Bay of Bengal.

Feelings were again running high. The constant mobility and frequent attachments left little time to establish any unit spirit. Amenities were almost non-existent. There had been the occasional invitation to the Bell Institute of the railway company at Kanchrapara while they were there but at Agartala there was nothing. The concrete runway was in the throes of being completed as a priority and domestic accommodation was hastily constructed bamboo bashas.

In spite of the uncertainty of its future, the main task of salvage continued and during December 1942 they had salvaged twenty aircraft and undertaken fifteen repair jobs, no mean feat under the circumstances.

Sqn/Ldr Bennett had not been at all happy with the somewhat erratic salvage and servicing policies of the unit since its formation and had frequently made his feelings known quite emphatically at Group Headquarters, only to have them fall on deaf ears. He submitted a somewhat radical policy paper, outlining a more efficient use of the unit's facilities and to everyone's astonishment, it was accepted almost without question. It did, however, sound the death knell of 60 RSU in its current form.

By 3 January 1943 the unit was accommodated, again in tents, on Chittagong airfield. Without waiting for the Garrison Engineer to make arrangements, the men took it upon themselves to organize the immediate building of the domestic site, using their own enterprise and technical skills, supplemented by whatever local labour that could be afforded.

For the first time since formation, an airmen's canteen was established and well stocked. Where the CO got the finance from is anyone's guess, though it was suspected that funds from Welfare for a unit Christmas dinner, which could only be attended by the few not on escort or detachment, was put to good use.

Aerial activity in the area was increasing, air raid alarms began to continually interrupt the unit's work and the airfield was bombed on 16 January. Only minor damage by bomb splinters was caused to Hurricane BN212 of 135 Squadron. This aircraft, transferred to 1 RIAF, was subsequently to catch fire in mid-air and crash land at Kuhatur. The following day, Hurricane BN567 of 79 Squadron was badly damaged after hitting one of the bomb craters and crash landing. Following repairs, it was written off after hitting another Hurricane during an attempted overshoot at Chittagong some months later. Two Mohawks of 5 Squadron (BJ441 and BS788), both shot up after a sortie, were patch repaired and returned to Agartala.

With its headquarters now firmly established at Chittagong, the unit was radically reorganized to overcome the difficulties presented by communication and distances. Though desperately short of personnel, mobile units were formed to deal with the southern area. One was sent to Ramu, another to 'Reindeer', a satellite east of Ramu, one to Feni and one to another satellite at 'Ritz' near Maungdaw.

The idea was to maintain maximum mobility of independent sections so that any future moves due to changes in operational commitment, could be carried out without upsetting the basic organization of repair. At the same time, they would give back-up to salvage crews where necessary. Chittagong was to be the control and workshop centre for the forward areas, while detachments, as far as possible, would be self-contained and provide a pool of allied tradesmen to assist mobile units, a sort of 'Flying Squad' of tradesmen.

The unit was also to have a flight of thirty-six gunners, drawn from 60 and 130 RSUs, under the command of F/O Garnett of 130 RSU. They would operate in the southern area and provide defence for any salvage crew in that area. This somewhat unorthodox scheme needed not only a large number of personnel but men with a high degree of skill and initiative for it to succeed. To accomplish this by 16 January 1943, 130 RSU was disbanded and merged with 60 RSU under the command of Sqn/Ldr Bennett, the originator of the scheme. The new set-up appeared as follows:

Bengal Maintenance Wing
Headquarters, RSU, Forward Areas
Chittagong

RSU HQ Detachment (Agartala)		RSU HQ Detachment (Reindeer)	
Mobile Parties (Agartala)	RSU Detachment (Feni)/ Mobile Parties (Feni)	Mobile Parties (Southern Area)	RSU Detachment (Ritz)/ Mobile Parties (Ritz)

After 60 RSU, still under the command of Sqn/Ldr F. N. B. Bennett, moved from Agartala to the airfield at Patanga near Chittagong in December 1942, along with the absorbed 130 RSU, it was simply referred to as Repair and Salvage Unit (Forward Area).

On 5 June 1943 Sqn/Ldr Bennett was posted to 226 Group and A/Sqn/Ldr L. G. Raspison, a Tech E, assumed command, until four months later he was posted on medical grounds to 320 MU at Karachi. His place was taken by Sqn/Ldr G. M. Tiffin on 3 November 1943 but a month later he too was posted to 143 RSU at Bishnupur and replaced by Sqn/Ldr F. J. Winfield who had been a P/O when the original unit had been formed at Padgate in 1941. A year later he was repatriated, his place being taken by Sqn/Ldr Welch, and the HQ moved to Mambur, south of Chittagong.

Whether a unit without a clearly recognizable prefix was creating complications for those responsible for admin and technical matters at 186 Maintenance Wing is not known, but a year later the unit was renamed 126 RSU (Mobile), following the arrival and formation of this unit in Calcutta in July. Apart from some of the officers and the new postings from Calcutta, it had the same personnel still doing the same job, with men on detachments at Comilla, Chiringa, Mambur, Cox's Bazar, Hathazari and Dohazari.

The final entry in the Operational Record Book of the former 60 RSU, now theoretically non-existent, states: 'The formation of R&SU Forward Areas is nearing completion and this completes the Operations Record Book of 60 R&SU which is now fully embodied in R&SU Forward Areas.'

This embodiment of units, and in particular the former 60 RSU, seems to have suffered from a lack of any account of their activities in spite of eventually serving east of the Brahmaputra for three and a half years. It may well be that their records are still mouldering away in some long-forgotten filing cabinet, for it is hard to believe that a unit, taking the trouble to record the following incident would not also record other events.

A signal had come in to 126 RSU based at Ramu that a Hurricane of 261 Squadron (HV646) had crash landed two and a half miles north of Goppe Bazar. Cpl Smith, LACs Stewart, Parks and Cullen were dispatched in a 15-cwt. truck to investigate the crash and to salvage whatever spares they could. Running short of rations, Parks and Cullen set out to collect some extra rations from the RIASC Depot at Goppe Bazar, leaving Cpl Smith and LAC Stewart to carry on working.

Half-way to the depot they were stopped by an Army patrol who informed them that a large Jap force was proceeding in their direction from Taungbazar. Without further ado they returned to the crash site to warn Smith and Stewart of the imminent danger and prepare for evacuation.

When they arrived back at the site they were surprised to find that the aircraft, tents and equipment were on fire, but of the two airmen there wasn't a trace, nor was there any message or indication of what had happened.

Fearing the worst, they made their way post-haste in the direction of Kyaundaung Bazar to an AMES camp north of the crash site. Since there was still no news of their colleagues, there was nothing else to do under the circumstances but to return to Ramu the following day.

On reporting what had happened, they were informed that Wg/Cdr Ellisdon, the CO of 169 Wing, had flown over the site in a Spitfire and dropped a message telling Cpl Smith to abort the salvage and get out fast, for it had also been reported to him that the Japs were only about four miles south of the crash site.

Cpl Smith was to destroy the aircraft, bringing back only that equipment which could easily be carried. Cpl Smith had waited as long as he deemed prudent for Parks and Cullen but when they didn't turn up he assumed that they had run into trouble and the only thing left was for Stewart and himself to put as much mileage between themselves and the oncoming Japs.

When they arrived at the RAF wireless post near Kyaundaung, he asked them to inform the unit that all was OK and that they were moving north again. Shortly afterwards, they met a Gurkha patrol and as it was getting near nightfall, the officer i/c advised them that it would be wiser to stay with them till daybreak when he would give them a guide to lead them back to Bawli Bazar. From there they could return to the unit in comparative safety.

When they finally arrived back at base they were relieved to find that Parks and Cullen had also made it safely.

Sadly, having survived this close shave, Cpl Smith died a month later of malaria and cardiac failure in 62 MFH at Ramu. LAC Stewart, who was an electrician, had an unfortunate accident four months later at Tulihul when he climbed into a Hurricane of 42 Squadron being repaired by 132 RSU. He switched on the wireless and, for some inexplicable reason, the accumulator exploded in his face and he sustained severe burns.

On 1 July 1945 the unit was ordered to move across the Bay of Bengal to Cholavaram near Madras. Whilst there, orders were received for all the MT vehicles and personnel to proceed to the transit camp at Madras prior to embarkation for an unknown destination.

On arrival at the camp, no accommodation was available. It was full to capacity with other RAF units and Army personnel, all standing by for embarkation and all wondering what was going on. As it turned out, it was the follow-up of Operation Zipper, the invasion of Malaya. After kicking their heels for almost two months, they embarked on 9 September at Madras on a New Zealand Lines ship, the *Tamaroa*, bound for Malaya, again with a new CO, Sqn/Ldr H. M. Louch, MBE.

The conditions on board were atrocious, with overcrowded mess decks and grim food. After a very rough trip, the convoy arrived eight days later at Morib Beach at 0300 hours. It was pitch dark and, fully laden with kit and weapons, they had to clamber down landing nets into a landing craft. Unfortunately, because of the tide it could not get close to the shore and they had to transfer to a Buffalo, a mechanized landing craft, which took them to within twenty yards of the beach.

After wading ashore through chest-high water, no one seemed to know the destination of the unit and they were directed to make do for themselves and camp for the time being in the nearby rubber trees. All they had for protection were monsoon capes and 'mozzie' nets. The scene as dawn broke was one of utter chaos: landing craft stranded on sandbanks, vehicles just yards off shore, immobile and awash, with a hospital ship perilously close to being grounded.

Subsequent accounts of the landings reveal that someone had not taken into account the large sandbars and the high tides in that area and that the landings should have been further along the coast.

Three days later they were still under the trees without any news and it appeared as if the unit's presence had been overlooked in the general pandemonium of the landings. The Advance HQ of 224 Group, who had come ashore with the original landings a week earlier and were ensconced at the airfield at Kelanang, finally signalled that the unit's destination was to be Port Swettenham and that they would be transported by No. 59 MT Company.

On arrival, after reporting in, they were again informed that the destination had been changed to the all-weather airfield at Kuala Lumpur. Arriving at the airfield, much to everyone's surprise, they were greeted by a Japanese guard of honour who presented arms as they passed through.

Various units and squadrons had by now moved into the area and the accommodation had become congested. The only site available was on the south-east end of the airstrip in a vacated tin mine warehouse which stank like a pigsty and had been left in a filthy condition by the departing Japanese troops.

They were informed by the locals that it had been used as a slaughterhouse, which seemed to be confirmed by the bloodstains on the walls. They were also told that it had been the scene of various executions. The chaps positively refused to occupy the building and on pointing out that there was an empty bungalow further away, were informed that it would be required for officers. In spite of vehement protests, the billeting officer was adamant, but as a compromise they were issued with tents.

A week later they were rehoused in billets on the domestic site. As it turned out, they might as well have stayed in their own tents or back in Madras for that matter. After spending the following month unpacking ground equipment, getting trade sections organized and helping to re-establish the airfield, the unit was suddenly informed, as if it was an afterthought, that under Disbandment Order No. 158/45 dated 20 November 1945, the unit establishment was cancelled and that from 21 November all personnel were to be absorbed into No. 390 MU (SRD) at Seletar, along with all their MT and equipment.

Worse was to follow, for on arrival they found that Seletar was bursting at the seams with over 3,000 men awaiting demob plus almost 2,000 civilians and Jap POWs employed on the site. With all the permanent buildings crammed to capacity, they were accommodated in one of the two tented camps which had been set up to house over 1,000 men.

The food was poor and inadequate, with only six cooks expected to cater for everyone. The off-duty facilities were almost non-existent and along with the rest of the personnel, morale began rapidly to deteriorate. By this time, the feelings on the station had almost reached boiling point and 126 RSU found themselves caught up in the beginnings of a strike action which had been orchestrated by some of the more disgruntled and militant personnel.

Like all RSUs they had become just another statistic, their efforts unrecorded or recognized, except in the minds of the men who, since picking up their first Hurricane in 1942, had serviced or salvaged hundreds of aircraft in the three and a half years of the unit's existence.

Chapter 4

No. 82 Repair and Salvage Unit (FRD)

This unit was formed at Cawnpore under AHQ SEA Order No. 100 dated 2 April 1944. Its function was to be that of a Forward Repair Depot undertaking major inspections or minor detail repairs to heavy bomber aircraft in the north-east on a 'fly in' basis. All that was known at the time was that a unit was to be formed at Cawnpore, in all probability for the maintenance of Liberators, and additional personnel would shortly be arriving from UK.

Sgt Andrews, an F2A from the Liberator repair section of 322 MU at Cawnpore, was to liaise with F/O Page, an equipment officer from 75 ASP, with the object of organizing the equipment necessary for the efficient running of the unit when formed. Considerable progress had been made in this direction by 19 March 1944 when F/O Page fell ill while on a visit to 226 Group and a temporary replacement, F/O Hunter, was posted in from 101 RSU.

Wg/Cdr Scullard, the CO of 322 MU (ARS) was contacted to try to ascertain the policy of the new unit and requested to find some office accommodation to begin the admin formation of 82 RSU. Although Wg/Cdr Scullard had received a copy of the Formation Order, there was still some uncertainty as to the actual requirement and policies of the unit. Not until the end of March, almost a month after the original Formation Order, was it found that the Central Registry of 322 MU was not only in possession of the original order but that a large quantity of stationery and mail for 82 RSU personnel lay undelivered. No doubt some Orderly Room wallah, never having heard of 82 RSU had assumed a misdirection of post.

With this discovery, the general policy could now be clarified and two officers were allocated, one to deal with engineering and the other as i/c Orderly Room/Central Registry. A F/O Rees-Griffiths was temporarily attached from 313 MU, Kankinara to assist with the organization.

F/O Page was still ill at 226 Group so it was decided that Rees-Griffiths should continue setting up the equipment section, and two buildings were provided by 322 MU for this specific purpose. The strength of the unit was now two officers and ten airmen, including an SNCO and a general duties clerk. There was still a pressing need for an Adjutant but a more urgent requirement for MT.

By the beginning of May 1944, various tradesmen were posted in but they were mainly electricians. As there was no immediate work for them, the CTO of the MU arranged for them to be temporarily lent to the MU to gain experience on Liberators and Wellingtons.

On 17 May the first batch of MT personnel arrived — without transport! The need for vehicles now became even more pressing due to the amount of equipment arriving at the local station. The MT section of 322 MU was stretched to the limit with their own duties and having to help with the needs of 82 RSU.

Sqn/Ldr A. A. McLaren was posted in from 170 Wing as OC on 25 May 1944 and F/O Hunter assumed duties as MT officer.

The expected transport finally arrived towards the end of May and comprised eight 3-ton Thorneycrofts and five 15-cwt. Chevrolets.

F/O Rees-Griffiths, who had only been with the unit for two months, was taken ill with gastric malaria and was replaced by F/O Allward, posted in from 143 RSU. F/O Page in the meantime, having recovered from his illness, had been posted to 305 MU in Bombay. By 30 June, the unit strength was three officers and 270 BORs and Flt/Lt A. P. Pearce from 140 RSU and WO A. W. Whatling from 301 MU at Karachi were posted in as Engineering and Armament Officers.

With the policy now established, it was planned to produce, for the first time, work on ten major inspections, but the work was delayed by the monsoons and violent storms striking the area on 26 August. Air testing of the five aircraft which had completed their inspection prior to the storms, also had to be cancelled. Apart from inspections and servicing, all the Liberators passing through were being fitted with paratroop attachments.

By this time the unit strength had now risen to five officers and 383 BORs. Although they had originally had a surplus of electricians and had lent them to the MU, they had not been returned and in consequence they now found themselves somewhat short of these tradesmen, including instrument repairers. A further fifty-four BORs were posted in from UK but since none had any experience of Liberators they only added too the unit's problems.

As a recognized unit it justified an inspection on 19 September 1944 by AVM G. C. Dawson, CB, OBE, AVM C. W. Weedon, CBE, the CMO, and Air/Cdre Iles, the AOC 226 Group. Two days after the visit, on 21 September, a signal was received stating that it had been decided to move the complete unit to Dalbumgarh, about a hundred miles west of Calcutta. It was to be accomplished in three parties, one by road and two by rail.

A party of eighty-eight men and NCOs were to be left behind at Cawnpore to complete the work that had already started on some of the Liberators.

The road party with F/O Taylor and a F/Sgt with twenty men plus ten prime movers and trailers left Chakeri for the 450 mile road trip to Dalbumgarh, arriving five days later. The advance rail party left the following day with an ETA of midnight on the 24th, a journey of some fifty-two hours. The rear party left a day later. However, when the special train carrying the essential spares and equipment did arrive at Dalbumgarh, it could not be unloaded for two days owing to violent storms which again swept the area.

The unit was finally ensconced in its new surroundings by 5 October, the whole move having been accomplished in exactly fourteen days. As a treat, arrangements were made for all personnel to visit a special film show at the US base at Chakulia, as the nearest town with any amenities was Jamshedpur fifty miles to the west.

Technical sections were established in canvas hangars to handle six Liberators at a time on a 'production line' basis. The first Liberator (BZ997) of 356 Squadron based at Salbani, arrived for a major overhaul on 30 October 1944, with a further two aircraft completed in the first ten days of November. The only snag encountered was that armament work was held up by the lack of experienced American turret personnel.

Althought the unit stayed at that location for a year, very little remains of its work record and one can only assume that it continued to function as an MU.

In August 1945, signs of a major change began to appear when the unit was suddenly converted to a Mobile Repair and Salvage Unit to support a fighter wing. In October, they were informed that they were to move to Calcutta immediately, where details of their final destination would be available. It was all very hush-hush for some reason and it was assumed that they could only be going to one of two places which could cope with heavy aircraft, Asansol or Dum-Dum.

With the urgency explicit in the signal, personnel had to set to and crate all the ground equipment; the servicing of aircraft became a secondary consideration as they prepared for the move.

By 11 October, everything was ready and Flt/Lt Clift and a road party of twenty-three vehicles carrying all the equipment left for Calcutta via Asansol and arrived eighteen hours later. The main party of personnel left by train the same day and on arrival at Howrah Station were taken to 35 PTC where the CO, Sqn/Ldr Paterson, was informed that they would now be going to Singapore. Much to his surprise, he was also informed that it was immediate and that F/O Gates and forty-nine men would embark at once on the *Dunera* anchored at Alipore Docks. The remainder of the airmen would stay at 35 PTC to await the arrival of the main party.

The following day, the road party arrived and without further ado some of the road party and a large proportion of the personnel embarked on the SS *Salween* for an uneventful nine-day trip to Singapore. The remainder would follow after supervising the loading of the equipment and MT aboard the SS *Ammla* and the SS *New Chang* which were due to arrive at the docks in two weeks' time. Rather foolishly, as events proved, it was to be shipped unescorted. On arrival in Singapore, following the unloading of the vessels by the unit, due to a dock strike, it was immediately obvious that a great deal of pilfering had taken place in Calcutta and many airmen had lost all their personal possessions.

For the IORs of the unit who travelled on the SS *River Crest* it was rather a traumatic experience, for the ship struck a mine in the Malacca Straits, only a few miles from their destination. Fortunately the casualties were not heavy, only two having been injured seriously enough to warrant detaining in hospital on arrival, though most of their kit was lost in the explosion below decks.

The rear party which had stayed behind to supervise the loading of the equipment, embarked on the *Derbyshire* on 21 November.

Unlike other units who found themselves in substandard accommodation on arrival in Singapore, 82 RSU were fortunate enough to be billeted in relative comfort in the former married quarters at Seletar and, while waiting for a decision as to their future, occupied their time in helping to clear the hangars of debris.

The unit was now being steadily depleted of personnel who were time-expired or Class B release. One party of armourers was flown to Batavia in a Liberator, to saw off bomb fins so that they could be used by the Thunderbolts of 60 and 81 Squadrons that were now operating against the Indonesians.

In the meantime, the CO, Sqn/Ldr Paterson, had been informed by Wg/Cdr T. Clare, OC 390 MU (SRD), that as from 21 October the unit had been absorbed into 390 MU and that the effective date of the disbandment would be 21 November 1945.

It seemed an odd state of affairs that the unit should only find out that it had actually been officially disbanded while still in India and that all the trauma of moving to Singapore could have been avoided, an admin peculiarity that many other units were to experience. It is partially understandable, for no doubt the authorities, in their anxiety to conform to the 'Quit India' policies and with the ensuing unrest as politicians wrestled for power as soon as the war was over, saw Singapore as a convenient and safe haven.

Chapter 5

No. 1 Airborne Salvage Section/ No. 85 Repair and Salvage Unit

Although originally formed at Dum-Dum in October 1943 under 228 Group Bengal Maintenance Wing, No. 1 Airborne Salvage Section had been operating in an *ad hoc* capacity since June 1943, but just how it operated is rather obscure. However, five months later with Formation Order No. 104, and an effective date of 23 March 1944, the unit was transferred to the control of Headquarters Air Command South-East Asia, but still within the admin control of 230 Group at Dum-Dum. It was posted to Barrackpore immediately to begin operations.

The unit's salvage policy was to fly in tradesmen to do makeshift and patch repairs specifically on Cat. BC Dakotas in order to allow them to be flown back to 322 MU at Cawnpore for further servicing and repairs.

The CO was Sqn/Ldr S. Kureishi, posted in from HQ ACSEA. F/Os A. R. Lebans and L. C. H. Halley, both Canadian test pilots from 322 MU, Cawnpore, and F/O L. A. Greatorex from an R & D unit were posted in at the same time. They were followed by another Canadian, WO Robinson, together with two New Zealanders, WOs Hyde and Dormer, who had recently converted from Blenheims. The only navigator was F/Sgt Dave Waddington until he was joined by F/Sgt Eric King from No. 1583 Calibration Flight based at Chittagong.

WO Pound, 511011, a Fitter 1 of the old school, from an R & D unit took up the post of Engineering Officer until the arrival of Flt/Lt D. W. Rimmell, a Tech E from 126 RSU at Chittagong, who was tragically killed in a Mosquito crash at Bishnupur later in October.

Fifteen airmen, most of whom had been promoted for meritorious service on similar work on Wellingtons were posted in to convert to Dakotas. Because of the shortage of aircraft at this time, the 'fly in' policy was not always available and ground crews travelled by road to the crash sites. Test pilots would then fly in on completion of repairs, more often than not leaving the ground crews to make their own way back to base. As it was only a small unit, this was to prove both a time wasting and costly exercise to have men travelling by road when they could be better employed working on aircraft and it defeated the object of the original intention.

Up to this time, aircraft had been 'borrowed' from other squadrons until two Dakotas (FD854 and KG504) were allotted to the unit specifically for its own purpose. Another Dakota (KK109), allotted a while later, unfortunately force landed in the Sunderbans during bad weather. Although the crew managed to get back without a great deal of trouble, the aircraft was never recovered as it was too far from solid ground to enable any salvage equipment to get near it.

The routine could now be to fly in crews and equipment, assess the damage and the time it would take to effect repair to a 'fly out' condition, or dismantle the aircraft and fly out the stripped spares in their own aircraft to the MU for recycling.

Mainplanes were of course a different matter. They could not be loaded inside the aircraft because of their bulk so those that were serviceable had to be conveyed by road, which again defeated the original purpose of the unit. To overcome this, experiments were carried out to see if mainplanes, held in place by straps, could be carried beneath the fuselage. The original cradle was, to say the least, something of a Heath Robinson affair. Flt/Lt Greatorex, the test pilot for the initial test flight, soon realized that, though a practical and viable proposition, it could prove extremely hazardous in an emergency unless the mainplane could be jettisoned quickly.

After further experiments, a sling was designed which enabled the mainplane to be jettisoned by means of a control in the cockpit. Basically they were glider release latches attached centrally beneath the fuselage. The mainplane was levelled and made rigid by adjustable jacks. In addition to this, an aerofoil cowling of canvas and wood was fitted over the root end of the mainplane to reduce drag.

During one of the test flights in Dakota KG504, flown by Flt/Lt Halley accompanied by the CTO of 322 MU, one of the suspension cables snapped. This released the jettison clips and the mainplane was dropped seven miles from Chakeri where it was later recovered as a write-off. A similar incident occurred at Agartala when a mainplane broke adrift as the aircraft was taking off. Fortunately, the aircraft was sufficiently airborne to allow the mainplane to fall clear. Had it not, then without doubt a major accident would have occurred.

However, one of the snags in the original design was that the slings could only be used for either starboard or port mainplanes and change-over from one to the other took about sixteen man-hours. Eventually the design was modified so that either mainplane could be attached at will with minimum effort.

By the same token, the Pratt and Whitney engines caused some problems in stowage inside the aircraft unless the reduction gear was removed. With the same ingenuity that had produced the mainplane carrying modification, a portable engine stand was designed by WO Pound which permitted the complete power units to be carried without the need for dismantling.

At the same time, he and his crew, confronted with a Dakota of 117 Squadron (FD896) whose undercarriage had been badly damaged on landing, designed a modification kit to strengthen the undercarriage and leave it in the locked down position. It saved time and extensive repairs on site and allowed the aircraft to be flown back to the MU by Flt/Lt Halley. As a show of confidence, WO Pound also flew back in the aircraft. The design was sent to the DGA for approval and accepted and was subsequently used on a number of occasions on aircraft with suspect undercarriages.

At this time, apart from the officers, there were only thirty airmen on the posted strength of the unit, including a DMT, but strangely enough no cook. The establishment did not provide for a cook or enrolled followers because it was anticipated that many of the personnel would be continuously away from the unit and therefore attached to the nearest unit for rations.

Messing for the unit on site was in the hands of 4 CMU, which worked quite well with reduced numbers until forty airmen of various trades were posted in in June 1944 to deal with the increasing workloads. The cooks at 4 CMU, whilst not exactly mutinying, made it quite plain that they could not cope with the extra messing.

After the problem had been resolved between Sqn/Ldr Kureishi and the CO of 4 CMU, another anomaly arose which bordered on the ridiculous. The unit was allocated, on a temporary basis, a 3-tonner, a 15-cwt. lorry, a water tender and a workshop trailer, but no drivers. The unit still had only one DMT! Though the vehicles were a valuable asset, they had to be driven and serviced by aircraft technicians taken off essential work.

Air operations in Burma were increasing dramatically and, as with other salvage units, 1 Airborne found it difficult to keep up with the rising tide of crashes and servicing. The only way to maintain output was to work at night. In order to do this, a Wisconsin lighting set and floodlights were borrowed from the USAAF base at Piadoba which of course had everything in the way of sophisticated tools and equipment.

The personnel were now split into three gangs, one on props, the second on the removal and repairing of engines whilst the third concentrated on installations. The latter group began work at 0600 hours and kept going until the aircraft was ready for air testing. In some instances this meant that men worked sixteen to eighteen hours a day. This shift system, however, caused further messing problems and once again a compromise had to be reached. Although the need for extra hours was accepted without question, morale flagged a bit at the irregularity and occasional absence of meals.

In spite of Sqn/Ldr Kureishi's continued request for some action to be taken in a matter that was becoming serious, Group would not bend from the establishment requirements. Instead, in the interests of maintaining adequate records, which up to now had been undertaken by the Tech officers, they posted in a qualified GD clerk to handle the admin. Their priorities obviously did not coincide with the unit's pressing needs for a cook.

Following a visit by Gp/Capt Blockey, Wg/Cdr Smethan-Jones and Sqn/Ldr Riley, the unit now changed from the operational control of DGA to 230 Group. At the same time it was decided to extend the periods of major inspections of Dakota airframes from 720 hours to 1,020 hours, though engines and propellers were to remain the same. It was an attempt to reduce the workload but, in the event, the hours saved on airframes were simply spent on the increasing number of damaged engines and prop changes.

By the end of June the monsoons were in full spate, adding to the problems of the unit, both in working conditions and in flying. In a message to Group, Sqn/Ldr Kureishi stated: 'The weather is a serious handicap to the "fly in" operations. Most of the 400 hours flown by this unit in the past few weeks have been in bad weather. As we have no wireless operators, we have to rely on visual means of navigation and in monsoon weather this is rarely possible. Consequently the trips are unnecessarily hazardous... We are making continuous and urgent demands to remedy this deficiency of wireless operators.'

This handicap is recalled by one navigator, Eric King, who recalls: 'Any trip over the Chin Hills during the monsoon was pretty hairy. Although I had a valley route worked out to get us in and out of Imphal below cloud base, it was always a very "twitchy" journey. The route into Burma was also somewhat dicey. The Daks weren't too keen on going much above 10,000 feet with anything like a full load which, of course, we always had.'

In spite of the problems of cooks, drivers and wireless operators, the unit continued to give a good account of itself in the salvaging and return of aircraft. By the end of April, a month after arriving at Barrackpore, twelve Dakotas had been patch repaired and flown back to the MU.

The initiative and enterprise of one salvage crew was stretched to the limit when they were called out to a Dakota which had crash landed at Chaklala. When they arrived at the scene, the aircraft had been used as a Christmas tree by other Dakota squadrons anxious to get their hands on spares for their own aircraft. Except for the shell and the engines, hardly anything remained and under normal circumstances the aircraft would have been seen almost as a write-off.

In spite of its condition, WO Pound was instructed to do the best he could by whatever means were at his disposal to get the aircraft serviceable again to fly back to Cawnpore. It seemed an impossible job but, undaunted, he and his crew set about the task. Parts of Wellingtons, Hudsons and other aircraft were used in lieu of Dakota spares until it was deemed airworthy.

The aircraft was now indeed a flying Christmas tree. It had a few serviceable instruments, including tachometers and boost gauges, but the electrical system was unserviceable. Satisfied that with a bit of coaxing the aircraft would fly and supremely confident in WO Pound's expertise, Sqn/Ldr Kureishi and Sqn/Ldr Blackwell, the CTO of 322 MU, took off for Cawnpore.

A similar act of faith in ground crew abilities was in the case of Dakota FD821 of 194 Squadron which had crash landed at Nolighat, sustaining damage to both spars and the port mainplane. The skin was wrinkled and the tip bent down to about ten degrees ten feet from the end, which had also buckled the ailerons. A fabric patch was doped over a twelve inch hole in the leading edge, not an unusual aircraft repair except that this one was in fact a khaki shirt belonging to one of the crew in lieu of the correct fabric.

Flt/Lt Lebans, who only had about forty hours on Dakotas, flew it off, accompanied by Sqn/Ldr Kureishi and WO Pound. After a somewhat dicey take-off, it was observed that the port mainplane had an air bubble which was working in a peculiar and disturbing manner at the point where the mainplane was bent, causing wrinkles to ripple along the entire length of the mainplane. It appeared that at any moment the rivets would pop and the skin would begin to peel back.

It was decided to abort the flight and land at the nearest airfield which happened to be Agartala. On approaching the landing, the port mainplane stalled at about 100 miles per hour and the pilot had great difficulty in getting it up with the rudder. After successfully touching down, it was found that the brakes were also defective and it would probably need a very long landing run. It did, only just stopping short of the end of the runway and the monsoon trench which spanned the airfield.

With the mainplane cradles and engine stands now a proven success, experiments were conducted to see if the same tactics could be applied to the salvaging of Spitfires so a similar cradle to that for the Dakota mainplane was designed and built. The fuselage minus the tailplane would with patient manoeuvring fit snugly in the cargo hold. Again the enterprise of the unit came to the fore in designing a special cradle to hold the fuselage securely and allow it to be fastened to anchor bolts in the floor of the aircraft.

The initial test flight in FD800, borrowed from 31 Squadron, was flown by Flt/Lt Halley and Sqn/Ldr Kureishi, carrying parts of a Spitfire VIII of 81 Squadron (JG199), which had crashed at Agartala, to Dum-Dum.

With the number of Dakota sorties engaged in supply dropping increasing, so did the number of accidents, and spares to repair them were scarce. It was often a race between 1 Airborne and the nearest RSUs to get to the crash site first. Invariably the RSUs won. Salvage allocation was ignored as resident RSUs, sometimes having to wait weeks until demands from MUs were met and keen to maintain their output record, took advantage of the bonus on their doorstep. The one benefit, however, which 1 Airborne had over other units was that they could nearly always fly in their own spares.

It was a silly situation and rather than improve things, it more often than not created extra work. In spite of protests, the habit persisted; providence and temptation were difficult to ignore.

On one occasion, a 117 Squadron Dakota (FD895) made a single-engine landing at Tulihul. It had been badly shot up and was riddled with bullet holes. Both mainplanes were damaged beyond repair, the undercarriage was damaged with the landing and the trim cables had been shot away. It also required a double engine change. It was a miracle that it had got back at all, let alone land. It looked a sorry sight and at first glance it seemed a virtual write-off. Even 132 RSU, after dragging it clear of the runway, were not interested.

Undeterred by its condition, 1 Airborne flew in two new mainplanes, two engines and props, along with their own salvage crew and within seven days, an aircraft which had been deemed fit only for the scrap heap had been repaired to a fly-out condition, with the damaged undercarriage supported by the modification kit designed by the unit. After a preliminary air test it was flown directly back to 322 MU at Cawnpore by Flt/Lt Halley and Sqn/Ldr Kureishi.

The patch repair with a shirt mentioned earlier was not unusual. It was often adopted by RSUs to repair the fabric of Hurricanes in the absence of the correct material. One of the ploys to get a new shirt was to say, 'I had to use mine for patching.'

Here again, the indenting system quite often bore no relationship to the reality of the situation. Dope would be available but no linen, conversely material was always available even if it wasn't always the authorized material. It was always assumed that there was no alternative to dope, until one day at Pinlehu a Dakota of 1 Airborne, which had been flown in to pick up a Spitfire to take back to the MU, while manoeuvring to a better position for loading, collided with the dismantled Spitfire and damaged its starboard elevator.

'Here goes my shirt,' said one of the riggers, but having got the patch ready, he found there was no dope available. It looked as if the aircraft would have to wait until some could be obtained. A Burmese, who had been watching with some interest, suggested trying some 'Zu', an unfermented rice wine. Although rather sceptical, but with nothing to lose, it was tried and it worked, producing a really taut patch.

The aircraft was loaded and flew back to Barrackpore. Two weeks later the aircraft was undergoing a forty-hour inspection when the navigator of the aircraft, Eric King, wandered down to the dispersal. There he found the ground crew replacing the port elevator. He mentioned that it was the starboard one which had been damaged. 'Oh, that's OK, we've just put some more dope on it,' replied the NCO i/c.

That's how it remained until the aircraft came in for its major service and the complete elevator was changed. (There is no evidence to suggest that Zu was henceforth indented for as a permanent substitute for dope.)

The unit was to break new ground when a Sunderland flying boat was allotted for salvage. It had sunk at its moorings on Willingdon Reach on the Hooghly River near Calcutta and was twenty-seven feet below the surface. Considerable preparation was required to make an accurate survey and collect suitable equipment. In this the naval authorities in Calcutta were particularly helpful, even lending the unit their diving personnel and river launches.

Unfortunately, the presence of a very swift current hindered the survey and preparations, making the possibility of a salvage impossible and the work had to be suspended until such time as the river subsided sometime in October.

The demand on the unit steadily grew throughout 1944, not only in its allotment of salvage and major servicing at its base, but in the supply of essential spares to other units. As the Army moved further into Burma, followed by the fighter squadrons as strips were retaken, it was found that replacement engines could hardly be supplied quickly enough by road and it became the unit's task to take in three Merlins at a time to keep the Hurri-bombers airborne. Added to this, motor transport was taking a pounding due to the difficult terrain. Army transport depots were being overwhelmed with broken-down gharries with seized engines and the unit's expertise was called upon to convey up to ten engines at a time to ease the hard pressed situation.

Its days as No. 1 Airborne Salvage Section were numbered and its unique role was to change through reorganization at Group. It was deleted from the SHQ establishment with the transfer of this HQ to the control of Headquarters 229 Group and re-formed, on paper at least, as an entirely separate unit. It would now be under the administrative control of Headquarters RAF Burma but still remain under the functional control of 230 Group for equipment.

It was to remain at its present location at Barrackpore which it had occupied since March 1944, but with effect from 20 January 1945 it would be known as No. 85 Repair and Salvage Unit. Its CO, Sqn/Ldr Kureishi, was posted and replaced by Flt/Lt R. Servos (C20878 GD pilot).

The success of the unit to this point can be judged by the fact that since its formation on 23 March it had salvaged, repaired, serviced and returned to squadrons no fewer than fifty-eight Dakotas, had changed forty-seven engines and carried out major servicing of two Liberators. It had performed countless delivery sorties into Burma, of passengers, engines, charpoys, cigarettes, anything in fact that was required by the advancing forces. The only thing that couldn't change in spite of official formation orders and establishment policies was its proud record which was to continue under a new hat.

In spite of a change of name and identity, right up to the time it disbanded it was repeatedly referred to by its former title.

The primary task, as before, was to provide facilities for the repair of crashed aircraft on a 'patch and repair' basis on site so that aircraft could be flown back to an MU for further repairs and servicing. However, as time went by the original policy became less of a priority. The main function became the supply of forward areas with urgently needed aero-engines and spares, along with other freight as operational units continually moved down into Burma.

With the increased distances came additional navigational hazards. The Dakotas were still short of wireless operators and still had to rely on visual navigation over unfamiliar territory. Whilst not solving the problems of navigation entirely, a welcome gift came from 132 RSU who presented them with all the computers they had salvaged from various aircraft.

The situation improved when new aircrews were posted in from the now disbanded Communications Flight of 230 Group, along with a number of wireless operators from 159 Liberator Squadron which had been operating from Digri.

With this new role, the unit was becoming less of a salvage unit and more like a transport unit. The main occupation of the tradesmen was now the servicing of the unit's Dakotas and others from various squadrons.

In May, the unit was informed that a move to a new location was imminent and that the unit would be more or less self-contained. This move, presumably to Burma, was welcomed as the unit had been flying increasingly back and forth between Barrackpore and Rangoon and other forward airstrips in Burma. The practice of returning the same day became increasingly difficult as the weather worsened and entailed an average of nine hours' flying time, putting an added strain on the aircrew and the limited number of aircraft at their disposal, apart from adding to the problems of the servicing resources. As far as the CO was concerned, an aircraft held over was an empty aircraft on the ground not earning its keep.

Expectations were shattered, however, when they learned that the move was to Kanchrapara. It was difficult to even begin to understand what lay behind the thinking for this move. There was simply no advantage whatever in moving all the equipment from a well-established site, only to have to start reorganizing again just twenty miles away.

Throughout June and July, urgent meetings were held between the CO, Sqn/Ldr Touch, AFC who had been the Chief Test Pilot of 230 Group and had taken over from Flt/Lt Servos on his repatriation, Gp/Capt Culley, DSO of HQ 228 Group, and Air/Cdre Blockey of HQ Burma to discuss the unit's future. The move, which at best would only be temporary, was finally resolved when it was decided that after all it would be in the best interests of efficiency to move the unit directly to Mingladon.

The unit strength at that time, including aircrew, was seventeen officers, twelve warrant officers, seventeen SNCOs and ninety-nine allied tradesmen, a small unit considering the future policy envisaged by Headquarters. To ease the shortage of tradesmen, ten airmen were to be posted in from 132 RSU, but again communications along the line were somewhat lacking and highlighted how divorced from reality the admin authorities were. Unknown to them 132 RSU was already in Mingladon and had been there since January with various detachments at other forward airfields in Burma.

Fortunately this oversight was discovered in time and exchanged for nineteen tradesmen from 143 RSU based at Bishnupur. The 132 RSU personnel would join the unit when it finally arrived at its new location. In the event, even this intended arrangement proved a non-starter, for it was 85 RSU who found that they had to supplement 132 RSU.

On 17 August 1945, an advance detachment flew in to Mingladon to prepare for the main move. A week later the HQ of the unit moved in, and technical and domestic sites were set up at both Mingladon and Insein about ten miles to the south of Mingladon. The technical site, because of lack of accommodation in the area, was a tented camp but the domestic site and admin block were hutted accommodation with running water and electricity, a very welcome facility after Barrackpore. The move was welcomed by all ranks and morale improved considerably. No less happy were the aircrew at the prospect of covering new and interesting routes.

Although still desperately short of tradesmen, a detachment was left behind at Barrackpore with F/O Wilding, DFC to complete the servicing of some aircraft still undergoing repairs and to liaise with 313 MU at Kankinara regarding freight. As if this wasn't enough to contend with, they also had to act as a maintenance and loading party to any of the unit's aircraft delivering or collecting spares and to co-operate when necessary with a detachment of 101 RSU from Agartala under the command of Flt/Lt F. B. Morley, their CTO.

In spite of the trauma of preparing for the move and the weather conditions, the unit handled just over one million pounds of freight and clocked up 778 flying hours up to that time.

The ground crews had been pushed hard with sixty-hour inspections and sundry malfunctions. The latter, strangely enough, contained a high proportion of tyre changes due to severe cuts caused by empty 'K' ration tins, of all things. Nevertheless, as always, they were immensely proud of the unit record and their own contribution.

Just prior to the move to Burma, the unit was called upon to take a Liberator (EV949) to be used for instructional purposes by No. 15 School of Technical Training to Bishnupur. The aircraft was in a very poor condition so the CO, Sqn/Ldr Touch, AFC, a very experienced test pilot, decided to do the job himself. Soon after take-off the oil pressure on No. 1 engine fell to the danger mark so to save the engine he feathered it. On entering the circuit at Bishnupur, No. 4 engine, whose boost had been fluctuating erratically, also decided to fade out with an accompanying smell of burning. This engine was also feathered immediately and the aircraft was quickly circuited on the two remaining engines and landed safely.

As far as Sqn/Ldr Touch was concerned, the aircraft was now delivered but to forestall any accident in the future, he had the aircraft recategorized as Cat. ES, suitable only for spares or ground instruction.

A second occasion when his skill was put to the test was when the pilot of a Mosquito (RF749), on a ferry flight to Agartala, felt violent vibration in the aircraft and thinking that the tailplane was coming adrift, selected the grass field some thirty miles short of his destination and made a wheels-down landing.

One of the unit Dakotas, again flown by Sqn/Ldr Touch, landed in the same field to enable F/O Blick, one of the Tech Es, and a de Havilland representative to carry out an inspection of the aircraft to try to locate the cause. It was found that the magnetos on the starboard engine were behaving erratically, causing the vibration and that the airframe was in fact OK.

The following day, Sgt Rogers and a working party were flown in by Flt/Lt Bilsland in a Dakota. Within a few hours the malfunction had been corrected and in the afternoon, Sqn/Ldr Touch was flown in to test the aircraft. Despite only having a total run of 900 yards and skirted by trees thirty feet high, he made a successful take-off — but only just — and the aircraft was flown 350 miles to 82 RSU at Dalbumgarh for further checks and servicing.

Although rapport has always existed between ground crew and aircrew in all squadrons, the relationship on this unit was to some extent unique, partly because of its unusual role and partly because many of the ground crew flew regularly with the Dakotas and felt in some way that they were part of the flying team. These were their aircraft and any problems were a joint responsibility. This relationship was strengthened by the fact that when not on flying duties, every officer had some other domestic duty, be it welfare, sports, education or just lending an ear to personal problems, which brought a closer understanding of each other's roles. In return for this personal interest, airmen felt part of the combined team and were prepared to do whatever was necessary to maintain the unit's commitments and image.

With the unit now firmly ensconced in its new surroundings, a large amount of welfare and sports amenities were obtained and Rugby, badminton, cricket and football competitions were held with neighbouring units. The unit football team, who had combined with 228 Group to form the RAF Bluebirds, were in fact in the Second Division of the Calcutta Services League and were the runners-up in the final of the GK Sports Shield, losing to Hastings Rovers 1–0 on the Calcutta football ground.

With the initiative and motivation which seemed to predominate over all RSUs, a very dilapidated wooden hall was commandeered and after some very enterprising work by the unit carpenters and some of the airmen, a canteen was opened. The unit now had its very own canteen for the first time in its career. A committee was formed and funds from Welfare were obtained to purchase goods. Furnishings were cadged or 'borrowed' from various sources. Gradually regular supplies, including American candy and Martin's cigarettes began to trickle in by courtesy of Mr Manterfield, a civilian welfare officer at AHQ Burma, supplemented occasionally by books and further gifts from the Overseas League of Friends in London.

Liberty runs to the Paramount Cinema at Insein and the ENSA concerts at the Garrison Theatre in Rangoon became a regular feature. The Adastral Cinema of 85 ASP, who shared the site, also allocated a number of tickets each week to the unit. Even the SNCOs, no doubt inspired by the efforts of the airmen, did wonders in the construction of their own mess, including, of course, the mandatory bar.

By the end of September, the unit also had its own chapel which was named St Andrews. The opening service and dedication were conducted by the Assistant Chaplain-in-Chief, Canon R. F. Diggle, MC. On the same day, 23 September 1945, the Secretary of State for War, Mr Jack Lawson, visited the unit on his way to Singapore and his aircraft was given a 100 per cent inspection.

Another important event that week, at least as far as F/O Wilding, DFC was concerned, was his wedding to Miss Barbera Livingson of Calcutta at St Thomas's Church, Calcutta.

The CO of the past five months, Sqn/Ldr Touch, AFC, was posted to No. 27 Beaufighter Squadron at Mingladon. His place was taken temporarily by Flt/Lt Markland, until Sqn/Ldr G. W. Topping, a Tech E, from 82 RSU at

Dalbumgarh, arrived to take over. His tenure was short-lived, for within ten days he was posted to No. 3 FEU and Flt/Lt Markland had once again to come off flying duties to take the chair, where he remained, alternating with Flt/Lt Wood, DFC until 10 December 1945 when he too was repatriated on age and service release. Flt/Lt Wood was to remain as CO until the unit disbanded on 31 May 1946.

Apart from its continued role in delivering spares to the forward areas, the unit was now helping with the evaluation of ex-POWs from Bangkok and Singapore as well as conveying an increasing number of VIPs to various destinations such as Singapore and Hong Kong.

With increased distances and flying hours, the number of engine changes also increased. In order to maintain continued serviceability, ground crews were again called upon to work all night, as they had done at Barrackpore. Their task was not made any easier by the repatriation of personnel under Class B and age and service releases now that hostilities had ceased. Many of the replacement personnel were relatively inexperienced as far as the working environment was concerned and the high number of skilled and experienced tradesmen leaving resulted in greater responsibility for the few remaining.

This shortage was further aggravated when, because of the long flights, it was decided to send detachments to Singapore and Hong Kong to deal with any minor malfunctions prior to the return trip of the aircraft. At the same time, although the Civil Government of Burma had now resumed control, it was found necessary to mount guards at night on the dispersals, due to an outbreak of pilfering by locals, no doubt intent on trying to recoup any losses suffered under the Japanese. This additional duty only served to add further problems to the unit's now fully stretched resources.

The supply of cargo began to diminish in early 1946 though there was a marked increase in the long hauls of passengers to and from Saigon, Singapore and Hong Kong. The urgency of maintenance eventually became less of a problem as aircraft from other units operating Dakotas were released. Spares, once at a high premium, became readily available; the need to make do and mend was over but it was too late to be of any real benefit.

The unit's activities were drawing to a close. The unit's strength was now down to sixty-eight officers and NCOs and seventy-three airmen, almost as many chiefs as Indians. On 31 May 1946 the unit was finally disbanded; those airmen who were not time-expired were absorbed into various MUs, either in India or Singapore.

The final paragraphs in the Operations Record Book of No. 85 Repair and Salvage Unit give little indication of the work which went into achieving such great results, but its motto of 'never fly an empty aircraft' was true to the very end.

Note: Although the designation of No. 1 Airborne Salvage Section had been deleted on 20 January 1945 and the unit disbanded in May, it was to re-emerge in November 1946 when the authorities at 390 MU at Seletar thought it would be a good idea to have an Airborne Section and allocated three Dakotas for the purpose.

Chapter 6

Nos. 101, 125 and 142 Repair and Salvage Units

On 22 January 1942 a signal from the Air Ministry was received by Flt/Lt P. C. Crowell, the OC of 75 MU, Manchester, posting him as OC 101 RSU on its formation.

On 20 March 1942 about 120 men embarked at Liverpool on the *Empress of Russia* and disembarked at Clairwood before being entrained for Durban to board the *Ile de France*. They arrived in Bombay on 20 May 1942 where they transferred to the SS *Yoma* and arrived at Drigh Road, Karachi on 28 May 1942.

As a unit they had little to do but kick their heels until a final policy decision was formulated. Not until 155 Squadron arrived with Mohawks from Peshawar on 1 July did 101 RSU commence to do any servicing of aircraft.

On 20 July 1942, it was decided to move the whole unit to Calcutta at an early date, as it had been proposed that the grass *maidan* and the adjoining Red Road would be an admirable site for an airstrip and workshops. It derived its name from the colour of its surface, not from any connection with a red light district. It ran parallel to the main street of Chowringhee and was approached down Old Court House Street, over the Great Eastern Hotel.

It was about the same width as a Hurricane wing-span but the camber of the road required some skilled steering because the concrete balustrades which flanked the road created a hazard to any aircraft veering from the centre line and wing-tip repairs became a regular feature of the unit's activities.

Aircrews waiting to scramble found a convenient crew room in the lounge of the Grand Hotel with all its amenities close by a link road.

As a preliminary to the move, the Armenian College in Kyd Street, quite close to the proposed site, was requisitioned on 11 August for domestic use. A month later on 7 September, the main party moved by train from Drigh Road to take up residence. Within twenty-four hours of arriving, the unit had its first salvage call-out when a Hurricane of 17 Squadron (BN684) crash landed on Red Road. Its pilot, Sgt A. R. Schwaighart, was tragically killed as the aircraft cartwheeled. While at Dum-Dum, one of 146 Squadron's Hurricanes (BH152) required urgent repairs following a glycol leak.

Within the first few weeks of arrival, without having time to settle in and with the minimum of equipment, the unit had salvaged three Hurricanes and a Blenheim as well as effecting repairs to six Hurricanes and a Hudson at Red Road, Alipore and Dum-Dum.

A signal requesting the highest priority for all Hurricanes to be modified for the fitting of jettisonable long-range tanks was received on 28 October. Unfortunately, many of the modification kits arriving from the Air Stores Park in Karachi were either damaged in transit or incomplete and the unit workshops had to set to immediately to rectify these deficiencies, using local resources where necessary, before the modifications could be carried out.

It was not long before the powers that be realized that sending out mod parties to these sites was impractical. Not only was it wasteful in man-hours but it depleted the unit's capacity for salvage work, so it was agreed that the aircraft would fly into the unit two or three at a time. The first squadron in for this mod was 135 Squadron. However, facilities at Red Road proved to be inadequate for this type of servicing so the PRU hangar at Dum-Dum was made available and a permanent mod party attached for the purpose of dealing exclusively with the work. Such was the urgency that a night shift was employed and the work proceeded round the clock with additional personnel posted in from the newly arrived 125 RSU.

The unit was to get its first taste of salvage in somewhat less than pleasant surroundings when they were called upon to salvage a Mohawk of 5 Squadron (BS735). This had crash landed several weeks previously at Naipit, a jungle island in the Sunderbans at the mouth of the River Hooghly. Enormous difficulties had to be overcome in getting the aircraft back to Calcutta because of the strong tidal currents in the vicinity and the complete absence of any local labour.

The excuse of the native 'crew' of the hired barges when called on to lend a hand was always, '*Hamara kham ne hai.*' ('It's not my job.') No amount of coaxing or threats would stir them into action. To make matters worse, the hostile environment was home to large cobras and giant crabs. It was a somewhat nerve-racking experience for anyone relatively new to India and not something one could readily get used to.

A similarly hazardous experience, this time with a different party, was the salvage of a Hurricane of 146 Squadron (BN214) which had crash landed near Contai. This was about eighty miles from Calcutta, some twenty miles south of Midnapore and during the height of a cyclone which caused huge floods in the area. The aircraft had to be dismantled in four feet of putrid water and carried in small sections for almost five miles before it could be loaded on to vehicles. The bloated bodies of villagers and animals which floated by as the crew worked were stark evidence of the disaster that had swept the Midnapore area.

As a consequence of this salvage, the unit received a letter from Air/Cdre Wilson, OC 224 Group, expressing an appreciation of the work carried out in such appalling conditions.

In common with many units at that time, basic equipment was at a premium and even though in the heart of the city and convenient for local purchases, they too soon found out that the local merchants were quick to exploit the scarcities and prices rocketed sky high.

Though heavy equipment continued to arrive by sea to the Kidderpore Docks, with the falling of the first bombs on Calcutta, thousands fled, leaving a dearth of coolies for unloading the ships. When a consignment of thirty much-needed bowsers arrived, they had to be offloaded by the unit personnel themselves, under the supervision of the white management staff and the Army.

As No. 101 RSU, it ceased to exist on 16 January 1943 when, under a Short Term Policy issued by AHQ, the unit was amalgamated with No. 125 RSU who had recently arrived in Calcutta. The new formation would be known as No. 1 (Fighter) Forward Repair Depot, still in the same quarters at the Armenian College with the airstrips on the *maidan* and Red Road. There were no officers on the strength of 125 RSU, so Flt/Lt Crowell would remain as CO, with P/O N. Taylor as Adjutant, P/Os A. G. Darroch, J. C. Boylan and R. A. Billson as Tech Es and the unit would be under the control of 226 Group.

During its brief existence as 101 RSU between 9 September 1942 and 16 January 1943, the unit had salvaged thirty-four aircraft of various types and repaired a similar number.

It had never been the intention that the *maidan* and Red Road should become a major centre for repairs and servicing, as well as dealing with salvage work, and the limited space began to create problems for the dispersal of aircraft. Although it had been proposed that four new hangars be erected on the *maidan*, progress by the Garrison Engineer was causing such grave concern at AHQ that fifty-six Hurricanes waiting for repairs and servicing were transferred to No. 1 CMU at Kanchrapara, despite the fact that their facilities were also at full stretch. It was simply a question of space and expediency to relieve the congestion of aircraft in Calcutta which also presented a target for Japanese air raids.

The unit strength was somewhere in the region of 500 officers and men. The billets at the Armenian College were stretched to the limit and some of the men were in billets in and around Calcutta reminiscent of the seaside guest-houses of Blackpool. The situation was becoming more acute as time passed, but according to the requisitioning authorities, they could find no buildings suitable for their needs.

In the meantime, to rub salt in the wound, three new huts were erected in the vicinity of Red Road to provide accommodation and messing for twenty-four RAF Regiment men who were to take over guard duties on the airfield and its approaches. The fact that this was done speedily by the Garrison Engineers in spite of the new hangars being incomplete, was brought to the immediate attention of the AOC, Air/Cdre L. M. Iles, CBE, AFC and Air/Cdre Mason, the AOA AHQ, when they chanced to visit the unit with Wg/Cdr Chacksfield.

It is surprising how 'scrambled egg' on a cap can motivate even the most dilatory admin paper-shuffler, for in a remarkably short time the hangars were complete and 'by coincidence' arrangements were made by the requisitioning authorities to take over St Thomas's School as additional accommodation for the unit.

At the same time, an approach had been made by the CO, now a squadron leader, to Brig. Williams at HQ 352 L of C, on the subject of improved dispersal areas contained by the strip and Fort William. The usual promises to look into the matter were given though never materialized.

Alterations were made to St Thomas's School and men moved in but within a week or so of settling down, the CO was informed, on 30 October, that No. 1 FRD (101 and 125) was to move forthwith to Singabil, some 400 miles away in Assam. The target date for the completion of the move would be 12 November and on completion of the move, the unit would absorb the 126 RSU attachment already at Agartala. It would, however, leave behind in Calcutta personnel and equipment corresponding to that which was already at Agartala. The purpose of this was to form the nucleus of a unit to remain in Calcutta and known as No. 1 Repair and Salvage Section. (This eventually became 134 RSU.)

In 101's second chapter of eight months as 1 FRD it had received for repair or servicing no fewer than 159 Hurricanes, salvaged twenty-nine more plus a Spitfire, a Hudson and several Mohawks, including a Mohawk of 5 Squadron (BB977), piloted by F/O Dick Tovey, which had spun into the ground near Agartala after an engine failure. The pilot was killed. This same aircraft had also force landed at Dum-Dum only a month previously with engine malfunction, again piloted by Dick Tovey.

On 2 November, the final preparations for this sudden and unexpected move were finalized by the CO and Wg/Cdr Bushe-Crawford of the RAF Movement Control.

Because of the problems involved in organizing a troop train to convey some 400-odd men, and partially for safety, it was decided to send the personnel in six drafts of about fifty men at two-day intervals on the normal train services. As an added safety precaution, the trade groups were also divided into separate parties. They were to travel to Goalundo, then by steamer down the Brahmaputra to Chandpur to pick up the train again for Agartala before being transported the final four miles by MT to Singabil.

For some reason, all the ground equipment would go under escort the long way round via Santahar to Bonapara then on the branch line to Tistamukh, across on the ferry to Bahadurabad, thence to Mymensingh and Tangi and over to Bhairab and yet another ferry trip, before arriving at Agartala. It was a slow and laborious trip and almost twice the distance.

All the MT and heavy workshop equipment was to go by an even more round-about route, by sea across the Bay of Bengal to Chittagong, followed by a two-day road journey on arrival.

It was now all systems go. The unit had an almost impossible task of packing and moving to Singabil in just twelve days. It was a task not made any easier as aircraft still arrived for repairs and personnel were hard pushed to keep abreast of the demand. To add further to the problems, personnel detailed to stay behind and carry on with the servicing often found that equipment they needed had been packed ready for shipment. Arguments occurred and tempers frayed with frustration. The upheaval was creating a general chaos.

On 5 November, just three days after the initial Movement Order, WO Bailey and an advance party of cooks, store bashers and admin staff, along with a number of enrolled followers left for Singabil to prepare the way for those who were to follow. By the time the second party arrived, the unit HQ had been opened. As far as AHQ were concerned, the target date had almost been achieved, the flow of 'bumph' could now commence. The fact that there was no equipment or transport made very little difference. Another flag could be pinned to the wall.

Meanwhile, the MT and heavy equipment had been held up at Kidderpore Docks because of an acute shortage of coolie labour. Although the remaining drafts still continued to arrive at Singabil, the ground equipment taking the long way round still had not arrived before the final party had left Calcutta. The situation was further aggravated when aircraft began to arrive for servicing. No doubt a signal had gone through indicating that the unit must be operational as it now had its HQ and Orderly Room organized!

Very little could be done. The 126 detachment at Agartala had hardly anything in the way of spare gear. Aircraft, other than those which only required minor checks, had to be stacked.

Finally, on 23 November, the MT arrived from Chittagong and was met by the CO who led the convoy of vehicles for the long and dusty two-day journey to Singabil. With the eventual arrival of the ground equipment, the unit began to settle down into something approaching an organized routine.

Instructions were received from 186 Wing that the unit would be limited to the maximum of ten-day repairs on aircraft; any that were estimated to exceed this schedule were to be put up for reallocation to a third line repair depot. Just how this would be accomplished is not quite clear. It can only be assumed that having done an estimation, the aircraft would fly on to an MU if the repairs exceeded the allotted time. Otherwise it would have been an enormous task to convey them by rail and river to Kanchrapara on the already overloaded rail system.

At the beginning of December, the CO was informed by Wing that a specialist unit, known as No. 3 Cylinder Block Servicing Unit, was expected to arrive direct from the UK and it would be located at Singabil under the control and supervision of 1 FRD. This type of unit, hitherto unknown on the Indian scene, duly arrived with Sqn/Ldr Elworthy, a Tech E from SEAAF, accompanied by Messrs Redfern, Morgan and Bradley, three civilian specialists from Rolls-Royce, plus a sergeant, two corporals and seven airmen who were to advise on the techniques and running of the unit.

As yet unaware of how they would be received by the local population at Singabil, airmen and enrolled followers had the additional task of mounting guard duties for the first time, though eventually they were to be relieved of this onerous task with the arrival of No. 4426 AA Flight of the RAF Regiment under the command of Flt/Lt Dutton.

A month later, having got used to being referred to as 1 FRD, in accordance with AHQ Order No. 11, the unit's number was again changed, this time to No. 142 Repair and Salvage Unit. It was to remain so for almost ten months, until October 1944 when No. 101 RSU, which was supposed to have ceased to exist, suddenly re-emerged with the arrival at Singabil of 350 men, to be temporarily accommodated at No. 9 RIAF before moving to Agartala.

To add further to the confusion, at the beginning of 1945, the unit's number was again changed, to No. 125 RSU, the unit which it had originally amalgamated with in Calcutta two years previously. Added to this, they would now also take over the servicing commitments at Kumbhirgram of 124 RSU based at Masimpur. They were moving to Tulihul to take over from 132 RSU, now moving down into recaptured airfields in the wake of the Army.

It is difficult to comprehend the thinking behind these somewhat fragmented arrangements, with detachments and attachments continually crossing each other's path. There seemed to be no clearly defined policy or strategy between Wings and Groups. The endless permutations must have left some personnel and equipment in a state of perpetual motion on the rail network.

Nevertheless, at ground level, work pressed on regardless and by the end of January the unit had handled 126 aircraft of varying degrees of servicing category, eighty-seven of which were Hurricanes, the rest being Spitfires, Beaufighters, Mosquitoes and Vultee Vengeances.

Flying became severely curtailed by the onset of the rains and perpetual fog. The camp was awash with deep mud. Roads in the camp became rutted and when they eventually dried out the ruts had to be filled in to make them passable again. Air tests became a matter of high priority when the opportunity presented itself and two further test pilots, F/O A. A. Crosse and F/Sgt Villa, arrived on attachment from No. 22 Ferry Control to help out the hard pressed P/O G. A. Hanson, the unit's only test pilot, who had formerly been with the Armament Practice School at Karachi.

On 3 March 1944, eleven Hurricanes of 60 Squadron returned to Agartala after sorties over Ramu, only to find that the runway had been blocked by a USAAF Mustang which had crashed, so they were diverted to Singabil to land in the dark at 1900 hours on a very muddy strip lit only by a single line of goose-neck paraffin flares, with everyone standing by, keeping their fingers crossed. Although log book comments suggest it was a very dicey situation, no mishaps occurred and the following day they staggered off the mud and took off for a remote airfield at Dergaon in northern Assam.

A week later, Singabil was hit by a cyclone that appeared without any warning. Before it had passed it had flattened over half the bashas, scattering debris far and wide and damaging several aircraft. Following in its wake came torrential rain and except for an odd day or two, the strip was unusable for almost three weeks, seriously curtailing the flying.

In spite of repeated requests for perforated steel planking to help solve the problem of flying in wet weather, the demands of forward airstrips exceeded the supply and Singabil was way down the list of priorities. Eventually, sufficient supplies did arrive to resurface the strip but, of course, only after the rains! In spite of the appalling conditions, a further 136 aircraft were received and returned after servicing, no mean feat considering they had to be worked on in the open, in parking bays surrounded by earth blast walls, the only protection from the unpredictable weather being tarpaulins or rush matting slung on rickety bamboo poles or amongst the mangrove trees.

One airman recalls a Hurricane being fitted with a new tail unit. It happened to be a fine day and was getting hotter as the day wore on, so it was decided to push the rear end among the trees to afford some shade. All went well and the tail was assembled. It suddenly dawned on the crew that they couldn't get the aircraft out from between the trees. No one dared cut the trees down so the whole unit had to be dismantled and started again. The Chiefie insisted that it was their own fault and they should carry on until the job was finished even if it took them all night.

Arrangements had been made in the meantime for the erection by a local contractor of some Bellman hangars on the Hurricane site with materials supplied by the RAF. Though he coped reasonably well with the brickwork, the lifting of the roof trusses was a different proposition and it took him almost two weeks, using bamboo scaffolding, to lift just two into position. As there were forty-five of these trusses, the war might well have been over before even one hangar was ready for use, so the unit decided to take over. By using a borrowed Lorraine crane from Agartala, they were swung into position in a matter of a few days and the hangars completed. They were a godsend and certainly made servicing a little more tolerable.

In common with many other units, spares were always in short supply, heavy reliance having to be placed on cannibalizing aircraft, although this was limited to Cat. E accidents in and around the airfield. As the unit's main occupation was servicing and not retrieving aircraft which had crashed out in the blue, these valuable sources were somewhat curtailed.

During a particularly bad patch with irregular deliveries from the MU, troubles began to be experienced with spares being already defective when they did arrive. Remould Hurricane tyres bulged on inflation, new fuel tanks were contaminated, long-range tanks were damaged in transit and there was the ever present problem of poorly balanced propellers.

As if these technical problems were not enough, a number of fires began to break out mysteriously on the domestic site. One burnt the cookhouse, dining halls and ration stores to the ground. When a fortnight later the Sergeants' Mess suffered the same fate, it was suspected that the fires were started deliberately. Although the locals had been reasonably friendly and quite willing to take advantage of the rupees they could squeeze out of the station and the men, there were signs of unrest in the district, largely due to Chandra Bhose and the activities of his Nationalist followers.

In an attempt to nip any further instances in the bud, an armed party went into Singabil and intimated that should any other fires or similar acts of sabotage break out, similar mysterious fires might start in Singabil. It seemed to have the desired result for no more occurred for the remainder of the unit's stay.

Sqn/Ldr Crowell, who had been the CO since the unit's formation in January 1942, was posted to No. 13 War Course at the ME Staff College. His place was taken by Sqn/Ldr Moody who naturally also took over Crowell's personal Harvard. This aircraft had been the pride and joy of the former CO and although it was supposed to be a communications aircraft, no one else was ever allowed to fly it unless accompanied by him. It was always kept 100 per cent serviceable by Geoff Lockwood and Fred Pears, ready for what was loosely described as a 'haircut run' to Calcutta. Strangely enough, on his return, his shattered appearance would usually indicate something other than a visit to a hairdresser.

With the new CO, there also arrived a WO Bujakowski, a Polish test pilot, who had been a civil pilot in pre-war China. Known by all and sundry as 'Boogie', he was a popular member of the unit although most thought he was slightly mad, especially when it came to air tests. On one occasion, while air testing one of the Harvards, he decided to 'shoot up' the Maharaja of Tripura's palace. As he did so, the cockpit canopy flew off nearly decapitating Fred Pears, the airman who had accompanied him. He was subsequently sent cap in hand, like a small boy asking for his ball back, to the palace to request its return.

Entertainment on the station was very limited. There was the usual housey-housey in the canteen and regular football matches. Liberty runs were usually organized to the Gremlin Theatre at Agartala for film shows arranged by the RAF Cinema Welfare Unit. On one occasion, an ENSA concert party was flown in from Sylhet and presented 'Love in the Mist'.

At a smilar concert given by Vera Lynn, the cinema simply couldn't accommodate the number of men who turned up. Anxious not to disappoint anyone, she had the piano hauled out of the cinema and placed on a 3-ton lorry and gave the concert outside.

Although there was a canteen with a dartboard and a gramophone, plus a tiny library of battered books, there was no church at Singabil. With typical RAF enterprise and ingenuity, one of the bashas was converted, using anything that could be scrounged from the scrapyard and decorated with whatever coloured dope was available. It became known as St Martin's in the Paddy Field.

Unlike Singabil, Agartala, where most of the servicing and repair activities of 101 RSU took place, was an all-weather runway, one of four in the Surma Valley capable of handling medium bombers and transport aircraft. It was well equipped with workshop facilities and the aircraft of the various squadrons were dispersed over a wide area in pens surrounded by large earth blast walls. Major servicing and inspections were carried out in bamboo and brick hangars.

It had the added advantage of a metre gauge spur line which ran from the Bengal Assam Railway into the camp and was a convenient means of transporting aircraft and spares to the ferry junction at Aukaura, for onward transmission to Kanchrapara.

The all-weather concrete strip was about 5,500 feet long, running from north-east to south-west, with a very large monsoon ditch at one end. The western half was flat but the eastern half had a dip about a third of the way along its length and approaching from this end was like landing up the brow of a hill and rather hazardous. Ground crews watching the aircraft take off and disappear from view into the dip would keep their fingers crossed until they came into sight again at the other end of the strip.

With about fifty operational Hurricanes, Beaufighters and Dakotas on station, with yet more to follow when the Americans came in, it was inevitable that there would be an increase in accidents and malfunctions. Many would occur with tragic results, some were simply overshoots that finished up in the large ditch at the end of the runway. This was the case with Sgt Sweet of 60 Squadron in Hurricane KX115, who survived with little more than bruising but he was tragically killed in action the following year.

On another occasion, a Beaufighter of 27 Squadron swung on landing and collided with the crash tender, cutting itself in two in the process, one half demolishing the Duty Pilot's hut. The aircraft, crash tender and hut were all categorized Cat. E.

Hardly a day passed without some incident or other and the expectations of worse to follow were not without foundation when the Dakotas of 31 and 62 Squadrons moved out to Comilla and their place was taken by the Curtiss Commandos of the US Combat Cargo Group who seemed to have a complete disregard for Air Traffic Control and would land at will from whichever end of the runway seemed appropriate at the time.

On one occasion their brashness created real panic stations with red flares fired left, right and centre when a Beaufighter of 27 Squadron was confronted by a Curtiss Commando making a similar approach from the other end of the runway. Fortunately the Beaufighter managed to open up and veer away from a head-on collision.

On 6 April 1943, the strip was attacked with HEs, anti-personnel and incendiary bombs by eighteen Army 97s, escorted by a dozen fighters. Very little damage was done to the runway and it was serviceable again within hours. However, the raid accounted for one Beaufighter, a visiting USAAF Lightning, two petrol bowsers, a tractor, its only motor cycle and burned out the Flight Office, the watch-tower and stores. Only two of the squadron personnel were injured with shrapnel but sadly twenty-five Indians were killed and fourteen injured.

The monsoon ditch, and in particular the dip in the runway, were still claiming victims in rapid succession, not least of which were Mohawks of 5 Squadron for whom it seemed to have a fatal attraction.

By this time, apart from servicing the fighters, the unit had established a reputation for the repairs and major overhauls of the Dakotas of 31, 62, 117 and 194 Squadrons, with the occasional Liberator and Wellington thrown in for good measure.

After the dropping of the 'Bomb' and the surrender of the Japanese on 12

September, everyone assumed that the work of the unit was now over and that they would be disbanded and sent home. Their optimism was short-lived when on 16 October 1945, a signal was received from HQ BAFSEA ordering the unit to Calcutta lock, stock and barrel by the 24th, prior to proceeding to Singapore. Following the Movement Order came a message of congratulations from Air Headquarters on the work they had done.Although the letter gave some satisfaction at being recognized, the intended move was shattering news and morale which had gone sky high with the cessation of hostilities, dropped to an all-time low.

Apart from the blow of having to move over 2,000 miles away, the unit had only eight days in which to organize their affairs. There were units in the Chittagong and Cox's Bazar area, some as far south as Mingladon. All these detachments were given instructions to drop everything which could not be repaired in a couple of days and to prepare reports on conditions for any unit that was to take over their tasks and return to Singabil at short notice. Similarly at Agartala, a number of aircraft were in the final stages of repair, including a Liberator with chronic engine problems, one awaiting air test and several other assorted aircraft as well as ten turrets which had been presented to the unit by 290 ASR for packing and dispatch.

In spite of the problems that the sudden Movement Order must have created, HQ sent further signals emphasizing the need to be in Calcutta by the 24th.

At Agartala all the work was to be taken over by 136 RSU and all the ground equipment was to be transferred to that unit. Meanwhile, back at Singabil, all serviceable aircraft had been flown out, either to squadrons or to Kanchrapara to await relocation. All that was left was the ground equipment and assorted aircraft in various stages of repair, including Spitfires, Hurricanes, a couple of Vengeances and a Beaufighter. These were ordered to be struck off charge and scrapped. Under any other circumstances, such an order would have been the opportunity to gain some valuable spares but the Christmas tree concept was no longer appropriate.Squadrons had moved on, the MUs had no need of engines to rebuild and return to service; adequate supplies were now coming in from the UK. Even the Cylinder Repair Unit, seen as innovative only six months previously, was now redundant.

The area was becoming deserted and took on the air of abandonment. To add to the problems, the local inhabitants, sensing that a valuable source of revenue was coming to an end, began wholesale and systematic looting at every opportunity. Other than being extra vigilant, very little could be done to prevent it. No men could be spared for extra guard duty. The main preoccupation was packing for the move. The question was, what was to be done with the surplus and once valuable gear? The only answer was to destroy it completely, so a party was left behind to carry out this task and ensure that what was left would be of no real value to the locals.

Tyres were slashed or burned, instruments were stove in, brand new alkali batteries, so precious a few weeks before, had their cases broken and engines were simply smashed with sledge-hammers. Fuselages were 'dismantled' with axes or a couple of gallons of fuel were poured into the cockpits and set alight with a Very pistol. It was an official form of vandalism on a gigantic scale. One of the quirks of the wrecking exercise was that only a week previously an MT driver had been charged with negligence for backing into the mainplane of a parked aircraft. The same aircraft was now receiving the attentions of a wrecking crew.

Although the demolition was designed to ensure that no one profited from what was left, it was an almost impossible task. The mountains of tangled material would inevitably yield profit to anyone enterprising enough to lay claim to it.

An almost brand new American Case tractor, used for towing aircraft, was the only piece of equipment that didn't fall into the hands of the wreckers. The driver, told to drain off the oil and run it till it seized, could not bring himself to wilfully sabotage his pride and joy. He just abandoned it under a tree. No doubt the eventual finder couldn't have believed his luck and is probably running it to this day. Even more difficult to believe was that those selfsame airmen who had spent the previous three years repairing and salvaging aircraft, begging for spares and having to make do, should now be in the position of destroying equipment; a complete reversal of their former roles.

On 24 October, the appointed time of arrival, the unit was once again west of the Brahmaputra and back in Calcutta after two years in Singabil. The NCOs and airmen were quartered at No. 35 PTC and the officers at the Grand Hotel.

The unit equipment had arrived at Kidderpore Docks, was loaded on to rail cars and shunted to Kankinara where it was unloaded into the railway sheds and prepared for the voyage to Singapore. The MT had arrived on time and was sent to Alipore, the drivers remaining with them as there were no adequate and safe parking facilities in Calcutta, much to their disgust.

Although the unit had sweated blood to get to Calcutta as ordered, 35 PTC could or would not give any date for actual embarkation. All the unit equipment had been handed over to No. 54 EU for loading on to the *Ocean Vespa*, including the personal kit of the airmen. This was to cause an uproar, especially as an ACSEA order had said the unit was not to embark without personal kit. However, 54 EU must have given a more persuasive argument to HQ and their insistence that personal kit should be loaded was upheld, though no reason was given.

On 10 November, all the enrolled followers were posted to other units, leaving the strength at ten officers, four WOs and SNCOs, 170 BORs and 110 IORs. The living conditions at 35 PTC left something to be desired. They were overcrowded and somewhat squalid. The men were disgusted and whilst prepared to accept basic living conditions in the back of beyond, were not prepared to tolerate such conditions in a big city.

WOs and SNCOs were quartered and messed along with the men, irrespective of rank. There were constant complaints about living conditions in general and daily complaints about the food and the conditions in which it was served.

There was a near mutiny when the whole unit, as one man, refused to accept a meal as served. The CO of 35 PTC investigated the matter and as a result there was an all round improvement in both the quality and the conditions. However, this temporary appeasement did little to improve the general standard of the transit camp and before long it began to decline again.

There was still no indication of when the unit would move. The men had little more than what they stood up in because of the insistence in kit being sent ahead. They were beginning to get angry and frustrated, almost to boiling point and it would have taken very little to have created quite an ugly situation.

On 20 November, after the unit had been kicking their heels in this sordid situation for almost three weeks, a signal, M463, was received from HQ 223 Group authorizing the disbandment of the unit but as the Movement Orders could not be changed and the equipment had gone anyway, they would proceed as planned to Singapore and disband there. Following this signal, instructions were received from 35 PTC that nine officers, three WOs, 110 BORs and fifty-five IORs were to stand by for embarkation on HMT *Derbyshire*.

Sixty of the airmen, a WO and an officer had been repatriated as time-expired, as well as some of the IORs, and as the unit was now reduced in numbers it was to go in two groups. No. 1 party embarked on HMT *Derbyshire* along with some Army personnel on 21 November and arrived at Madras on the 24th.

Although the vessel was not filled to capacity, complaints immediately began to arise about conditions on board. This was further aggravated when on arrival at Madras, large numbers of other personnel also began to embark. This was just too much for the airmen who had already had enough of sordid conditions and being treated like cattle. As a protest, along with all the NCOs, they walked off the ship and gathered on the quayside to be joined by other units in sympathy, all refusing point blank to stay on board until conditions were improved.

Being addressed by the ship's captain who implied that charges of mutiny could be brought against them if they didn't return to the ship immediately, did little to improve the tempers of the men, especially when the threats were from a naval officer. Even when about twenty officers went ashore and talked to the men in small groups about their grievances it had little effect on their mood. Finally a group captain from RAF HQ Madras addressed them and after promising that conditions on board would improve, everyone reluctantly boarded the ship shortly before it was due to sail. One of the unit officers, F/O Coltart, was appointed troop deck commander in order to keep the peace and there were no further incidents.

A week later, No. 2 party embarked on HMT *Rajula* at Kidderpore Docks whilst the MT party plus the escorts embarked on the SS *Ikauna*. During the loading, the CO's car was dropped in the harbour and was never seen again. Whether it was accidental or done as a protest is not known.

The *Derbyshire* docked ten days later at Singapore and the party proceeded by road to Seletar. The Rajula arrived on 6 December and No. 2 party was also conveyed by road to join the rest of the unit. When the SS *Ikauna* finally arrived a week later, in spite of having an MT escort on board, it was found that wholesale looting of equipment had taken place. Most of the cases had been deliberately smashed, the contents either ruined or missing. Some of the cases had not even arrived and it was apparent they had never even been loaded at Kidderpore in the first place.

The *Ocean Vespa* must have done a cruise of the Bay of Bengal for it didn't turn up till much later. When this too was finally unloaded, the amount of kit missing was beyond belief. Many of the men's possessions had disappeared; precious souvenirs, presents for home, letters, etc. had vanished for ever. The dogmatic insistence of 54 EU in not allowing airmen to carry their own kit had proved a bonus for the locals who had certainly taken advantage of the departing servicemen.

At Seletar, an Orderly Room was set up to deal with all the necessary documentation and the unit commenced to disband. With few exceptions, all ranks were absorbed into the recently formed 390 MU. The unit had now passed into obscurity and was merely one further statistic, another coloured pin which could be removed from the map. Apart from a few lines in the Operational Record Book of the unit, there was no farewell thanks or appreciation for their efforts:

> This is the end of the historical record of 125 RSU, recorded with some regret, which for three hard years has carried on the task of supplying aircraft from one of the world's most difficult climates and at a time when Great Britain's strained resources, manpower and materials received priority on other fronts.
>
> From the time when the unit arrived in India in September 1942 until the end of the war on August 15th 1,510 fighter aircraft had been sent to squadrons after passing through our hands for overhaul or repair.
>
> We are not without pride in this achievement.
>
> (signed) F/O Coltart

What is so difficult to comprehend about this unit and the variance in numbers, and in particular the effective dates of the changes, is they all seem so contradictory. In spite of the final entry being as 125 RSU, the message of congratulations which had appeared on the notice-board, dated the very day that the unit was ordered to move to Singapore, addressed to No. 101 RSU clearly highlights one of the many discrepancies of identification that beset not only this unit but many others which suffered the same inconsistencies during their life span.

Chapter 7

Nos. 122 and 143 Repair and Salvage Units

Although with less than adequate facilities, 60 RSU based at Kanchrapara was still potentially the only active Repair and Salvage Unit in India.

Singapore had fallen, followed by the evacuation of Rangoon on 7 March. The Japanese now had a firm foothold in Burma and were driving north to Lashio. On the face of it, the threat to India seemed fairly imminent and its defence would rely heavily on air power. The very nature of the activity and the vast area covered by any eventual sorties would mean that one salvage unit could not possibly cope with such a projected increase in the volume of work.

On 8 February, about thirty men arrived in India aboard the RMS *Andes* following the breakdown in Durban of their troop-ship, the *Duchess of Athol.* They were to form the nucleus of No. 1 Repair and Salvage Unit, with the suffix (India) in order to distinguish it from No. 1 RSU serving in Europe. It came under the direction of 226 Group, Maintenance Wing, Bengal.

They arrived at Asansol, about 120 miles from Calcutta, after a train journey which could hardly be described as comfortable, in carriages that at best were more befitting the conveyance of cattle, and lasting some ten days, broken only by a brief stay at the Jahat Regiment barracks at Bareilly. Met at the station by transport, they travelled some three or four miles along what was loosely described as the Grand Trunk Road which ran between Calcutta and Delhi.

It was a flat, featureless area on the site of a disused brickworks not far from the busy coalmines of Ningah. No accommodation had been made ready. There was only a mountain of rolled-up tents waiting to be erected. Sanitary arrangements were primitive, just trenches surmounted by the familiar 'thunder boxes' with water having to be obtained from a well at the nearby coalmine. Meals were prepared in a field kitchen and eaten alfresco in whatever shade was available to afford protection against the sun and the ever-present kite hawks waiting to pounce.

The 'airfield' was simply flat, open ground, suitable only for light aircraft and was still in the process of being improved by hundreds of coolies, both men and women, digging and levelling by hand the parched earth and removing hundreds of tons of soil by the basketful to the side of the projected runway. These large banks of earth were to be the cause of quite a few aircraft mishaps in the months to follow. The airstrip was consolidated by giant concrete rollers hauled by coolies, the earth being wetted by an endless stream of natives carrying large *chattis*.

With little to do as far as maintenance of aircraft was concerned and few tools to do it with in any case, the airmen were expected to lend a hand. This seemed an odd waste of manpower when vehicles could have towed the rollers far more efficiently. It was as if Air Headquarters, still staffed by the old school of Empire days, had failed to recognize the real urgency of the situation and although native labour was relatively cheap, airmen in the King's pay could not be allowed to be idle and get into mischief.

The heat was horrendous, at times reaching temperatures of 120 in the shade. Nevertheless, within a week or so, the strip was deemed serviceable enough to receive aircraft for servicing.

Slowly the unit began to get more organized: workshop tents were set up, trade sections began to appear though there was still a dearth of tools available. A compressor for the plug bay had been obtained from a local contractor who had been given the option of either selling it at a fair price or having it commandeered for the war effort. Needless to say, he sold it.

By early May, the influx of aircraft really began to escalate. 60 Squadron, who had re-formed at Lahore after seeing action in Singapore and Burma, had flown in with their Blenheims under the command of Wg/Cdr C. B. Wallis, DSO, who was tragically killed in a fatal accident at Dum-Dum when the port engine of his Blenheim (Z7647) failed and he swung off the runway and collided with a steamroller being used on the airfield. 113 Squadron, also with Blenheims, had come in from Fyzabad as well as 'Wimpies' of 99 Squadron from Ambala and some Lysanders of 20 Squadron based at Jamshedpur plus sundry Tiger Moths and other Comm Flight aircraft for servicing.

With this increased activity, it was inevitable that the number of accidents and malfunctions would also grow, not only on the strip but in the surrounding region. More and more personnel began to be posted in to deal with the upsurge of work. Many of them were airmen who had been evacuated from Singapore and Java, which were now under Japanese domination. Airmen were having to work flat out from daybreak until noon with a break of a couple of hours because of the intense heat, then they would carry on till almost dark.

Asansol was very prone to dust storms which covered everything and everyone. Dust mixed with sweat ran in muddy rivulets down the faces of the airmen, making them almost indistinguishable from the locals. On 11 May, Mother Nature, not content with what she already provided in the way of discomforts, pulled a cruel stroke. Without any Met warning one such storm developed into a violent cyclone. It lasted about ten minutes with torrential rain that stung the face, accompanied by hailstones as big as eggs. Although personnel endeavoured to secure all the aircraft, they were hampered by simply not being able to stand against the wind.

The devastation left in its wake was indescribable. Aircraft were flung about like leaves in the wind, six Blenheims of 113 Squadron were damaged, some seriously. One which broke away crashed into a Wellington of 99 Squadron which had only just been repaired and was waiting for an air test. A Blenheim of 60 Squadron (V5513) which had recently been serviced and was awaiting air test was damaged while a Hurricane was lifted clean off its trestles and tossed to the ground. It was a heartbreaking sight and was to take four months' work in field conditions to rectify the damage of a ten-minute freak storm.

One airman had particular cause to remember that day. A Tiger Moth had been 'borrowed' by the CTO from the Comm Flight and was used as a 'hack', locating crash sites, fetching spares, etc. On this particular day it had flown to Ranchi to pick up some bits and pieces. Accompanying the pilot was Stan Charman. On the way back, he happened to look over his shoulder and spotted a dark swirling cloud rapidly approaching. He told the pilot who made haste for the airfield at Asansol. Landing quickly, they both jumped out and ran to the dispersal to warn everyone of the impending storm, but they were too late. It struck before anyone could prevent any damage.

When the storm finally abated, they went back to where they had left the Tiger Moth. It was miles away from where they'd landed and was a complete write-off. It had been lifted and thrown like a paper dart on to its back, its wings were crumpled and the undercart buckled. It was a sad sight and a rather ignoble end to what had been a very useful workhorse.

Although the unit had only been in existence a relatively short while, the prang locations began to look like a Thomas Cook's itinerary.

On 4 May, a Lysander (N1315) developed engine trouble at Barka Kana near Ranchi in Bihar Province. It gave an opportunity to use a newly acquired Queen Mary for the first time and the aircraft was recovered by Cpl Brady and party and returned to Asansol. A week later one of the first of the 60 Squadron Blenheims (Z7990, 'Grumpy') piloted by Lt Beesley (SAAF) developed engine trouble and crashed four miles north-east of Asansol, injuring the crew, but was recovered successfully. A few days later another Lysander of 20 Squadron (P1732) had an engine failure at Jamshedpur and was brought back by road five days later.

As this recovery party came in, so another was dispatched to salvage a Wellington of 215 Squadron (DV576) which had force landed on a bend of the Brahmaputra River at Tulsa Bari about twenty miles from Dhubri over the border in Assam. Because of the distance, it entailed a journey by road and rail. Tragically, during the salvage in the river, one of the team, LAC Dodds, was drowned. He was the fifth man to die from unnatural causes in the past ten days, thousands of miles from home and in places they hadn't wanted to be in in the first place.

With the rout of the British and Indian forces in Burma by the middle of May and the Japanese continuing their thrust further north, so the raids on their supply lines increased. With the additional aerial activity, the number of crashes rose, putting a further load on the already stretched resources of the unit.

By this time, the unit's number had been changed to 122 RSU. What lay behind the change in numbers is difficult to understand. There appeared to be no logical reason. The first anyone knew that they were now members of a different unit was when it appeared in DROs. The resultant chaos in delivery of mail seemed of little concern to those who made the changes. Even less thought was given to the change causing delays in indents for equipment. Pending trays became fuller than out trays and much needed spares were often held in limbo for weeks awaiting identification of units.

Nevertheless, the change of identity did not lessen the ever-increasing workload. The lack of communication, however, often created unnecessary and duplicated salvage journeys, as in the case of Sgt Smith and a party who set out from Asansol to repair a Blenheim of 113 Squadron (Z7987) which had force landed at Baigachi, only to find that 60 RSU had already been to the site and completed the repair.

A similar occasion arose over a Blenheim (Z9613) which had been reported as having landed at Asansol a month previously to await repairs. Urgent signals demanded to know where it was. The unit knew nothing about it nor could they find it. It was subsequently found at Kanchrapara, perfectly serviceable having been kept in reserve as a unit hack ready for immediate use should the Japs land in Calcutta. It was a somewhat fanciful idea, but Fred Rogers, one of the fitters, recalls quite clearly that every time a query was made as to its state, the F/Sgt i/c always found an excuse to put it unserviceable.

So far, the unit's main occupation was the salvage and continuous repair of Blenheims. They were elderly and tired, effectively worn out before they arrived. They had been in operation in Europe, the Middle East and at the defence of Singapore before finally retreating from Rangoon into India. By the end of the year, forty-three Blenheims had needed either major repair or were written off completely.

In point of fact, it is extremely doubtful if any of these aircraft could still be classified as original. They still looked like Blenheims but the number of transplants made their pedigree open to question. Credit for this technical cross-breeding must go to the salvage unit for their ingenuity which sometimes was stretched to the limit. There were times, of course, when all the hard work and enterprise were of no avail and it was quite disheartening to see or hear of an aircraft which had probably only been repaired a day or so before being brought in. This was the case with a Blenheim of 34 Squadron (Z7490) which had force landed at Ondal, was brought back, repaired and made airworthy, only to be written off a few days later at Asansol. Even a Tiger Moth of 221 Comm Flight (Z-02), piloted by P/O Richard de Mestre on an air test following servicing, suffered the same fate when it dived into the ground from a hundred feet at the east end of the runway. The pilot suffered a broken leg whilst his passenger, LAC McKeon of 113 Squadron, lost an eye.

By the middle of June the monsoons had begun and the heavy rains increased the difficulties of servicing and salvages.

The CO, Sqn/Ldr Lockhart, on assessing a Blenheim of 34 Squadron (Z7976), piloted by Sgt Cecil, discovered it had crashed in the bed of a tributary of the river at Sainthia. Unless it was salvaged quickly it would be submerged in the rising waters. As it was, three rivers had to be crossed in order to effect the salvage and, for the first time, the front-wheel drive winch vehicles which the unit had recently acquired, proved to be invaluable and the aircraft was recovered successfully. Unusually, because of the acute shortage of airframe and engine fitters, an 'instrument basher', Sgt Shrives, was i/c the salvage.

There were occasions when a party might go out to salvage one aircraft and come back with two.

F/Sgt Webb, accompanied by Phil Sansum and five others were detailed to salvage a Blenheim of 113 Squadron (B9801) which had force landed at Gafargaon, about twenty miles from Dacca. When they arrived at the site, it was found that the Blenheim had landed on the dry mud flats of a tributary of the River Banar. It was on its belly. The blades of one prop had folded with the impact, the other had sheered off.

The monsoons had broken in Bengal and it was a matter of extreme urgency that the aircraft be salvaged or removed to high ground before the river became flooded. Work commenced almost immediately to remove the mainplanes which posed no real problems and they were dragged above the high water mark. Sheer legs and block and tackle were set up, the port engine was removed and dragged to safety. However, during the course of removing the remaining engine, the monsoon broke with a vengeance and before the crew had time to complete the dismantling, the aircraft was almost submerged and the job had to be completed by working chest high in murky water.

With the flood waters came the inevitable flotsam. All seemed attracted like a magnet to the artificial island created by the aircraft in mid-stream. Every day the crew had the unenviable task of continually having to clear away bloated carcases and vegetation from the fuselage as they worked. Men were having to dive continually under the aircraft to disconnect fittings before the engine could be finally dragged ashore along with the sheer legs.

The river was almost in full spate and it looked as if the aircraft would be swept downstream with the strong current. To prevent this from happening, lines were attached and coupled to the winch vehicle in an attempt to drag it nearer to the bank of the river. Try as it may, the winch could make no impression on the waterlogged fuselage. Its wheels would not grip on the soggy ground. All it could do was to act as an anchor and prevent the aircraft from being swept away until some alternative means of getting it ashore could be found.

Someone, probably one of the many native onlookers who had gathered to watch the activities, had the bright idea that elephants from a nearby factory might succeed where mechanical devices had failed. With nothing to lose, F/Sgt Webb negotiated the loan of four fully grown animals complete with their own mahouts and pulling chains. Unperturbed by the swirling waters and almost as if it was a commonplace occurrence, the elephants, accompanied by shouts of encouragement from all the onlookers, slowly began to haul the aircraft from its watery grave until it was finally on solid ground.

From then on it was a comparatively simple task to complete the dismantling and loading on to gharries, aided by local labour. Under normal circumstances, the loaded vehicles would have been driven directly on to flat cars at the nearest rail link for shipment back to Kanchrapara. In this instance, however, a message had been received that a Wellington of 215 Squadron (BB514), piloted by Sgt A. N. McClean had blown up in mid-air just four miles south-east of Gafargaon after taking off from its base at Pandaveswar. As the vehicles would be needed for this second salvage, the Blenheim had to be offloaded on to the rail cars.

When they arrived at the site of the Wimpy prang, there was very little in the way of salvageable items and what remained was scattered over a wide area. Only the engines were recovered. The fuselage was little more than tangled metal. Of the six crew members very little remained that could be readily identified.

Around this time anti-British feelings were still running high; Chandra Bhose and Ghandi were still both striving for independence, one by militant means, the other by passive resistance and was fasting to death to achieve it. In Bihar State, around Patna, lawless mobs incited to violence by Bhose were rampaging, looting, burning down stations and tearing up railway lines and generally creating mayhem. Blenheims of 60, 34 and 113 Squadrons were sent out almost daily to patrol and protect the vital rail link. On one such sortie, a Blenheim of 60 Squadron (V5642), piloted by F/O Muller-Rowland had a very lucky escape when it hit a signal gantry during a low level run. It lost about five feet off its wing-tip but managed to limp back to Asansol and land safely.

Two other Blenheims on similar sorties were not so fortunate. On 18 August 1942, F/Sgt Stanley Goss of the RCAF, a US citizen and former member of 45 Squadron attached to 113 Squadron, suffered a malfunction and crash landed his Blenheim (T2245) not far from Kotihar. The crew survived the crash but were immediately surrounded by a mob howling for blood. As evidence of good faith they handed over their pistols, a decision that was to cost them their lives, for they were immediately set upon and beaten to death.

Twelve days later a similar fate befell the crew of a Blenheim of 113 Squadron (Z7943), crewed by F/Sgt Julian, Sgt Greaves and P/O Thwaite, a South African. Two accounts have been given as to their fate. One is that they were rescued by natives in a boat and murdered out of hand there and then. The second is that they managed to elude the mob and take refuge in a small wayside railway station at Rohias. The mob, having cornered them, apparently threatened the stationmaster who, fearing for his own life, allowed them to be taken.

So outraged were the authorities at these horrendous acts of murder that a party of Green Howards was sent to the scene. When they arrived, they were also confronted by a menacing rabble bent on trouble and they had to open fire to disperse them, killing some of the mob in the process. The patrol also razed a village as a reprisal and a warning against any future rioting and acts of violence against the British.

Because of the violent circumstances surrounding the two crashes, it was some time before arrangements could be made to ensure the safety and security of a salvage inspection. Eventually a team did go to the sites. It was led by P/O Sorrell who reported that one aircraft was submerged and the other hardly worth salvaging.

A month later, a salvage crew of twenty-four men and vehicles set out by rail from Asansol. Unloading at Patna, they went the remainder of the way by road. When they arrived it was evident that the salvage of the two aircraft was going to present something of a problem. The aircraft were on opposite sides of the river, so some of the salvage vehicles had to cross by ferry and drive to Parroha to the site of the first Blenheim, the intention being to use the winch vehicles to drag what was left of the aircraft to the railway for loading. Unfortunately the floods had breached the banks of the river and before any progress could be made, coolies had to be hired to repair the gaps in order to allow the transport to get to the site. What greeted the crew was an amazing sight. The aircraft had been torn to pieces by either the mobs or looters and was scattered over a very wide area. It looked for all the world as if it had blown up on impact. Very little, except for the engines, remained to be salvaged.

In the meantime, the other Blenheim presented a very different picture. It was partially submerged not far from a railway bridge which spanned the river. Obviously it would have to be winched on to dry land before any dismantling could be attempted.

Both winch vehicles were attached to the fuselage and began to pull but without much success. They could not get a grip on the soft ground and made no impression on the waterlogged aircraft. In spite of repeated attempts, it proved a hopeless task. The only alternative was to add sheer muscle power and after some negotiations over payment, some 150 coolies were recruited. Further ropes were attached and after much chanting and heaving, the aircraft was slowly and steadily hauled on to firm ground. On examination, it was discovered that large holes had been hacked in the fuselage and one mainplane in an attempt to conceal the aircraft by sinking it in the river, but without much success as one mainplane remained buoyant.

The crews immediately began to dismantle the aircraft. The only problem was how to get it to the railway line some fifty feet above their heads. There was no alternative but to seek the help of the railway authorities and get them to provide a mobile railway crane and load from below the bridge directly on to the flat cars brought in for the purpose. To get the engines and fuselage to the bridge two boats were hired and with improvised staging they were loaded and floated into position under the crane. During the entire operation, conscious of the fact that it was a very hostile area and that without a doubt, amongst the onlookers and hired coolies there may well have been many who had been involved in the massacre of both aircrews, weapons were carried with 'one up the spout'.

The remains of the murdered crews were never discovered although a skull, complete with teeth and fillings, was found not far from the site and taken back for possible identification.

One of the longest and most difficult salvage operations, thanks largely to the monsoons, was a B-52 which had crash landed in the River Adjai near Pandaveswar on 28 June. It was in the centre of the river with no road bridge in the immediate vicinity. Access was by a bone jarring drive across the railway bridge. Following a frantic operation lasting three days, the engines were finally dismantled and dragged ashore by the winch vehicles. It was not a moment too soon, for the following day the river rose rapidly and completely submerged the aircraft. Not until August had the waters receded enough to allow the recovery of the aircraft to be completed.

Not one single Blenheim V, or Bisley to use the correct name, of 34, 60 and 113 Squadrons escaped without mishap. Some were relatively minor malfunctions, others more serious. One aircraft had just been serviced and was being air tested when 'Tex', the pilot, decided to 'shoot up' the convent in Asansol. His aircraft hit the stone cross on the roof and brought down tons of masonry. Luckily, he managed to maintain control and land safely but the ground crew were not amused at having to carry out repairs caused by the escapade.

Sadly, human error was to cause the death of three aircrew of 113 Squadron on 11 October. Blenheim Z9598 was piloted by F/Sgt H. Peters, known as 'Joseph' because of his habit of wearing his multi-coloured dressing-gown wherever he went. Having been discharged from No. 65 Combined Military Hospital in Asansol after an illness, he was required to have his flying skills checked. During the first flight, accompanied by an observer and air gunner, he had to 'shoot up' the No. 1 Gun Site at the end of the runway. Unfortunately he misjudged the height and crashed into a tree. The aircraft broke up, the cockpit was sheered from the fuselage and landed some way from the main wreckage.

Two airmen, who were driving in the same direction, hurried to the scene to render help. What greeted them was a sickening sight. The observer and gunner had been catapulted from the aircraft and their clothing torn off. They had been physically joined together with the impact, the leg of one protruding through the body of the other. Still strapped in the cockpit was Joseph, dead, with his eyes wide open and without a blemish on his chalk white face. The following day three more coffins passed through the gates of Asansol Cemetery, bringing the total to nine in as many weeks, the term of 'Flying Coffins' being applied to Blenheims beginning to have some significance.

Up to this time, the technical skills of the unit had been concentrated mainly on Blenheims and Wellingtons with the odd Lysander and Tiger Moth thrown in but Lockheed Hudsons of 62 and 353 Squadrons now appeared on the scene. They had to be serviced and repaired by some tradesmen who had never even seen this aircraft before and expertise had to be gained in the field, conversion courses being unheard of. Their home base was at Cuttack, in Orissa and because their flight patrol paths were over the Bay of Bengal and the Sunderbans, their crash sites were usually in or near rivers and seldom with convenient access.

One aircraft of 62 Squadron, returning to base at Cuttack having aborted a raid on the Arakan coast because of engine trouble, jettisoned its bomb load in the Bay of Bengal and force landed on the dried-up bed of the Mahanadi River. The recovery party would normally have travelled the 300-odd miles in twelve hours on the Madras mail train but the rail authorities classified the load as goods. In consequence it took twenty-four hours and being shunted into sidings at various stations along the way.

Arriving at Cuttack in the early hours, the wagons were uncoupled and shunted into a siding to await the arrival of the RTO, a rather pompous captain who was obviously not expecting them and who went to great lengths to explain how the travel system should work.

After consulting the quarter-inch survey maps, which were useless, it was obvious that there was no way in which transport could get anywhere near the site, a fact which seemed to have escaped the notice of the CTO back at base. By dint of flannel and hinting at what an important function RTOs played in the recovery of aircraft, the captain negotiated the hire of a rather dilapidated launch and a barge from a local rice merchant. The salvage crew had 500 rupees impress money to pay, primarily, for the hire of coolie labour. The rice merchant wanted about this much to start with but the circumstances seemed to suggest that a great deal of local labour would be needed and require all the allocated cash. After a great deal of arguing and bargaining with the help of the RTO, he accepted a promissory note. Whether he ever got his money is another matter.

The vehicles were left on the flat cars in a siding and the salvage gear was loaded on to a barge which had seen better days, as had the launch with its tattered canopy strung on bamboo poles. The 'living quarters' stank to high heaven and were little short of a pigsty. Rather than share the squalor, all the chaps opted for the less smelly barge. The toilet facilities aboard the launch were, to say the least, primitive, comprising a precarious frame over the side. Using it would have required acrobatic skill which would have been a source of amusement, not only to the crew but the interested spectators on the banks. The brass *chattis* hanging on strings were for the exclusive use of the crew's ablutions. Finally, to the amusement of the onlookers, the convoy set off slowly down the river and finally arrived the following evening at Jagatpur Lock, the nearest point to the scene of the crash.

Fortunately, the site was not very far from the lock because the aircraft was Cat. E and unable to be repaired and flown out. It would appear that it had made an emergency landing on the dry mud flats, hit a soft spot or an obstruction and the undercarriage had collapsed. In skidding to a halt both props were bent, one mainplane crumpled and a considerable amount of damage done to the underside of the fuselage. The monsoons were imminent so, obviously, the salvage would have to be completed as quickly as possible before the aircraft was submerged.

Without winch vehicles a great deal of local labour would be needed. Fortunately, Eric West, one of the salvage team was born in India and spoke

Urdu and to him went the task of organizing the labour. The local babu, or headman, who could speak a little English, was bribed with 100 rupees, a small fortune by their standards, to control the labour. His badge of office was a large manufacturer's plate from the aircraft to hang round his neck and as a baton he used the aircraft's whip aerial. He accepted this authority with extreme enthusiasm and his zeal had to be restrained on more than one occasion.

As the river was quite shallow and safe at the edges, most days the blokes went in for a dip to cool off. One day, some of the chaps, seeing a flock of vultures on the river edge, went to investigate. On chasing them off, they found two bodies, both Indians, a man and a young woman. Rather shocked at the sight and not knowing quite what to do, it was decided to bury them. However, the babu didn't seem at all perturbed at the sight and explained that it was an accepted part of the Indian scene so they decided to leave well alone. It was a pretty nauseating sight to see the vultures back at work within minutes. Within a day, nothing was left except a pile of bones and some trinkets which the babu collected. He said he would offer them to the gods in the local temple. Perhaps he did.

One night they were roused by the sounds of shouting and footsteps running towards the campsite. Grabbing their weapons, they went outside to see what all the commotion was about. Pursued by a crowd of villagers was a native, stark naked and brandishing a large knife. Seeing the chaps standing there, he turned towards them. It looked as if it could turn into an ugly incident. There seemed to be no alternative but to fire some shots into the air to deter or calm the situation. Unfortunately, in the heat of the moment, someone must have fired low and he was hit by a stray bullet and dropped in his tracks.

Everyone suddenly stopped. There was a deadly silence, like the calm before the storm. No one moved, not knowing what to expect or what to do next. From amongst the crowd stepped the babu who explained that the man had gone berserk and killed all his family. He went to great lengths to explain the gory details and told the airmen not to worry. Had they not stopped the man, the villagers would have wreaked retribution and killed him anyway. The following day the local police appeared to make inquiries and take statements. That appeared to be the end of it except for reporting the matter back at Asansol.

A few days later the aircraft had been stripped of everything of value. With the added weight of the salvage, it was a very slow trip back to Cuttack.

Since the arrival of the Hudsons nearly three months previously, no fewer than seventeen required to be salvaged. One from 353 Squadron (FH338), piloted by P/O R. G. Hoyer, returning to base with a petrol shortage in bad weather, landed in the river near Salipur. It submerged in twenty feet of water and was never seen again. Another of the same squadron (FH364) suffered a tragic accident while coming in to land at Cuttack at the same time as six Hurricanes of 135 Squadron on their way from Vizagapatam to Dum-Dum were preparing to land for refuelling. As Sgt Hargreaves, the pilot of the Hudson, made his approach, one Hurricane (BG973) approached from a slightly higher altitude and they collided at 100 feet above the airfield. The Hurricane pilot managed to maintain control and was thrown clear as he crash landed. The Hudson dived into the ground. Three of the crew died instantly, the fourth died from his injuries later in hospital.

Tragically another of 353 Squadron (FH213) piloted by F/O D. C. Bhaj Deo with an Indian prince on board, trying to locate the airfield during a cyclonic storm and failing to receive diversion signals, flew into the ground at Tangi Lyacundi killing everyone.

One of the last three Hudsons to be flown in from England to join 353 Squadron (FH339) swung into an earth barrier at Asansol and gave the unit an opportunity for one-upmanship. On inspection it was found that the starboard fuel tank had been holed. The guns, ammo and pyrotechnics were removed and the salvage deferred for a while because of the fuel leak. The fuel tanks were an integral part of the wing and supposedly irreparable so a complete mainplane change would be necessary but none was available. After consultation with Mr Webb, the Lockheed representative in India, it was decided to attempt a repair *in situ.* It entailed removing a considerable portion of the skin to get at the damaged area. Within a couple of weeks the task was satisfactorily completed and the aircraft returned to service.

The civil disturbances created by Ghandi and Bhose's demands had not lessened and began to create problems for the unit. Apart from being stretched to the limit with aircraft repairs and servicing, armed guard duties had to be undertaken. Meanwhile the amount of work was still escalating. The unit had been in operation about six months and had already dealt with seventy aircraft.

One of the biggest flaps, not connected with anything so dramatic as aircraft, was when the Orderly Room wallahs discovered that ants were beginning to enjoy the taste of the all-important unit files. It invoked an urgent signal to HQ to expedite the delivery of the metal filing cabinets which had been on order from Godfrey & Boyce of Calcutta for six months. Such was the alarm that hallowed bumph was being destroyed without authority that the cabinets were delivered in a matter of days.

Because of the heat, chaps learned to move slowly to conserve energy. Not so one day in September when two Blenheims of 113 Squadron (Z7369 and Z9749) piloted by Sgt Taylor and Sgt McLennon, taking off abreast, bound for Agartala and a sortie over Burma, both bombed-up, touched wing-tips, crashed and blocked the runway. Both aircraft caught fire immediately but the crews managed to get out before the bombs and ammo went up. Debris and splinters went everywhere, liberally spraying everything in range including a Blenheim of 60 Squadron which was badly damaged by shrapnel. Never did so many people dive for shelter so quickly, conservation of energy forgotten. No spares could be salvaged from either aircraft.

The banks of earth piled alongside the runway were still causing problems. Not only did they create a dust cloud as aircraft took off, partially blocking the view of the following aircraft but they formed an impenetrable barrier for aircraft which had the misfortune to swing off in that direction. In one incident,

Chinese Air Force Vultee Vengeances were on their way to Dum-Dum and had put in to Asansol for refuelling. Within minutes they were taking off again, two abreast. On opening up for take-off and beginning its run, Z6864 swung into the earth bank and began to career out of control towards a group of airmen who were standing at the edge of the strip. As it veered past Glyn Edwards, the wing-tip missed him by a hairbreadth as he dived to the ground, whipping off his topi in the process. Onlookers felt sure that Glyn's head was still inside the topi as it bounced down the runway. The aircraft eventually came to a standstill in a stack of oil drums alongside the strip with its undercarriage collapsed and the prop sheared.

It was not until another relatively new aircraft suffered serious damage by this obstruction that someone decided to do something about it. The aircraft, a Hudson (V9188) which had only recently had a major service and was on its way back to Cuttack, suffered serious damage to its starboard side. The undercarriage collapsed, the mainplane and tail fin were crumpled, the prop bent and the starboard engine caught fire but the crash crew managed to get that under control. Thousands of pounds worth of damage had occurred within a week or so, not to mention the man-hours spent, for the sake of a few hundred coolies to clear the rubble at a rupee a day.

Although many of the crash sites were in the back of beyond with primitive living conditions, there were exceptions as Cpl Alderson recalls.

He and five airmen were detailed to salvage a Vultee Vengeance of 84 Squadron (AL917) which had suffered engine failure and crashed in a paddy field near Madhaiganj, about thirty miles from Asansol. They left Chapui around 0900 hours and arrived at the site around 1430 hours. Under normal circumstances they would either find a suitable campsite or hire a basha in the local village. In this instance they had a remarkable stroke of good luck. Geordie, one of the lads on the team, was acquainted with a member of staff at a paper-mill near Ranigangh, only a few miles from the crash site. When his son had been in the Army and stationed in England he had been shown hospitality by Geordie's parents. The father wished to return the goodwill and the whole salvage team were invited to share some bachelor quarters used by staff who were on night shift. The offer was readily accepted.

These bungalows had two bedrooms, two bathrooms, a large living-room, a dining-room and an outside kitchen. There was a bearer for each room and a shared *khanasama*. Each morning they would be woken with a cup of tea. The bearers would run a bath for them and lay out fresh linen and towels. An unopened tin of fifty Players cigarettes was provided every day for each of them as a gift from the mill. They breakfasted with the returned night-workers and joined them for dinner in the evening before they returned to work. As an added bonus, the wife of one of the staff asked each one in turn what his favourite after-dinner sweet was back home in England and went out of her way to provide this reminder of home.

The Chief Technical Officer at Asansol was obviously not aware of the sumptuous lifestyle the crew were leading but he had previously given permission to take advantage of any accommodation that was available provided it did not cost the RAF any more than the allowance allocated for the purpose, which was about three rupees a day (20p today). As it turned out, it didn't cost the RAF a rupee and the money saved was put to good use.

The job itself was a straightforward dismantling exercise and was not rushed unduly though they had no desire to outstay the welcome at the mill, however pleasant. After about a week, with the help of local labour, the aircraft was loaded on to a Queen Mary and dispatched to 327 MU at Cawnpore.

On another occasion, a salvage crew left Bishnupur to pick up another Vengeance at Giridih and on arrival were met by a representative of the local white community who invited them to make use of an empty bungalow which belonged to the nearby brickworks. Although they didn't have the benefit of a resident cook and bearer it was only necessary to think about breakfast and tiffin, for not long after settling in, the priest brought along invitations to dine at a different bungalow each night and to use their club at any time. Their hosts went out of their way to make them feel at home, wanting nothing in return other than news from England.

A third instance was when Roy Alderson had taken a party of twelve airmen, a Dodge truck, six-wheeled Studebaker and a low-loader to pick up a Wellington of 99 Squadron near Panagarh. Accommodation and rations for the salvage party had already been arranged for everyone at the base which was occupied by the 15th United States Air Corps, operating Liberators.

Arriving after a long, hot journey, they were allocated a basha complete with American style cots, a far cry from the sagging string charpoys which were usual for British troops. The food was unbelievable with a wide variety and plenty of it. Ice cream could be had by the gallon and rationing was a word they hadn't heard of. The most amazing sight, however, was what appeared to be a giant kit bag with a number of taps around its base suspended from a tree in the centre of the domestic compound. It proved to be a water container with a difference. It was kept ice cold day and night. This was achieved by typical American brashness in making special air journeys each day to Calcutta to collect blocks of ice. No doubt any flight plan would have been recorded as a special sortie! Their PX or canteen was even carpeted with rattan matting, in spite of the jungle surroundings, and provided the inevitable Coke and Hershey bars. When they finally returned to base, everyone was brought down with a bump.

Conditions in the original tented camp at Ningah had become far from satisfactory. The domestic facilities had been stretched to the absolute limit as more personnel were posted in so it was decided to move to Loretto Convent which had been commandeered for the purpose, along with St Vincent's RC School which was to house 113 Squadron and SHQ, whilst the equipment stores would be housed in a bungalow called Gillian House. The convent was a large brick building and although not designed to cater for a large influx of men, it was much cooler and to some degree more secure.

Cooking facilities still comprised the Brighouse trailer at the rear of the premises. The sanitary arrangements were not ideal, however, and in spite of repeated requests to the Asansol Municipal Authorities, no improvement was made and after a while conditions began to deteriorate quite rapidly. After consultation with the Garrison Engineer in Calcutta, it was agreed to create a purpose built camp at Chakulia near the village of Chapui and convenient for the airstrip on the north side of the Grand Trunk Road. By the middle of June the camp was completed and the men moved in, leaving the admin and stores at the school and Gillian House.

Four months later, in October 1942, they were to move again, this time to Kundulia, nearer the airstrip on the south side of the Grand Trunk Road. A move that was supposed to be the last. However, at the beginning of December there were rumours that some further reorganization would be taking place. Exactly what it would entail was not clear but the camp bearers, who always seemed better informed, were almost certain that not only was the move imminent but that the 'Yanks' would be taking their place. Although only hearsay, this suddenly seemed to have some foundation when, on 18 December, a large detachment of tradesmen were posted to Jessore, about 130 miles south-east of Asansol, to form No. 2 FRD. Three days later the Blenheims of 60 and 113 Squadrons also flew to Jessore to complete the formation of 167 Wing. This move was closely followed by the official news that in January 1943 122 RSU and a newly formed 88 RSU would amalgamate to be known only as Forward Repair Depot (Bomber) with a combined strength of 500 officers and men.

Prices in Asansol escalated sky high almost overnight. Whether it was due to the possibility of the reduction in revenue by the departure of masses of men or the prospect of the huge sums from the free-spending Americans if they did take over, is not certain.

The weather by now had become almost intolerable with temperatures reaching 120 in the shade. Men with heatstroke were being rushed to No. 65 Combined Military Hospital in Asansol to be packed in ice. Sadly, some did not survive, including WO Hopkins who died of a heart attack before reaching the hospital.

To add to the miseries, Mother Nature struck again without warning, as she had done ten months before. Though mild in comparison to the previous storm, three Wimpies, six Blenheims, due to join their squadrons at Jessore, a Hurricane and a Hudson had their fuselages and control surfaces damaged by hail.

The rumours became a reality when, towards the end of 1943, it was decided that 122 RSU would be renumbered 143 RSU and move *en masse* to Bishnupur, about fifty miles south-east of Asansol, to join forces with 326 MU. On 7 December 1943, F/O Nolan and seventy-eight flight personnel, accompanied by WO Webb and forty-four enrolled followers moved by road to Bishnupur, leaving the site at Chapui at 0820 hours and arriving at 1400 hours. Three days later, F/O Davies arrived with the remaining transport and the flight personnel arrived the following day by rail.

Within hours the unit was in full spate. The primary aim was now to be the major servicing and modification of aircraft flown in for the purpose, in conjunction with 326 MU. The salvaging of aircraft, other than those in the immediate vicinity was now of secondary importance. The Blenheims had more or less left the scene and the majority of work was on Vultee Vengeances of 82 Squadron based at Madhaiganj, about forty miles to the north, along with Beaufighters of 27 Squadron at Agartala and 177 Squadron at Feni, with the occasional Wimpy of 99 Squadron stationed at Jessore thrown in for good measure. By the end of December, three weeks after commencing operations, the unit had dealt with eighteen Vultee Vengeances, seven Beaufighters and five Wimpies.

A new CO, Sqn/Ldr G. M. Tiffin, arrived from 126 RSU at Chittagong to replace Sqn/Ldr R. D. Briggs who had been posted to the newly formed 132 RSU at Barrackpore. In mid-December valuable hours were taken up for 'bull shine' pending an inspection by Air/Cdre Garrity, Gp/Capt Blockey and Gp/Capt Benson. They had already had a visit from Gp/Capt N. L. Fisher a few days before and were not amused at another interruption.

So intense became the workload that men were working twelve hours a day and simply could not be spared to marshal and deal with the increasing number of visiting aircraft. It was decided to form an R & I Flight, comprising three test pilots, a WO i/c, six NCOs and twenty-two airmen, to deal specifically with these visitors. In the first five months they had handled no fewer than 182 aircraft of different marques and categories.

Unlike Asansol, there was a pukka parade ground complete with that symbol of military occupation, a flagpole, which, apart from its regulation ensign, at various times had pyjamas, dhotis and socks suspended from it until, as a protest against the bull and PT initiated by the SWO, it was chopped down one night by persons unknown. Although an inquiry was made and the pole replaced, PT and square bashing ceased, except on special occasions, and the WO was posted, probably to the North-West Frontier where peacetime aura and bull still prevailed.

By the middle of June 1944, Mosquitoes began to appear on the scene to stretch the technical know-how of the unit even further. Because of their all-wood construction, these aircraft were presenting problems in the Far East with the failure of the adhesive bonding breaking down through heat and humidity. For some reason, Americans referred rather unkindly to this aircraft as the 'bamboo bomber with a built-in swing'.

Evidence suggested that a pilot with experience of Mosquitoes was needed for air testing after servicing. Accordingly, Flt/Lt R. A. Campbell, a Canadian of the RCAF, and F/Sgt Pridmore, a navigator, were attached from RAF Poona. Tragically, Flt/Lt Campbell was to die during an air test in a Mosquito less than a month after arriving at Bishnupur.

One of the airmen on 143 RSU had good cause to remember that day. Had fate not stepped in, he would not have been able to recount the incidents surrounding the tragedy. It was Tuesday 10 October 1944. Cpl Charles (Lofty) Courtney, an F2E, and his crew had just completed an engine service on an aircraft and were waiting for the next detail. It was blisteringly hot and the only shade was provided by a large mango tree. Glancing up, they noticed that an approaching aircraft was trailing white smoke from one of its engines. It made a successful dead-engine landing and was marshalled to where Lofty and his crew had been working.

It was a Mosquito Mark 6 Fighter/Bomber. These aircraft had only been on the Indian scene a few months and were still undergoing tropical trials. Within minutes of switching off, the Engineering Officer and Lofty, who had considerable experience on Merlins, had diagnosed an internal glycol leak. The simplest solution would be to change the engine completely. While some of his crew were dismantling the u/s engine, Lofty, who was also an experienced motor mechanic and a stand-by driver for the MT section, was detailed to take a Queen Mary and an escort to collect the replacement engine from 1 CMU at Kanchrapara.

Within a couple of days of collecting the new power unit, the comparatively straightforward task of installing the new Merlin 23 was completed. The blanking plugs from the new engine were fitted to the old unit and it was returned to the MU. After the usual checks and inspections, the pilot was informed that the aircraft was ready for air test. Satisfied that all was OK and the F700 duly signed, the pilot asked Lofty if he would like to go up on the air test. He jumped at the chance and drew a parachute from stores. As he was buckling up the straps, the Engineering Officer, Flt/Lt Rimmell, informed Lofty that he was going to accompany the pilot. With some reluctance he handed over the parachute and stood down, somewhat niggled at being deprived by rank of the opportunity of a trip in a new type of aircraft.

A few minutes after take-off, the aircraft reappeared over the airstrip. Suddenly without warning, in the clear blue sky at about 3,000 feet and in full view of the watching airmen, a three-pronged smoke trail, not unlike the Prince of Wales' feathers, issued from the aircraft. It was only too apparent that the aircraft was in serious trouble as it spiralled down out of sight some miles away. The time was 1215 hours. The CO, Sqn/Ldr Tiffin, took off immediately to locate the site of what was obviously a fatal crash. He located it just three and a half miles north-west of the airfield at Piadoba.

An immediate inquiry, headed by Sqn/Ldr C. J. Chabot, a World War I pilot and now a Tech E, was set up. Lofty Courtney was on tenterhooks but the investigation revealed that the actual cause of the disintegration was not a mechanical fault but a bird strike on the port wing and that break-up had occurred at a bad glue joint. It also revealed that the casein adhesive used in the laminated spar had become unstable in the heat, dangerously weakening the structure. Only then could Lofty relax and breath a sigh of relief. His title was changed to that of Lucky.

Sqn/Ldr Tiffin was posted to Base Air Force, SEA in December and replaced by Sqn/Ldr P. de L. Markham. Three months later he was repatriated and Flt/Lt H. Richmond, a Tech E, who had been posted in from 308 MU, Allahabad a month previously, took over.

With the announcement by Churchill on 8 May 1945 of the cessation of hostilities in Europe, the Indian unit contractor, M. A. Salam, financed a victory dinner for the unit. A week later there was a full turn out, including the IORs, for a ceremonial Victory March Past in Bankura.

It became apparent that the more militant of the population couldn't wait to see the back of the British and became pretty hostile in the ensuing weeks. Telephone wires were cut again and again and local police had to patrol the perimeter of the camp in addition to extra guards inside. The same hatred was mirrored throughout the country with mass demonstrations, vehicles being sabotaged, men being spat upon and stoned. Memories of relief given in the great famine which had swept Bengal and the enormous help given by the forces following the disastrous floods of Midnapore were conveniently forgotten in their haste to get rid of the British.

With the cessation of hostilities in Europe, the urgency for repairs and servicing began to reduce. New aircraft and equipment began to pour in from the Middle East and Europe for an all-out assault on Japanese occupied territory. Working hours began to take on a more acceptable pattern as they dealt with servicing of aircraft *en route* for Burma.

In June 1945, the unit was ordered to disband. All its documents were to be handed over to 326 MU along with all its equipment. Aircraft were struck off charge or handed over for reallocation by the MU. Many of the men were repatriated and those recently arrived were absorbed into other units.

In October 1944, No. 122 RSU was resurrected under a new guise, as a second line MU stationed at Koggla in Ceylon, under the functional control of 192 Maintenance Wing of 222 Group, RAF Colombo. The unit was commanded by Flt/Lt H. T. Robinson, the Adjutant was Flt/Lt Hamilton Smith, formerly of 615 Squadron at Baigachi. Their primary task was the servicing of Catalinas of 205 Squadron based at Koggla and 231 Squadron based at China Bay, for anti-submarine patrols, 212 Squadron based at Calcutta on air-sea rescue and the Sunderlands of 230 Squadron also engaged on anti-submarine patrols from Koggla. No record exists of their disbandment, though the unit's ORBs indicate that it was still in operation in the early part of 1946.

Chapter 8

No. 124 Repair and Salvage Unit

Although established on paper at Asansol with effect from 2 July 1943, 124 RSU did not commence to form until 3 September 1943 when Sqn/Ldr W. R. Middleton, who was then officating as the Station Commander, took over command. 122 RSU, who were already occupying Asansol, had begun to disperse personnel and reform other units, beginning with a detachment at Jessore to form 2 FRD. The remainder combined with 88 RSU in January 1943 to be known as FRD (Bomber).

On 20 November, 124 RSU began organizing the movement of all equipment to Masimpur, near Silchar, with the agreed allocation of fifty men. It entailed a great many signals to Calcutta to come to an agreement with 122 RSU as to what equipment should be allocated to the new unit from the existing stores held on site. No one wanted to release tools and spares accumulated over a period of time and MT arrangements presented their own particular problems. The arguments were causing considerable delays in the move until a token agreement was reached and it seemed the move would proceed without further delay.

It was easier said than done. There was still the important question of MT to resolve before the final move could be accomplished. By now the uncertainties were beginning to have an adverse effect on morale. In a signal to HQ, Sqn/Ldr Middleton stated 'morale somewhat low in the protracted idleness by enforced sojourn at Asansol'. He decided to go to Calcutta himself, confident in a higher authority's ability to get things moving when confronted by a personal appearance and to explain that no assistance could be expected from 2 FRD due to their almost simultaneous move to Bishnupur. His faith in higher authority paid off when twelve 3-tonners, a 15-cwt. and two Jeeps were finally lent to them by the Army.

To add to his troubles, during his absence all the WOs and NCOs had suddenly developed tonsillitis and had been admitted to hospital. Whether this was due to arguing or a silent protest has not been established! Nevertheless, the vehicles were loaded with equipment, ready for shipment by rail. It looked as if 124 was on its way at last. However, on arrival at Asansol Station, it was discovered that the same authority who had organized the MT had overlooked the simple fact that three railway flat cars could not possible accommodate such a large convoy, and in spite of the RTO wiring for further trucks, none was forthcoming. The CO again decided to bypass authority and enrolled the help of the local stationmaster who provided the necessary trucks and the convoy proceeded to Naihati the same evening.

At Naihati, however, on changing from the East Indian Railways to the Bengal Assam Railway, they discovered that no train drivers were available to carry on to Sealdah Station in Calcutta. The shift was probably over, and that was it! The whole convoy had to remain in a siding, though the stationmaster obligingly made some third-class carriages available for accommodation.

About mid-morning a train driver finally arrived and they reached Sealdah at midday. It had taken almost thirty hours for the 120 mile journey. To avoid further delay, Sqn/Ldr Middleton immediately contacted the resident RTO at Movement Control and insisted that the loaded trucks be shunted, there and then, on to Platform 5 which was the departure line for the ferry to Goalundo. All the men then dismounted and paraded on the platform. Washing facilities were organized and food brought in. Feeling human again and having little to do until the train pulled out some hours later, they gave an impromptu concert on the platform, organized and led by Sgt Allen, a musical saw player of some talent. The station echoed with community singing such as Calcutta had seldom heard.

Towards midnight, the special train steamed out, bound for Goalundo. Eight hours later, they arrived on the banks of the Brahmaputra River and within hours all the equipment was transferred to a river steamer and the unit cooks got busy preparing a meal on board. The journey up the river took seven hours and gave everyone a chance to relax in the cool river breezes, a distinct change from the hot plains of Bengal and the discomforts of the train journey. At Chandpur the unit entrained for Masimpur. WO Thorpe, who was in charge of transport, and thirteen drivers were left behind at Chandpur to bring the ground equipment by road. In the event, it was all transferred to eight-metre gauge trucks by coolie labour supplied by the RTO and No. 5 Motor Transport Company.

On 14 December F/O Tha, who had been posted in to Asansol as a Tech E at the end of October, arrived at Silchar with a second party of men. The RTO at Silchar provided an engine and some trucks for the short journey to Masimpur.

A signal was sent to 186 (Bengal) Maintenance Wing, repeated to 226 Group and AHQ: 'Request policy and area to be covered. Ready to carry out repairs on site. 23 December 1943.' It would seem, however, that Sqn/Ldr Middleton had served his purpose for he and Flt/Lt Norris were posted to 137 RSU at Dacca on 24 December, the very day after his signal. In their places arrived Sqn/Ldr R. F. J. Barber and Flt/Lt Ricketts from 137 RSU, formerly known as 4 RSS, in Dacca.

Sqn/Ldr Barber realized that 124 was relatively inexperienced so negotiated a transfer of 137 RSU personnel by arranging a conversion of these detachments to postings to 124 RSU. At that time, the Imphal Valley was serviced by a detachment of the former 4 RSS who had been there for about a year and were conversant with the problems of the area, including the hazards of the Dimapur Road. Naturally Sqn/Ldr Barber wanted to retain this experience in the interests of the new unit.

Similarly, detachments at Kumbhirgram and Palel were also converted to postings, retitled Salvage Sections and numbered 28, 90 and 57. In addition to this juggling with numbers and units, men and aircraft returns, a Sgt Innes was posted to Manipur Road Station with a small party to control the handling, dispatching and escorting of aircraft from Imphal and Palel by rail to either Dacca or Kanchrapara, near Calcutta. Given the grand title of Repsal, 885 AMES, RAF Manipur Road, it was accommodated in No. 52 Transit Camp, known by all troops as Penis Park because of the many monoliths which dotted the site.

The salvage and servicing returns of the new unit showed that from 26 December to 15 January thirty-eight aircraft had been serviced or salvaged. This was accompanied by a corresponding drop in aircraft servicing returns from 137 at Dacca. This unexpected loss of experienced tradesmen and nil return in servicing rather upset Sqn/Ldr Middleton and he requested that Sqn/Ldr Barber immediately arrange to replace these personnel. In the interests of harmony, Sqn/Ldr Barber tried to arrange, on a temporary basis, an attachment of four SNCOs and twenty-eight men of various trades, pending other postings. Gp/Capt Blockey of AHQ had other ideas. He had already decided that thirty BORs from 124 RSU would be needed to support 131 RSU which had just been formed at Ramree.

With this decision thrown into the argument, the relationships between the two units became somewhat fraught. 124 RSU still needed the facility at Dacca and they in turn wanted men. As the position became stalemate, Gp/Capt Blockey, some Tech Es and equipment officers met with the two COs at 94 EP and devised amicable arrangements for dealing with crashes east of the Brahmaputra.

At this time, the unit had no permanent test pilot. Any aircraft requiring testing remained grounded until a pilot could be borrowed. Finally, a Flt/Lt Constant arrived along with F/O John Chapman, a Canadian, to take up test duties. Sadly, Constant was killed three weeks later at Silchar when returning from a ferry flight in the unit's communication aircraft, Harvard FE973. He was trying to avoid three Spitfires returning from Imphal which were landing in the opposite direction. He struck a toddy palm and cartwheeled. His passenger, F/Sgt Marshall of 615 Squadron suffered a broken neck and died later in hospital.

A few days later, John Chapman, the remaining test pilot, had a lucky escape. He had been detailed to test a Hurricane at Pathakandi but the remaining Harvard had gone u/s and he could not get there in time. His place was taken by Flt/Lt W. J. N. Lee of 5 Squadron. During the air test, the aircraft, BN671 of 123 Squadron, suddenly dived out of control into the ground from 1,000 feet. There was nothing distinguishable left of the aircraft. A few days later, notification of the award of the DFC to Flt/Lt Lee came through.

Sorties in central Burma had escalated. Operation Thursday had commenced, taking troops by glider to the jungle airstrips of Chowringee, Broadway and Aberdeen, while other assaults were taking place in various areas. All required air support, either as escorts to supply dropping Dakotas or harassing the enemy on the ground with Vultee Vengeances and Hurri-bombers. Inevitably the number of crashes increased. At this time, the unit only had two Tech Es, F/O Kya Tha and Flt/Lt Kenchington, and they were hard pressed to keep up with the control of salvaging and servicing.

On 19 April, Flt/Lt Rimmell was attached from 126 RSU, based at Chittagong. He was to take charge of a detachment based at Johrat who were dealing with salvage north of the hill range. Not only would he be able to deal with on-the-spot decisions but it would considerably reduce the number of ferry flights by the unit Harvard. His contribution was short-lived, for hardly had he had time to settle in than he was recalled to his unit pending a posting to 132 RSU at Tulihul. He was to have two further moves in as many months, first to No. 1 Airborne Salvage at Barrackpore then to 143 RSU at Bishnupur where he was killed in a Mosquito crash a month after arriving (Chapter 7).

A second test pilot, F/Sgt Norman Gunnell arrived from 681 PRU Squadron at Dum-Dum. He had the distinction of being the first pilot to fly a Spitfire XI (MB896) from England to India in September 1943. His tenure as test pilot lasted only a month before he too was posted to 132 RSU at Tulihul, changing places with F/Sgt Stokes of that unit.

One morning at Masimpur, the Adjutant happened to look up from his desk and was alarmed to see a Vultee Vengeance 'shooting up' the Orderly Room almost at zero feet, before it pulled away and disappeared over the horizon. Although not aware of who the pilot was, he made a note of the incident and the time, intending to report the foolhardy exhibition. Just over an hour later, a very agitated Indian merchant from Masimpur was brought to his office with news that an aircraft had crashed near his house. Sqn/Ldr Barber and the Indian set off to view the wreckage. The Vengeance of 45 Squadron (AN656) was four miles from the nearest road and was Cat. E. The bodies had been removed by Flt/Lt Swanson and some medics from 94 EP and a guard was standing by to deter souvenir hunters. Sqn/Ldr Larney from Kumbhirgram arrived to see if the supercharger could be removed for examination as to a possible cause.

Unless a unit had had specific information that the crew had survived and were in safe hands, salvage crews always went out hoping for the best but prepared for the worst. Such was the case when Arthur Dyer, a Sgt F2A from Liverpool and an ex-Singapore Harrier, and a salvage crew were sent out from Masimpur in January 1944, to salvage another Vengeance of 45 Squadron (EZ879), piloted by P/O Jewell, which had crash landed in the Nowgong area some 150 miles to the north of Silchar.

The aircraft had buried its nose in the soft earth and was partially burnt. Although the aircraft had been there for four days, no attempt had been made to remove the body of the pilot. He was not in the cockpit but had somehow been caught up by his parachute lines as he left the aircraft, presumably having pulled his parachute too early and got entangled as the plane went down.

Although he had been covered up by some sympathetic person, it was still a gruesome sight. The navigator had managed to bail out successfully, suffering only minor injuries and was being cared for in the local hospital.

The subsequent inquiry revealed that the formation of Vengeances had become separated over the target area and failed to reformat. The aircraft had run short of fuel and become lost in 10/10 cloud at 10,000 feet over Imphal. Some confusion had also arisen over the radio frequencies and a wrong signal had been sent out by a radio station before informing the aircraft it had no homing facilities. The correct homer station failed to receive or answer any calls or SOS.

At the beginning of May, an urgent and unusual request for help came from the Brigade Headquarters at Silchar. A bridge had collapsed at Dorkinkeat near Silchar and the unit's Coles crane was the only vehicle capable of repairing it. The CO instantly dispatched WO Crozier with the crane, a Chev winch, a 3-tonner and a party of fitters to Kulaura to pick up a forty-three feet long girder and deliver it to the waiting party of Royal Engineers. Work on the bridge proceeded night and day, for the longer it took, the greater would be the delay in getting troops to all points on the Imphal–Kohima front.

On 5 July 1944, Sqn/Ldr Barber relinquished command of 124 RSU and was flown by F/O Chapman in the unit's Vengeance (AN900) to Kumbhirgram on the first stage of his journey to Quetta to attend a Staff course. Many of the men, having served with him since the early days at Asansol, were sorry to see him go. However, he re-emerged on a number of occasions, in his new role as Staff Officer, to sort out some of the problems which inevitably arose as RSUs changed places and moved down into Burma. Flt/Lt Kenchington, the Tech E, took over until Sqn/Ldr A. C. Ward, MBE from HQ 230 Group assumed command.

The number of crashes was still on the increase, particularly to the north and north-east and the unit was hard pressed to keep up with the demands for salvage crews. Many were Cat. EO and of no real value as spares. Though every attempt was made to recover engines, it was not the easiest of tasks when the aircraft was crumpled, burnt out and often half buried. Consequently, the Chief Maintenance Officer of AHQ signalled a change of policy that engines in this category were not to be salvaged. The order was received with some relief by the salvage crews.

In spite of the hard work, the unit had its lighter moments. When a tiger killed two people and began terrorizing the villagers, the elders approached Flt/Lt Kenchington to ask for help to get rid of this menace. He suggested to John Chapman, the Canadian test pilot, that they should tie a pig to a tree in the village and, armed with .303s, sit in the tree to wait for the tiger to take the bait. John Chapman, in as kindly a way as he could, told him he had no intention of staring down the throat of a tiger voluntarily.

Unperturbed by the lack of co-operation, Flt/Lt Kenchington decided to do the job himself. After spending a few nights up the tree without success, he decided he would give it one more night. His luck was in. The tiger turned up and as it made a swipe for the luckless pig, Flt/Lt Kenchington fired. Whether it was by luck or good judgement is a matter of opinion but the tiger dropped dead with the first shot.

On another occasion, having just air tested a Spitfire VIII for No. 81 Squadron (Ace of Spades) at Silchar, John Chapman saw six Dakotas on the airstrip. He recognized one of the pilots, Flt/Lt Phil Mahoney, who explained that they were on a return flight to Imphal with supplies and that only that morning had lost some of their aircraft after the Japs had jumped them. The Japs lost one aircraft when it struck the tail of one of the Daks. They had been expecting an escort from the Ace of Spades squadron to see them safely back to Imphal but most of them were away on a sortie. Chappie told them he would be only too pleased to escort them in the Spitfire he had just tested. Waiting until he could see that they had arrived at the mountains, Chappie took off and climbed to 18,000 feet and weaved in and around them, hopefully giving them confidence. No Japs appeared and everyone landed safely at Imphal just before dusk.

In the Mess that night, he was introduced as the 'guy who escorted us over'. All wanted to shake his hand until he told them, 'It's lucky we didn't meet any Japs as I had no ammo.' Most of them withdrew their offer to buy him a beer.

John Chapman was less than popular with authority on another occasion when he pranged a Vengeance (AN988) at Silchar. This aircraft, of 84 Squadron, had been in for servicing to cure its habit of turning in a dive. Being assured by Sgt Phil Sansum that the problem had been solved, Chappie suggested he show his confidence by coming on the air test. Against his better judgement Phil agreed and drew a parachute from stores.

Shortly after take-off, Chappie noticed oil was leaking on to the windscreen. He wasn't very concerned but as they were climbing to diving height, he noticed that the gill lever was creeping open. Turning it back to the closed position, it soon opened again. Once more he closed it. This slowed the aircraft's climb but it finally reached the desired height and he started to dive. The aircraft behaved perfectly. After pulling out of the dive, he went to close the gills and found that the control lever was too hot to touch. After attempting to correct it with his elbow to no avail, he left it as it was. Suddenly the windscreen was covered with a layer of black oil, with the exception of a tiny area about the size of a half-crown on the left-hand side. Chappie decided to come in low and turned steeply. All was fine and he touched down and started turning the trimming tab to get the nose down. Without any warning the aircraft was airborne again. He had landed about twenty feet from the end of the runway and hit a pile of bricks. Unwinding the trim tab to return to earth, the port wheel came off, complete with oleo leg. As the wing dipped, he applied hard rudder to starboard and applied starboard brake. All was in vain. The aircraft lost air speed, the wing hit the ground and it skidded to a halt, ending up on its nose off the edge of the runway.

Apart from some bruises Chappie was unhurt though Phil Sansum suffered a cut knee and had to extricate himself from some fifteen feet up in the air. Arriving with the 'blood wagon' was a squadron leader who began to take photographs. Asking for a copy for his album, Chappie was told they were for the court martial.

Towards the end of 1944, the Army were travelling much faster than anticipated in their offensive against the Japanese in central Burma. The increased distances meant a lower payload for the supply aircraft due to the increase in fuel consumption. Only more aircraft could redress the balance in order to maintain adequate airborne supplies. In spite of two more squadrons of Dakotas arriving on the scene at the specific request of Lord Mountbatten, transport aircraft were in very short supply and their services were still required on other fronts. The only alternative was to capture the airfields held by the Japanese in the Arakan and thereby considerably shorten the haul distances.

Plans were made for the capture of the island of Akyab. It would provide not only a short-haul base for transport and increased penetration for combat aircraft but would provide a port where ships could bring supplies direct for ferrying by air to the 14th Army. Little did 124 RSU realize what their involvement would be!

Flt/Lt Kya Tha, the unit's Tech E, whose home had been in Akyab, was called to Group HQ to be informed that it was to be his task to recruit a small group of twenty-eight 'volunteers' of assorted trades who were experienced in the servicing and maintenance of both fighter and transport aircraft and were used to working in field conditions. Given no hint of what would be involved or where they would be going but assuming they would be just another RSU detachment, the twenty-eight men, under the command of Flt/Lt Tha, set off by train from Silchar to Chittagong. Everyone thought it strange at the time that none of the usual vehicles or ground equipment accompanied them. On arrival at Chittagong, they were met and conveyed a few miles south, not to an airstrip but a beach at Patanga. On the beach were dummy landing craft and other strange looking structures built from bamboo with large landing nets hanging from them. They had arrived at a Marine Commando training camp.

After a fortnight of intensive training to prepare them for a possible seaborne assault on the Arakan coast, they were considerably fitter but not happy with the change in status from RAF tradesmen to Army privates. Early one morning they awoke to discover a ship waiting off the beach. It seemed that the assault was now real and not just speculation. Within a few hours of setting sail down the coast, they found themselves in the company of other assorted vessels off the island of Akyab, ready for an amphibious landing.

The expectation of having to do battle, however, was short-lived. Much to their relief, the Japanese had fled across the Kaladan River following a saturation bombing of the island by the RAF and bombardment from offshore cruisers of the Royal Navy.

The first Allied 'occupier' of Akyab was Wg/Cdr J. B. Bradley of the Royal New Zealand Air Force, who had flown in by light aircraft only hours before the unopposed Allied landings and was in fact a former judge on the island. After getting ashore, the first priority was digging slit trenches for although the

Japanese had abandoned the island, it was more than likely that they would still continue to harass the Allies. The Spitfires of 67 Squadron touched down very soon after and were serviced by the 124 detachment.

True to expectation, enemy bombers flew over to attack the naval convoys but were intercepted, losing five of their aircraft in the action, a sortie for which the CO, Sqn/Ldr Day, received the DFC. Undeterred, they still continued to carry out low level bombing raids on the airfield, using anti-personnel bombs. Fortunately many of these attacks were too low. The canisters hit the ground before they had opened and merely spilled out, a great many of them not exploding. Of those that did, very few caused any serious injury and none of the airmen was hurt.

Although the detachment was now on dry land there was very little they could do without tools and equipment. They spent much of their time in maintaining the serviceability of the airfield until a fully equipped detachment from 131 RSU at Chittagong arrived to take over and they returned to Masimpur. This was the first in the new role adopted for RSUs in Burma. Hilary St G. Saunders, in his book *The Fight is Won* described the landing of the twenty-eight men from 124 RSU as 'The first use of RAF Servicing Commandos' and they became an essential part of any advances made by the Army. Though the title might have been coined to show some operational difference between what was generally accepted as the role of an RSU, it is somewhat misleading as RAF Servicing Commandos did not arrive on the Burma scene until January 1945.

By the end of 1944 the salvage policies had changed dramatically, not only for 124 RSU but also for other units which served the area. Squadrons were now hopping from airfield to airfield as fast as they were reopened in Burma. These policies became haphazard with no coherent liaison between operational Groups. It was becoming a vicious circle with everyone denying responsibility when things went wrong but at the same time expecting the same degree of efficiency from the salvage units. It was almost as if everyone wanted to take the road to Mandalay and be the first to set foot in Rangoon.

On 21 January 1945, 124 RSU received orders to move immediately to Tulihul, previously occupied by 132 RSU who were moving down into Burma in the wake of the Army. Although it was scarcely a hundred miles due east by air, it was a circuitous route of 130 miles by rail and a further 140 miles along the Dimapur Road. Because no other unit was to replace them, all equipment had to be taken. Fortunately they managed to obtain the services of 1 Airborne Salvage who laid on a couple of their Dakotas to transport much of the essential equipment and personnel. Fifty tons of heavy ground equipment and vehicles, with Sgt Powell as i/c, went by rail. They arrived a week later having been held up by the inevitable shunting at Badarpur and Lumding.

On arrival, the unit was informed that detachments were to be sent immediately to Wangjing and Tamu, one to Imphal Main and another back to Kumbhirgram. It was over half the strength of the unit in one fell swoop.

Although 132 RSU had left behind a number of men for clearing up, many were due for repatriation. At the same time, forty men of 101 RSU, who had already been attached to deal with a number of Dakotas in the valley, were now needed back at Agartala. The unit establishment was simply a theoretical one with no relationship to the actual fact. Though Group had stated an intention to build up 124 RSU to its former strength and appreciated that the unit was having a rough deal, they were only words of appeasement. As the operational Groups altered the disposition of their units almost daily, so too did the so-called personnel reinforcement policies change.

The constant attachments and redeployments, coupled with the irregular arrival of mail which was forever being redirected, were having an effect on morale. Although fifty aircraft in the various locations had also been dropped in their lap without any previous history or requirements, no one seemed prepared to accept responsibility for them or strike them off charge.

To further complicate matters, when the squadrons moved out they had taken the telephones with them. Communications with Tamu had to be made by air should a problem arise and added another burden to the already over-worked test pilot, Flt/Lt Burton, while problems at Wangjing and Sapam had to be dealt with by road courier. Though repeated requests were made by Sqn/Ldr Ward for a second test pilot, his appeals were turned down, 'forward area priorities' being given as justification for refusal. However, thanks to the intervention of Sqn/Ldr Barber, the former CO and now a Staff Officer with AHQ, a test pilot from 135 RSU at Salbani arrived on a temporary attachment to assist. It was a very temporary assistance, for ten days later Flt/Lt Burton was posted to join 132 RSU at Tabingaung, putting the unit back to square one.

The situation was becoming intolerable. Even the unit transport and the Coles crane were demanded by HQ 181 Wing to assist with their own move south. To add further insult to injury, the enrolled followers, who had been left behind by 132 RSU, also departed and the unit was compelled to employ their own personnel on sanitary duties. It was an indignity which made the AOC's commendation of only a month or so previously seem almost worthless. Men felt that they were living in a house of cards and counted for nothing.

Although the unit had been stripped of its assets and were seen as a convenience for others whose need was deemed greater, they were still expected to deal efficiently with the servicing of 79, 146 and 261 Squadrons' Thunderbolts at Wangjing, 1 Squadron's Hurricanes at Imphal and the Beaufighters and Mosquitoes of 47, 45 and 82 Squadrons at Kumbhirgram, followed eventually by the Liberators of 215 and Dakotas of 267 at Tulihul.

To add even further to their problems, on 14 February 1945, at about seven o'clock in the evening, a terrific explosion shook the district, followed by smaller explosions that lit up the night sky in the direction of Imphal. It was the ordnance dump dug into the hillside at the back of the aircraft dispersals at Imphal which had gone up. It sounded as if the whole Jap army had suddenly returned and were making an all-out attack. Everyone took cover in the slit trenches as shrapnel and exploding ammunition filled the air while several unexploded shells landed amongst the billets.

The following morning one airman found the charpoy he had hastily vacated occupied by one of the missiles. Although considerably shaken, none of the 124 detachment was injured. The damage caused by the exploding shells, shrapnel and bursting ammunition to the Hurricanes on the strip was considerable, worse than any Jap air raid. It was a heartbreaking situation to have to begin repairing aircraft which had only recently undergone servicing. A signal to the AOC brought no replacement spares and the unit had to adopt a make do and mend policy.

If this wasn't enough to dishearten the most stalwart of men, an unexplained fire broke out on the domestic site at Tulihul. It was an identical situation to what had befallen 132 RSU only a couple of months before. There was little water available and although an American fire wagon from Palel was quickly on the scene and prevented the fire from spreading, seven bashas were gutted. This included the canteen and all its supplies plus a 15-cwt. lorry, while the airmen who had occupied the huts lost all their personal kit.

Although the unit's strength had been depleted to an all-time low by constant detachments, further demands were placed on it by requesting they now take over the commitment at Thazi and Kalemyo of 83 RSU who were moving forward. The only way to comply was to reduce the commitments at Kumbhirgram and deploy the attachment at Imphal to Wangjing.

Suddenly the penny must have dropped and someone at Group realized that they couldn't keep shifting personnel about without replacing them, for in February 1945 a F/Sgt Evans and a detachment of men arrived from 3209 Servicing Commando based at Singabil. Although adding welcome bodies to the depleted establishment, their arrival did nothing to rebuild the 'house of cards'. F/O Gilongly, the unit Adjutant, in the F540 of 124 RSU, commented, 'Welcome as they are, they would have been even more welcome had they arrived with tool kits.'

It would seem on the face of it, that the brief of the Servicing Commandos would now be to step in and provide solutions for all the problems of servicing aircraft in forward areas. The fact that many of the RSUs had already had this operational commitment from the very beginning, following in the wake of the Army as they pushed the Japs back and were well on their way into Burma, seems to have escaped the notice of the planning wallahs.

Many of the chaps felt somewhat incensed that the arrival of this unit seemed to imply that they could not handle the rapidly changing situation. Many were hardened veterans, some had been at Dunkirk, some in the Middle East, others in Singapore and Java and all had had considerable experience in servicing and salvaging aircraft under the most arduous of circumstances. Some had already undergone training in Commando tactics at Chittagong in preparation for the invasion of Akyab. Nearly all had been sniped at, bombed and strafed with regular monotony and were as *au fait* in jungle search and survival as the next. Yet here were these new arrivals to the scene, having landed in India only a month previously, although they had served a spell in Normandy, sporting Combined Ops badges to distinguish them as something unique and different. It had never been thought of as appropriate to afford the privilege of a shoulder badge to Repair and Salvage Units.

Nevertheless, after the initial animosity, which is almost impossible to sustain when men mess and work together, had died down, the work of servicing aircraft continued. Had they known then what their CO, Flt/Lt Wood, had written in a report to 230 Group, it is doubtful if such harmony would have reigned. His report suggested that working with RSUs was very leisurely and too soft an option for the SCUs: 'Long periods of comparative inactivity, such as working with RSUs and MUs are not conducive to the best results in personnel with a highly developed sense of unit pride ... and with a mentality moulded around the word Commando.' The co-operation was short-lived, however, for in April 1945, 3209 Servicing Commando were recalled to Singabil.

On 12 April, 124 RSU were also instructed to move to Myingyan, some sixty miles south-west of Mandalay, with a target date for completion of the move of 26 April. In spite of the upheaval and the work involved in packing up for the move, the unit was also instructed to supply an attachment immediately to Kalewa for servicing the Hurricanes of 60 Squadron. Flt/Lt Tha set off on 14 April with an advance convoy while Flt/Lt Howarth, the unit MO, set off a few days later with a larger convoy, arriving at Myingyan sixteen days later. The campsite was in a glade four miles from Myingyan North and in easy reach of 901 Wing and 908 Wing at Kynmagon. Sqn/Ldr Ward, the CO, in a signal to 221 Group, requested an airlift for the remaining men and equipment and was told that Dakotas of 435 Squadron RCAF would be arriving on the 27th to airlift everyone out.

In spite of all the trauma of having to move, they were still expected to carry out servicing and salvage commitments. One demand from BAFSEA HQ was to investigate a crash in the Lumpui area as a report on the crash had shown an unidentifiable engine number. The only person who could be spared was P/O Hartley. After a two-day trek, accompanied by an escort of Assam Rifles, the aircraft was located. It was buried nose first in the ground and the fuselage burnt almost beyond recognition and very little could be readily identified, least of all an engine number. It was common practice then for squadrons to mark one or more of the cannons with the aircraft number. Only three of the four cannons could be found, none of which had any number. Obviously the fourth had been looted so P/O Hartley and his escort made an immediate search of the surrounding villages and the missing cannon was found in one of the huts. It bore the number LD998 of 60 Squadron.

Operational changes were still having an adverse effect on the unit, for apart from moving forward, as a rearward RSU with no one to follow them, it meant that they were responsible for clearing up the strips as they vacated them. With the move of the unit's headquarters to Myingyan, communication with the Kumbhirgram, Wangjing, Tulihul and Thazi detachments became a real complication. Signals to 230 Group HQ were either going astray or simply ignored. Any urgent problem had to be dealt with by air. Without a test pilot, this meant that Flt/Lt Tha or the CO had to make repeated journeys to iron out any queries. The despondency felt by the unit at the way they had been overlooked and treated in the past few months seemed highlighted when, on 7 May, Sqn/Ldr Ward wrote:

> The Premier's speech on the end of the war in Europe is awaited on the evening broadcast on All India Radio. We should have liked all our lads around us, but as it is not possible, each in their separate ways will celebrate in the desolate isolation of the now deserted airfields on which they are working.
>
> We, and not alone, wonder if we are indeed at times overlooked by those in Government at home. It is true that we have had messages of congratulations on work well done.
>
> Like the lads of the glorious 14th Army and all the supporting elements, we do not think that it is enough. We shall carry on till our job is done, but we all deserve something tangible, like tour reduction or accelerated release for those entitled.
>
> The general feeling on camp today is one of remoteness. The fact that the Prime Minister failed in his speech to make any direct mention of the troops fighting in this theatre of war created a very bad impression.
>
> A lot has been written by higher command of the necessity of doing everything to maintain high morale and a great opportunity to carry this into effect has been lost.

Although his emotive letter probably echoed the sentiments of many others, it drew very little response and the less than satisfactory situation of the unit remained unchanged.

A signal was received informing the unit that a Warwick III of 353 Squadron had force landed somewhere near Pagan, about forty miles south-west of Myingyan and required salvaging urgently. When the crew arrived at the site, they found that the aircraft had been left unguarded and had been extensively looted by Burmese, with every vestige of fabric torn from the fuselage, though what use doped fabric as stiff as a board would be is anyone's guess. Apart from recovering the engines, very little of value was left to salvage and the remains were destroyed. This looting became widespread in the ensuing months and it was often a race to see who could get to the site first, the salvage crew or the Burmese.

The unit's detachment at Meiktila had been working closely with a detachment of 3 RSU but as this unit had now been ordered out, all the aircraft in the area had been handed over to 124 RSU. Obviously the unit would need reinforcing, but how? The only alternative was to abandon attempts to clear up at Kumbhirgram and Tulihul and recall those detachments. Unfortunately, they could not bring their vehicles by road as the Bailey bridge over the Chindwin had been removed in the face of the oncoming monsoons. Flt/Lt Svenson, who had been in charge of these detachments, was instructed to hand over the vehicles to 364 MU at Palel and arrange for an airlift for any ground equipment and the remaining personnel.

By the middle of May, the weather had worsened and on the morning of 21 May the detachment at Kynmagon woke up to find the repair dispersal cut off from the airstrip by a deep trench which had been dug by flood waters during the night. The domestic site was on slightly higher ground but only escaped immersion by a few inches. Although the floods subsided as quickly as they had come, the deep gully was a barrier which required the help of the Royal Engineers to bridge in order to get the aircraft to the strip.

Sqn/Ldr Ward, who had been the CO for the past ten months, was repatriated and his place taken by Sqn/Ldr F. W. May, a Tech E.

Although the unit was still beset by an acute shortage of tradesmen, its servicing and salvaging allotments were in no way reduced. To make matters worse, Flt/Lt Svenson, one of the Tech Es, was posted to 139 RSU in Madras, while WO Martin, MBE was attached to RAF Burma Communication Flight. The loss of these officers meant that their duties now had to be taken over by WO Wall who assumed the duties of Flt/Lt SD. Again an appeal was made to Sqn/Ldr Barber, now at 221 Group, for a definite policy regarding the unit's duties, the absence of which was making life extremely difficult. The CO, commenting on the lack of interest in the unit, believed that RAF HQ was involved in a different war.

In August the unit was airlifted from Kynmagon to Hwambi in support of 132 RSU dealing with Mosquitoes and Thunderbolts of 908 and 909 Wings. At the same time, the unit's number was erased and it was absorbed into No. 56 Forward Repair Unit in Rangoon, which was a holding unit for all disbanded squadrons as a pool for possible moves to Japan, but with the surrender of Japan, this unit was also disbanded.

The CO, Sqn/Ldr May, was posted in August to Baigachi and replaced by Sqn/Ldr Semple.

In November a signal from AHQ notified the unit that it would be going to Singapore by the end of the month. 124 RSU was finally disbanded in Singapore in October 1946. Some of the airmen were repatriated as tour-expired or on Class B release, others were absorbed into 389 MU which had just been formed. Some went to 60 Squadron in Java, a few joined 273 Squadron in Bangkok and Saigon.

Although not sharing the glamour, honour, prestige, or whatever one wants to call it, of being first to set foot in Rangoon, the unit's contribution as it passed down through Burma in the wake of others, was no less important. Treated as something of a convenience for all and sundry, nevertheless they salvaged hundreds of aircraft of one sort or another since their formation in Asansol.

Chapter 9

No. 132 Repair and Salvage Unit

Only two units, 4 RSS at Dacca and 124 RSU at Masimpur with detachments at Imphal and Palel, were dealing with salvaging and servicing and having to cope with the increased flying activities in Assam and the Burma border. In order to deal with this increase, another was formed at Barrackpore on 15 October 1943, under 226 Group and exercised through 186 Maintenance Wing Bengal. When formed, this unit, 132 RSU, would move immediately to Imphal.

Initially it was issued with a Jeep, three 3-ton four-wheel drive Chevrolet lorries and two 15-cwt. trucks. At this stage it was obvious that these assorted vehicles would be completely inadequate for an operational unit who, by December, comprised 350 assorted tradesmen, cooks and office staff. This situation became even more critical when this very small transport pool was depleted even further by a detachment of men with tools and Hurricane and Merlin spares being sent to 4 RSS at Dacca. Equipment was arriving almost daily at the stations at Howrah and Barrackpore but because of the shortage of transport it could only be collected in small batches. It was only after repeated urgent signals to Group that further vehicles were allocated.

After three months, the unit was still in limbo and it was not until 24 January 1944 that it was ready to move by rail to Imphal. It was to be in three convoys setting out at intervals. The first left Barrackpore at 0800 hours on 24 January. The second convoy with P/O Allsop, twenty-two men and transport left six hours later and entrained at Sealdah at 0200 the following morning. Meanwhile, the first convoy discovered that no Movement Order was available to allow them to proceed further and they were shunted into a siding to await the proper authority. It was to be four days before they were finally allowed to continue.

The third convoy was more fortunate, for in three days they had arrived at the railhead at Dimapur to find the other party still at No. 52 Rest Centre. No one had thought it necessary to organize transport for the final leg to Imphal, it being assumed that the three convoys would use their own vehicles. The fact that one party had been delayed for four days hadn't been taken into account. A signal was sent to the CO at Imphal, Flt/Lt Ricketts, requesting transport. They finally arrived at 1600 hours and were temporarily accommodated with 81 Squadron at Ghari village. Again, there were crossed wires, for, although it had been the intention to use this village as a base because it was close to the strip, somebody at HQ had blundered and overlooked the fact that it was already occupied.

The advance convoy, with all the vehicles, was even less fortunate and had been caught up in all sorts of rail hold-ups and did not arrive until a week later having been on the way for almost three weeks. Ghari village was now almost bursting at the seams. Something needed to be done quickly so it was decided to move the whole unit to Tulihul, about twelve miles further on.

By 13 February, they were firmly ensconced at the airfield at Tulihul. It had taken almost three weeks for the journey from Barrackpore and very nearly four months to finally establish the unit.

The airfield at Tulihul was new, one of three all-weather strips in the Imphal Valley. Due to a misunderstanding between the Americans and the British engineers, it had been constructed 4,000 yards long instead of 4,000 feet, though the error was subsequently to be of advantage.

As no billets were available, the men were temporarily accommodated in tents which they erected themselves. With the ritual reckoned to be conducive to good order and discipline, the tents had to be pitched in straight lines. Being in a forward area with the Japs almost on the doorstep, it didn't need a great deal of imagination to see they would be a sitting duck for any stray Jap aircraft. In spite of protests, those in command insisted. A day or so later a lone Zero came over and made a low level attack. No one was hurt but a Beaufighter parked on the dispersal was severely damaged. The same day, the surviving tents were dispersed among the trees and camouflaged. No. 132 RSU had had its baptism of fire.

It began operational activity almost immediately by taking over responsibility for various aircraft allotted to 124 RSU and its No. 28 Section which had been at the Imphal airfield for over a year.

All realized and accepted that the benefits of freedom from bull were based on the unit's capacity to get things done efficiently with the minimum of fuss. This independence was not a licence for laxity. Bashas were kept in good order and each took it in turn to be room orderly. There were no bugles to signal the start of the day but very rarely did anyone miss the gharry to the dispersal and turn up late for work. The unit was by no means a paragon of military virtue but a team spirit prevailed.

The autonomy of the detachment was soon to be changed with the absorption into the new unit. Notice-boards displaying Daily Routine Orders and Station Standing Orders appeared. Pay, which in the past could be obtained casually whenever there was a need, could now only be obtained at pay parades. There were to be kit and hut inspections and a CO's parade at various intervals. As if to reinforce the 'New Order' a discip. NCO was posted in from 15 STT at Poona. It was apparent right from the start that he intended to shake up what he thought was a sloppy unit. He would creep round the dispersals looking for any infringement of regulations and gradually became a major fly in the ointment of efficiency. Men began to look over their shoulders to see if he was around. He almost became the main topic of conversation. Even protests to the warrant officer, who was sympathetic, had little effect in curtailing his enthusiasm for fault finding.

There was, however, one flaw in his make-up. He had an inclination for the bottle. Where he got his supplies nobody knew but it was always evident when he had overindulged. One day the opportunity to get their own back arose. Someone had found out that he was going to Tulihul and suggested that as the unit Harvard was going there, he could fly in it. In a show of bravado, he agreed. What he didn't know was that the Harvard was going on an air test and that the chaps had arranged for F/Sgt Norman Gunnell, the test pilot, to put it through its paces including some which were not in the manual.

About thirty minutes later, the aircraft came back and out he stepped, ashen faced and wobbling at the knees and probably with skid marks on his underpants, if the truth be known. He made no comment to the crowd of grinning airmen though he was obviously seething with rage at the way he had been set up. Although the men knew he would make their lives hell in the coming days, they felt a great deal of satisfaction. Strangely enough, the experience must have made him realize what a thoroughly unpopular guy he was and although it would be wrong to say that his attitude changed overnight, over the ensuing weeks he spent more time in his office than he did in wandering around picking fault.

Needless to say, no one shed any tears when he was posted. The NCO who took over was the direct opposite and was well liked. He believed everyone had a job to do whatever their status and was not averse to lending a hand at clearing the strip when the occasion arose. Harmony descended on the unit once more.

By this time, it was obvious that something was afoot. Transports had been flying in and out of the two airfields almost non-stop, bringing in supplies of every description and ferrying non-combatants and wounded out. Jap air raids were becoming a regular feature and squadron sorties were increasing. With this increase of aerial activity the number of accidents escalated. Many were local, aircraft having limped back or suffered malfunctions during landing or take-off. Whatever the cause, the unit became hard pressed to keep up with salvaging and repairs. Inevitably, the supply of new spares began to dry up and, as with all RSUs, the unit began to rely heavily on cannibalizing other aircraft.

To add to the problem, a liaison policy had been organized between the USAAF and the unit in the salvage of their aircraft which crashed 'in the blue'. Those American aircraft which pranged on the strip were usually just pulled to one side to await the arrival of their own repair crews. Although these crews were usually extremely well equipped with the most sophisticated of tools and were the envy of most RAF fitters, they could only usually deal with minor malfunctions on the strip. Others which could not be handled on site were simply dismantled and picked up usually by Curtiss Commandos, the equivalent workhorse to our Dakotas.

There were many anomalies regarding the obtaining of spares. Some were readily available, usually those which were less in demand, others, like filters, magnetos and even simple washers were at a premium. One such anomaly was highlighted when Sgt Carn flew specially to Calcutta for urgent spares, including a Merlin engine spanner. All engine fitters will know that the spanner kit for a Merlin is unique, certain spanners being required for specific assemblies. In this instance Sgt Carn got all the spares required but was informed that the spanner he required was not available anywhere in India but given the required size and details, one could probably be made locally. A singular case of 'for the want of a nail ...'

A similar incident, though soon resolved, was when the unit was informed that a Coles crane was awaiting collection at Manipur station. These cranes are indispensable so without further ado a driver was detailed to collect it. It had, however, been dispatched from Air Stores Park in Calcutta minus the jib. It arrived a week later and entailed another two day journey to Dimapur to collect it.

At this point 132 RSU had only been active for a little over two weeks but apart from taking over the repair of six Hurricanes and a Mohawk from 124 RSU, they also had an input of three Blenheims, eighteen Hurricanes, an Anson and a Mosquito IX of 27 Squadron which was a relatively new aircraft on the scene.

In early March a great many Dakotas were seen in the skies above Imphal. Not all were dropping supplies but were assembling at Lalaghat to be used for the invasion of Burma by Gen. Wingate's Special Force, now known as Operation Thursday. More than eighty of these aircraft took part. Forty came from 31, 62, 117 and 194 (The Friendly Firm) Squadrons and the rest from the 27th and 315th Troop Carrier Squadron and No. 1 Air Commando USAAF.

Inevitably, some were to crash or suffer malfunction, as did two on 9 March when they collided when taxiing. The port wing of one and the starboard wing of the other were severely damaged. It was a relatively simple task to switch the undamaged wing of one to the other aircraft, the donor aircraft to await two new mainplanes or be used as spares.

Some of course did not crash in convenient places as in the case of a Dakota reported down in the hills near Manmon. The CO, Flt/Lt Bullen now promoted to Sqn/Ldr, and F/Sgt Stokes, a test pilot, flew in a Tiger Moth (DF725) to examine the wreck to see if it could be flown out. Unfortunately, they crashed on landing and wrote off the Moth but both were unhurt. The Dakota also proved to be a write-off. They set out to walk back and got to Johnson Camp, some fourteen miles away, well after dark. They stayed the night and left next morning, again on foot to BHQ, having to scramble through jungle and ford rivers, taking about eight hours for the fifteen mile trek. They obtained a couple of mules and a guide and finally came to a Jeep track. By sheer luck they managed to get a lift in an Army Jeep to Tamu where they stayed the night at the Motor Transport Company Depot. They were picked up next day by a Dakota which had been signalled in to collect them and deliver them back to

Imphal. The Dakota and Tiger Moth were both destroyed by strafing the following day, no doubt providing some target practice for one of the Hurricane squadrons.

Mountain searches very rarely recovered the aircraft, though they may well have yielded some small salvageable items that could be carried. The primary aim was to render any assistance to any aircrew who might have survived. In some cases they had but, sadly, in the majority of instances, very few did survive and often presented rather gruesome evidence when finally discovered and required a strong stomach to deal with. These searches or recoveries, unlike salvage operations on airstrips, in paddy fields or the mud of the Sunderbans, always presented their own set of problems. No two were ever the same and Mother Nature was always reluctant to yield up her victims without a struggle, be it an inanimate aircraft or a living being who had survived her grasping clutches.

In the majority of cases it was impossible to get transport to within miles of the area and the search would have to be concluded on foot. As everything had to be carried, including rations for the estimated time it would take, at times it required the nimbleness of a mountain goat combined with the expertise of a sherpa.

Occasionally crews would be escorted by either patrols from the Assam Rifles, the Gurkhas or would manage to pick up Naga guides and porters which made things considerably easier.

One essential item of equipment, odd though it may seem, when setting out from the Burma Plain pouring with sweat, was the need to carry blankets, a need which was only too apparent as the swirling mists on the ridges in early morning chilled the bone to the marrow until the sun burned off the dampness of the night.

Having struggled to the top of a ridge, one always hoped that there would be some visible evidence. Rarely was it so, the camouglage of the aircraft either effectively fulfilled its purpose or 'Murphy's Law' decreed that the crash was on the opposite side of yet another ridge.

There were times, after spending days searching without any success, that an expedition would reluctantly have to be abandoned and another aircrew would join the growing list of 'Missing in Action'.

One unsuccessful search occurred in early January 1944 when a message came through to 132 RSU that a Vultee Vengeance of 84 Squadron had crash landed in the Chin Hills, somewhere near Tiddim, about 150 miles away.

It was a somewhat vague message with no details as to the fate of the crew, merely that it had been seen going down some miles away by an Army patrol in the area. Almost certainly, it was returning to its base at Kumbhirgram after a sortie in Burma.

A Chevrolet four-wheel drive winch vehicle was loaded with rations and whatever kit was thought to be necessary, including weapons and ammunition. It would probably not be a full recovery in view of the remoteness of the reported sighting but whatever salvageable items there were would be brought back and the aircraft identified for the records.

The salvage crew were to report to an Army Transport Depot at Tonzang on the Tiddim Road where they would be given a more positive location.

The road to Tiddim, commonly referred to as the Tiddim Track, had formerly only been little more than a cart track through the mountains until it had been bulldozed and scraped out of the mountainside by the Royal Engineers and thousands of coolies. It was a single track about twelve feet wide with many steep gradients and only really suitable for dry-weather motoring and compared to this the Dimapur Road was a motorway. It was a really rough ride, the many pot-holes threatening to project any vehicles over the khudside into the deep valleys below. Mute evidence of those that had succumbed were still visible below as a stark reminder of the dangers.

After crossing the Manipur River by way of a Bailey bridge, they pulled into the Transport Depot in late evening and were given a meal and billet for the night. The following morning, one of the officers gave the general direction in which the aircraft had been seen to go down. The wave of his arm in the general direction of the Chin Hills was pretty noncommittal and about as informative as the quarter-inch maps they had been given.

In addition to the general vagueness, he added two points regarding the intended salvage. One was that the Chevrolet winch would be utterly useless for the purpose, as the tracks off the road were only negotiable by mule and Jeep, and the latter would only be with luck. Secondly, Jap patrols had been active in the area and he didn't set much store on RAF blokes being able to cope should a confrontation arise. Unperturbed by his pessimism and deciding they would have a shot, the crew negotiated the loan of two Jeeps. Leaving the Chevrolet as security, they set off to try to locate the aircraft.

The officer wasn't wrong, the tracks leading into the hills were little more than bridle-paths and required frequent halts to hack away vegetation to allow them to continue deeper into the hills. Before long it was apparent that they could go no further and would have to go the rest of the way on foot. Immobilizing the Jeeps and taking what rations and tools might be required, along with the weapons, they began the long climb to the summit. As they began their exhausting climb, they saw evidence of temporary cultivation in the shape of small clearings in the dense jungle where it had been *jhumed* or burned by the Nagas and showed up as lighter green of new vegetation. Near the top of the ridge they came across a small abandoned hut, built on stilts and used by the hill men as they tended their crops.

Having got to the peak, they were confronted with other ridges stretching as far as the eye could see, but there was no sign of the aircraft. It was decided to call it a day and bed down for the night, using the deserted Naga hut as protection from the chill mountain air and, conscious of the warning of Jap patrols, they cooked a meal before it got dark and took turns at keeping guard.

Breakfasting at first light, they set off for the next ridge, having agreed that if no sightings could be made, the search would be abandoned. Although only appearing a mile or so away, it required a long descent into a narrow valley before beginning another scramble to the top.

During the climb, they suddenly heard voices and without further ado, took cover with weapons at the ready. It seemed that the transport officer's warning had come true and they were to be faced with Japs. Much to their relief, round the bend of the track came four Nagas. They didn't seem a bit surprised at being confronted by four white men armed with Stens. They showed no fear but just stood looking curiously for some minutes until one of them, wearing a red blanket, stepped forward and by means of sign language and arm waving, indicated that there was a crashed aircraft not far away. It was obvious that they had been aware of the presence of the searchers for some time.

Following the exchange of some silver rupees and a couple of packets of cigarettes, they offered to lead the salvage crew to the site. 'Not far away' turned out to be descending the ridge and crossing the Manipur River over a very shaky bamboo bridge followed by another long climb to the peak of another, a journey which was to take the best part of twelve hours.

With the additional company, the Jap threat seemed to lessen. The blokes knew full well that the Nagas would be well aware of any strange or hostile movement and give adequate warning.

Sure enough, there was the aircraft, about a hundred feet from the top of the ridge. It looked as if it had hit the hillside sideways on and had cartwheeled. The impact had torn the engine from its mountings and it had rolled some way down the mountainside along with one of the mainplanes. It was a total write-off. There was nothing to show what had caused the crash or any evidence to show that it had been shot up. The fuel tanks were empty but whether he had run out of fuel or it had evaporated was not possible to establish and very little remained that was worth salvaging.

As he scrambled to the aircraft, one of the men caught hold of a tree to prevent himself from sliding. When he removed his hand he saw it was covered in congealed blood. Looking down into the undergrowth, he saw a head, or at least what was left of it. The pilot had obviously been catapulted out of the cockpit with the impact. Though they searched for further remains, none could be found except for remnants of a bush jacket with the breast pocket still intact and containing an identity card belonging to Sgt Edwards who was eighteen years old and hailed from Kent. Although they searched the undergrowth for some time, they found no signs of the second member of the crew. He may well have bailed out, though the chances of survival and walking out of this hostile territory were almost nil.

The remains were buried and marked with a small cross roughly fashioned from part of the aircraft fuselage. Little else remained to be done and the crew began to retrace their steps to where they had left their Jeeps, again escorted by their friendly Nagas.

Arriving back at Tonzang three days later, they handed back the Jeeps to the transport officer who actually seemed relieved at seeing them returned safely. Evidently, there had been quite a lot of Jap activity in the Chin Hills and he had considered organizing a search party for them.

Geordie Hopper, who had been one of the crew, afterwards said, 'I shall never forget the sight of that face looking up at me out of the grass. It haunted me for weeks and every time I went out on a prang in the mountains, I kept hoping I wouldn't see a similar sight.'

With the increasing call-outs to salvage aircraft and keep the airfield cleared from early dawn well into the night, what with the constant air raid alarms, the barrages by the Bofors guns and the Jap 'jitter' patrols at night, life became somewhat fraught. All were tangible evidence of the war surrounding the Imphal Valley, as was the cutting of rations, but lack of sleep was having an adverse effect on both morale and stamina. The situation was highlighted by the following message from 221 Group on 23 March:

170 Wing and all units in Imphal Valley

> All units from the AOC. Bands of the enemy in small numbers have been reported near the Imphal Valley. We have gone into our Defensive Boxes and must be ready and alert for sniping, sabotage or small scale attacks. These may never occur but we must be ready in all respects to meet and beat them if they do. Sentries and listening posts must keep quiet and keenly alert. Positions must be well sited and dug in. If shots are fired, maintain fire discipline and do not blaze away with no definite target, thereby giving away our own positions. If a Box is attacked it MUST repeat MUST hold out, reporting attack to Group and Corps who will send tanks which can mop up the enemy. We must keep our landing strips safe to use and our aircraft fit to fly. We can then beat them for certain. This may be the biggest opportunity yet to prove that our standard of discipline in the RAF is sound and that we can take it and fight calmly and with proper control. If the test comes I look to every Officer and Airman to act with discipline and determination. Air Force humour will beat the Jap who has none. Good luck and good shooting. Vincent.

The 'flap' at Imphal, unlike Ladysmith or Lucknow, was not a siege in the same sense of the word. Although it was cut off by the Japanese to the north and south and by the hills encircling the valley, there was an air corridor through which supplies could be flown in. Even in good weather this meant flying high over twisting mountain ranges and through valleys often shrouded in mist. With the coming of the monsoons, the hazards increased dramatically. This air supply line was known as Operation Stamina.

In the second month of the Siege, in spite of assurances that the Japs were being pushed back, or at least contained, further cuts in rations, now supplemented by energy tablets, had done little to dispel the distinct possibility that maybe, just maybe, the tide could change and the Japanese overrun the valley. After all, they had cut the Dimapur Road at Milestone 107, fierce fighting was raging in the Tiddim and Bishenpur area, Palel had been shelled and Wangjing had had to be evacuated. The unit personnel were forced to sleep in defensive boxes, large trenches covered in corrugated iron or tarpaulin sheets. They were cold and damp and had to be bailed out after rain, leaving evil smelling mud.

The likelihood of becoming front line troops became the main topic of conversation. Some airmen began to organize emergency packs, ready for a quick dash to the hills but the odd tin of bully or packet of hard tack biscuits would have been hardly sufficient to sustain a lengthy trek. Some simply packed their more treasured possessions and hoped for the best. Everyone had his own idea of a survival kit. For four airmen it was history repeating itself. One had survived the beaches of Dunkirk, another had been evacuated from Rangoon while the other two had narrowly escaped from Singapore and Java.

The opening of the Dimapur Road on 22 June ended the flap which had lasted eighty-one days. The first convoy through brought petrol, potatoes and beer. The latter was the first supply for three months and was rationed to one bottle per man. It tasted like nectar and the teetotallers became the centre of attention, open to all sorts of offers for their ration. Though probably not appreciated at the time, that simple bonus had only been made possible by the great sacrifices at the Battle of Kohima.

Even though the Japs had suffered a decisive defeat at Kohima, their activities to regain control of the valley did not lessen. The need for continuous alertness was highlighted when on 3 July a Jap patrol eluded the RAF Regiment guards and sneaked through the perimeter defences at Palel. Using limpet mines they blew up three Spitfires of 152 Squadron, two Hurricanes of 113 Squadron and two Harvards used as communication aircraft. To add insult to injury, they also broke into the office of Sqn/Ldr Courtney, the CO of 113 Squadron, and defecated on his desk. Maj. Teddy Kennington, the Army Liaison Officer of 113 Squadron recalls the entourage of VIPs from 221 Group who descended to view the damage and the words of Gp/Capt Henry Goddard who summed up the visiting card on the CO's desk by announcing, 'I think the damage incurred is commensurate with the missile employed.' It left everyone speechless.

Aircraft fuel was often unofficially used for other purposes from that for which it was intended. It was the habit every week to sterilize the latrines by the simple expedient of pouring a gallon or so into the pit and setting fire to it. It was a very effective way of destroying the millions of maggots which bred in this nutrient rich soup. Because the temperature vaporized the petrol very rapidly, the safest way to ignite it was by using a long bamboo pole with a piece of burning four by two tied to the end, thrusting it into the trench then retreating very smartly.

One day, one of the wise guys (every unit has one) decided his way was better and less fuss. He poured the petrol into the trench and laid a petrol trail as a fuse. Unfortunately, the trail fell short of the trench and burned itself out. By this time the petrol in the trench had well and truly vaporized and filled the trench with volatile fumes. His only resort was to revert to the bamboo pole and lighted cloth. He had no sooner approached than it flashed and the ensuing blast emptied the trench.

It took off the roof, hurled the thunder boxes in all directions and showered the site with the contents of the latrine, the offender taking a fair share, for which he received no sympathy whatever. The coolies, who were eventually called in to clean up the mess and repair the damage, had to be bribed substantially before they would begin.

Air raids were still an almost daily occurrence, though the unit suffered no casualties. The quick 'squirts' by the Japs were a source of irritation rather than a serious threat but a Beaufighter which had just been serviced was strafed and burnt out.

There was a limit to the work that any RSU could do and no amount of juggling could increase the number of man-hours. Understandable though it may have been, the worst misuse of skills and manpower was the removal of crashed aircraft from the strip in order to keep it open. The heavy rains turned the dust into mud and aircraft would skid almost out of control while ground crews held their breath, praying they would stay in a straight line and not come to a halt in the monsoon ditch. Vehicles became bogged down in their attempts to free aircraft which were also bogged down. The salvage of MT vehicles was almost on a par with that of aircraft. With most of the personnel occupied in extricating aircraft from the morass, dispersal and workshops were almost deserted and aircraft in various stages of servicing had to be abandoned.

The hiatus served to draw attention to the need for some sort of contingency plans to maintain continuity of servicing so the policy regarding the unit's handling of the different salvage categories of aircraft was changed. All aircraft requiring extensive repairs would now be dismantled and conveyed to the MUs where the tempo was likely to be less hectic. The problem could have been dealt with in two other ways: post in more men, which would create unacceptable demands on the domestic site, or work at night. Lighting would be provided by utilizing landing lamps salvaged from aircraft but it would be almost impossible to maintain adequate blackout. The workshops were merely bamboo frameworks with woven rattan mat roofs. Nevertheless, because of the urgency, this idea was put into practice but, as predicted, it attracted the attention of Jap snipers in the hills who began to take pot-shots at the illuminated area. Although it was a fair way off one airman did suffer a superficial wound and the whine of bullets became quite disconcerting.

One of the chaps suddenly remembered that his father, who had been in a similar situation during the Boer War, once told him that they used to hang up wet horse blankets over the trenches to stop stray bullets. Although rather sceptical, they draped a wet blanket over a frame and fired at it. Sure enough, even from a relatively short range most of the bullets fell harmlessly to the ground. As many blankets as could be found were hung on to bamboo frameworks around the work area, soaked with water and the lights switched on. The sniping started again but now the bullets had little effect much to the relief of the servicing crew.

However, a few days later Lieut.-Gen. Scoones, the GOC of 4 Corps, was inspecting the defensive boxes and on seeing the multi-coloured array of blankets, now dry and waving like washing on a line, demanded to know who was responsible for this unmilitary display. No one wanted the responsibility of informing this rather stern, unsmiling general of its true purpose. Finally, the chap who had had the idea provided an explanation. The general, now rather bemused at the thought of Boer War tactics being used in Burma and who had not been aware of the snipers, immediately became concerned at the jeopardy the chaps were placed in by working at night. He ordered the blankets to be taken down and Bofors guns from a nearby artillery emplacement were brought in.

When night fell, orders were given to switch on the lights and take cover. No sooner had they complied than the bullets started whizzing into the illuminated area. Following the line of flashes, the gun battery opened up and blasted the side of the hill, obviously finding their target for the sniping ceased and the unit was able to carry on with night-time activities unhindered.

In spite of all the hard, menial labouring work, the repairs and the abominable conditions of the previous months, never did the unit receive any thanks from the top. In fact, a signal received was viewed as a reprimand for it stated: 'Expedite repairs immediately as the present holding of forty-seven aircraft under repair is excessive and must be reduced.' Just how was never explained. Crashes were still a daily occurrence, men were still in the field salvaging and others still worked day and night repairing aircraft. The atmosphere was depressing and morale sank even lower when a smallpox epidemic broke out in a nearby village and the whole unit had to be vaccinated. The men were determined to vindicate themselves and, although an almost impossible task, within five weeks the so-called excess holdings had been reduced by thirty-five aircraft with a reduction of ten others as spares, at least on paper. What was not realized was that for every one struck off another took its place. It satisfied the office wallahs, however.

Additional help now arrived in the shape of 1 Airborne Salvage who had flown in to investigate the possibility of salvaging four Spitfires at Singkaling Khampti. Two could be repaired and were expected to fly out after repairs. The other two were found to be Cat. BC and Cat. ES and were dismantled and flown out in Dakotas. They did, however, leave fourteen of their men behind to be attached to 132 RSU.

With the easing of the situation, the unit began to take a more positive interest in its own welfare and amusement and had formed a concert party. Its first show, quite appropriately, was entitled 'Something from Nothing'. The significance was even more apparent when an outbreak of fire in the Sergeants' Mess, supposedly caused by an exploding pressure lamp, burned down three living bashas and the wash-houses, destroying everyone's kit in the process. The following day, fate took another hand in the drama when a number of the airmen's quarters were also destroyed by fire. Rumours had it that it was a reprisal. About this time, speculation was rife that the unit was to move on into Burma in the wake of the Army. It looked very much as if the unit was burning its boats behind it.

On the same day as the fire, 11 January 1945, an advance party, under Flt/Lt M. D. Hobbs, left Tulihul just after midnight in convoy for Ye-U, not far from Schwebo about 180 miles away, which had been captured by the Worcester Regiment a few days previously.

The mountain road beyond Palel to Tamu wound through hills for some forty miles. It was originally part of an old Assam tea planters' track over which thousands of refugees and the remnants of the British Army had escaped from the Japanese onslaught on Burma in 1942. It had now been converted by the Army engineers into a dual roadway which someone once described as a series of boulders held together with dried mud. Like the Dimapur Road it wound round and along the sides of high mountains covered in jungle, with deep ravines to trap the careless. The route beyond Tamu lay through the notorious Kabaw Valley which was aptly named Death Valley by the local inhabitants as it was one of the most malaria infected regions in Burma. It had taken its toll of thousands of refugees, too weak to offer any resistance to its contagion in their flight to freedom in 1942. As if in retribution, exhausted and starving Japanese troops had suffered the same fate as they fled before the British Army.

Anxious not to expose themselves any longer than necessary to the same pestilence, the convoy pressed on as quickly as conditions would allow. Frequent stops were required for repairs, mainly due to tow-bars becoming distorted with the continual changes of directional pull caused by the inclines and twisting nature of the road. Even worse was to follow when one of the Holmes wreckers broke down. Rather than abandon a valuable vehicle it was decided to try to tow it to an Army Recovery Depot. There Flt/Lt Hobbs obtained a reconditioned V8 engine and left three fitters behind to effect repairs.

No sooner had they arrived at Ye-U than Flt/Lt Hobbs was instructed by Gp/Capt Goddard of 906 Wing to take a fully armed party, escorted by men from 2961 RAF Regiment Squadron, to the Myiama area to salvage a Japanese Oscar 2 which had been reported to have landed almost intact. In the meantime, the main body of the unit, which had left ten days after the advance party, finally arrived. All the vehicles now moved on to Sadaung, leaving detachments at Ye-U, Onbauk and Tabingaung. While at Tabingaung a district court martial was set up to charge two sergeants with conduct prejudicial to good order and discipline. The suspicion was that they had instigated the burning of the airmen's billets at Tulihul in retribution for the loss of their own quarters. Nothing could be proved and the investigating team flew back to Imphal without any conclusive evidence.

The site at Sadaung was situated among Buddhist temples and surrounded by palm groves. The Japanese 'jitter' patrols could be heard either shaking tins filled with stones, shouting orders in English or firing at nothing in particular. Guards opened fire on shadows that did not respond to challenge. On 1 March the atmosphere became quite tense when it was reported that about 500 Japanese had been sighted about fourteen miles north-east of Sadaung. Unlike Imphal and Tulihul, there were no defensive boxes. It was just a question of doubling the guards, keeping a constant look-out and hoping for the best. Nothing happened, however, and it seemed they were going in the opposite direction.

In their retreat, the Japs destroyed airfields by digging large trenches across strips or blowing huge craters in them. This was where the Sentinel L5 came into its own for it could land and take off in a very short space. It was also relatively easy to salvage. The light structure and a Lycoming engine, only a little larger than a car engine, once dismantled could be manhandled on to trucks with ease. Two, K3392 and B3393, in different locations, were salvaged by WO Eldridge and a party who, in order to get to the sites, had to cross the Irrawaddy over the Ava bridgehead which had been established at Ywathitgyi. This bridge had been blown up by the British in their retreat from Burma and was now spanned by a Bailey bridge mounted on pontoons, each section towed by a Dukw and could carry three 3-ton lorries plus two Jeeps. One of the L5s was repaired on site and flown out, the other was a write-off. Only the engine was recovered and brought back.

Leaving a detachment at Ondaw, the unit moved southwards, crossing the Irrawaddy at Nagzun and bypassing Mandalay, which was still occupied by the Japs, before arriving at the airfield at Dwelha. Meiktila had fallen on 4 March though it was unusable for ten days after occupation because of enemy action. Squadrons had now moved within striking distance of Mandalay which was still fiercely holding out. One of the unit drivers, AC Cashman, was among the first to enter Mandalay and had watched while Fort Dufferin was being attacked by Hurricanes and Thunderbolts supported by American B-25s.

After leaving another detachment at Meiktila, the unit finally arrived at Kwetnge, ten miles further south, while the HQ of 132 RSU moved to Sinthe which was now the main airfield for No. 4 Corps. It had been occupied by the Japanese but had been rebuilt in about ten days by Army engineers. It was a small air town, complete with miles of roads and dispersals. It even had an irrigation system to keep down the dust on the airfield. There were ordnance dumps for petrol and oil, medical centres under canvas and complete operating theatres underground. Severely wounded men could be back in Comilla within two hours of receiving first aid treatment. The facilities even included a psychiatric unit.

By the end of March, feelings began to run high among the airmen, not because of the work and the environment or the dicey situation regarding the proximity of the Japs, but because another month had passed without an issue of beer. The last had been at Tulihul at Christmas. Army units in the area had received theirs on a regular basis while other RAF detachments had, in some cases, received two months' rations.

Appeals by the CO, Sqn/Ldr Davies, to Group HQ and personal assurances by Gp/Capt Goddard that it was on its way from Imphal did little to lessen the grievance felt at the neglect of this very basic amenity. In spite of promises of giving the matter priority, it was a further two weeks before they were fulfilled.

It is strange that whilst willing to submit to all sorts of discomfort and hazards, the one thing that could almost cause a rebellion would be a simple bottle of beer.

One of the detachment's first jobs at Kwetnge was to fit a new engine in a Hurricane. F/Sgt Gunnell, the test pilot, was to fly it out but was concerned at the unevenness of the ground. The airfield had been bombed regularly by the RAF and although the craters had been filled in by the Army, the filler was still soft. To overcome these hazards an airman stood by each filled-in bomb crater to mark out a suitable flight path. The sight of an aircraft rapidly approaching required not only strong nerves but absolute faith in the skill of Norman Gunnell.

A month later, the unit was again on the move, this time to Kalewa, north of Toungoo. On the first night there was pandemonium when a lone Jap, no doubt in a gesture of defiance and anxious to please his Emperor, got through the guards and blew up an L5 and himself with hand grenades. The prospect of further attacks was ever present and quite clearly indicated by the enemy camp-fires on the hill on the opposite side of the airfield.

In the meantime, other detachments had spread out to Pegu and Hwambi, just north of Mingladon, and on 2 June 1945, the HQ arrived at Mingladon from Sinthe.

The final entry in the F540, dated 1 March 1946 at Mingladon, was to instruct 132 RSU to take over the Spitfire XIVs from 273 Squadron which had been disbanded. Although the war had been over for some months, the amount of work did not seem to abate and many airmen were beginning to get a bit disenchanted. This disillusionment must have been widespread for suddenly Dakotas and other aircraft were flying in with messages chalked on their fuselages encouraging airmen to revolt. It was treated as a bit of a joke until one of the chief culprits was finally arrested and went the way of all mutineers.

Unfortunately, there are a great many gaps in the records between 1 April 1945 when the unit arrived at Kwetnge and 15 August 1945 when 85 RSU (Airborne) arrived to join them from Calcutta, and for good reason. Unknown to the personnel, on 31 March 1945 all the documents of the unit had been transferred to 56 MU (Forward Repair Unit) HQ for retention and the unit had now become 56 FRU (No. 1 Detachment) Mingladon and commanded by Sqn/Ldr W. W. Pink.

Strangely enough, in spite of this change-over, no reference to this new title was ever made in relation to the unit's activities and it continued to be referred to as 132 RSU in its dealings with other units in the area, right up until the end when it was finally disbanded in Rangoon on 31 March 1946. Nevertheless, however it was described by the admin wallahs, in its advance through central Burma, the unit had salvaged and serviced hundreds of aircraft of every description at almost every airfield which had been opened up by the Army, many with tongue-twisting names which will be unknown to many but never forgotten by a few.

Landing stage at Dacca built by 4RSS

Wellington HE131

Dakota whose wing was 'dismantled' by Gurkhas

Holmes wrecker and MT crew Imphal

Levelling airstrip by hand

113 Squadron Blenheim damaged during storm

Elephant help at Gafargaon — B9801

Repairing banks of the river to get to site

Z7943 being recovered

Brighouse trailer at Loretto Convent

Loretto Convent

Before and after the Siege

On the road to Tamu

132 RSU MT Section

Curtiss Commando of US Combat Cargo

The Dakota victim of the Commando at Imphal

Spitfire F–LY, but it never did again

Ready for trouble

Japanese surrender

Patrol of Assam Rifles at the recovery site of the B–25 engine. Mr Lengkuingum, an eyewitness, is in the centre

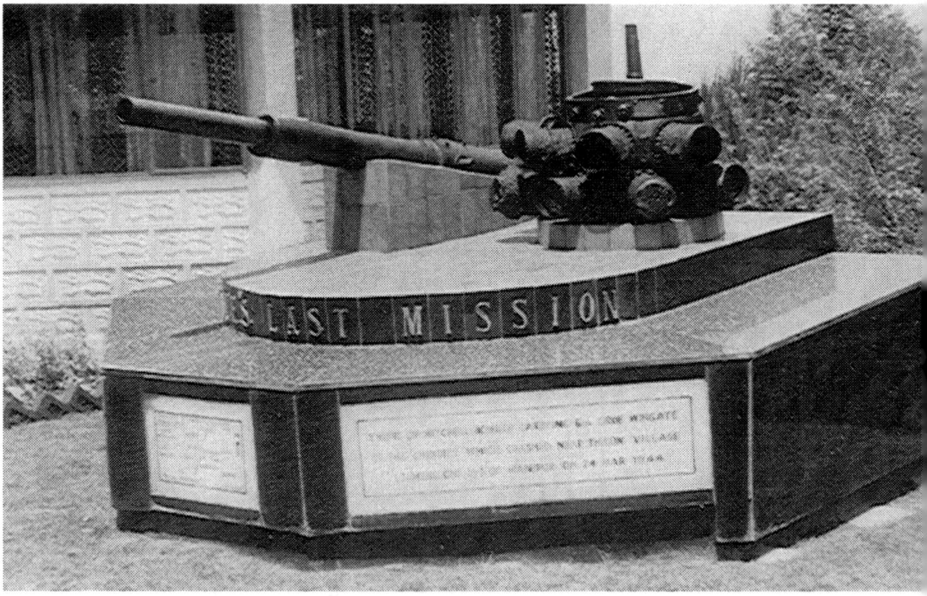

Engine and cannon from Wingate's B–25 outside Officers' Club at Shillong

Lord Louis Mountbatten addressing the troops in 132 RSU scrapyard

Darjeeling/Himalayan Railway

Mod cons Far East style

Chapter 10

Wingate's Last Flight

A great deal of controversy has surrounded the events before and after the fatal crash in which Gen. Orde Wingate lost his life. The times of take-off, the location, the so-called sightings in the last few minutes before the crash, the weather conditions prevailing at the time, even the position and state of the wreckage when it was found two days later and, of course, the probable causes of the fatal crash are all debatable.

The following eyewitness accounts, in describing the day leading up to the arrival and departure of Wingate's aircraft, point to many discrepancies in the so-called factual accounts of the tragedy, including the denial that Wingate was NOT advised against flying, that there was no discord prior to take-off, that the weather was relatively fine with only isolated storms which could be avoided and that he took off in late afternoon in broad daylight.

For 132 RSU stationed on the Imphal Plain, 24 March 1944 began much the same as any other day. There was a clear sky with little cloud and it was hot and sticky. The chota monsoons were as yet no real threat though storm clouds had been gathering on top of the surrounding hills in the evenings for some time. The Japanese were reported to be only twenty or thirty miles away, closing in from the north and south, and the predicted attack to capture the Imphal Plain seemed imminent. We had been told that Ukhrul had fallen and that the salvage crew which had brought the 28 Squadron pilot back had been lucky.

Flying activities had increased dramatically with transport planes bringing in supplies in a never-ending stream. Those that landed to discharge their cargo would return to their bases in the Surma Valley with wounded and non-combatants. Hurricanes and Spitfires were flying in at first light from rearward bases ready to scramble.

No one could foretell that the next twenty-four hours would see the death of a general who was a legend in his own lifetime, who was seen as an eccentric mixture of warrior and prophet, who had compared himself with Gideon and whose unconventional military tactics seemed to ruffle the feathers of the more traditional school of military strategy, or that Friday 24 March 1944 would be an important date in military history books.

After the usual breakfast of soya sausage in one of its many unimaginable guises surrounded by a glutinous dried egg concoction supplemented by a sour tasting bread made locally, upon which, if it hadn't liquefied, one could spread a substance known as Oleo margarine, supplied in seven pound tins, all of which was washed down with *chai* so brown and thick it was almost like varnish, the airmen began their allotted tasks. Some serviced aircraft in the dispersals, others repaired those which had survived minor prangs or had been shot up. Others went to the strip to carry on clearing away the previous day's casualties. The primary object above all things, was to keep the airfield clear for the day's sorties.

On this particular morning, two Hurricanes of 28 and 113 Squadrons were awaiting the attention of the salvage crew. Both had been shot up the day before but had managed to make it back safely and had been hauled to the side of the runway. By 0930 hours both aircraft had been towed back to the dispersal. The airfield was once again clear of obstruction and normal flying could resume. Not for long, however, for at 1030 another Hurricane returning from a sortie had slewed across the runway and run into soft ground. Fortunately, it suffered no material damage and after towing out and an inspection, it was able to taxi under its own power to the dispersal.

Transports, which had been stacking, began once more flying '*in anum*', some barely touching down before taking off again. Bales of fodder, drums of fuel, crates of all sizes and descriptions were unceremoniously kicked out of the cargo hatches by the dispatchers, to be loaded as quickly as possible into IASC gharries to be taken to the supply depots at Imphal. It was a dicey situation with supplies bouncing all over the strip and one had to keep a wary eye open for these dangerous but welcome missiles.

It seemed, at last, that the day might now be relatively free from any further panics for a while and normal servicing could continue. The optimism was short-lived!

After about four hours of incident-free flying, around 1530, a Curtiss Commando of the USAAF Combat Cargo Squadron, bringing in supplies, developed brake failure and veered across the runway, colliding with a Dakota of 194 Squadron (FL511) parked on the side of the strip. This aircraft had got itself bogged down but after being pulled out with the Holmes wrecker and checked over, was awaiting the arrival of the crew to take off back to Agartala. The Commando finally came to a halt straddling the main road which ran alongside the airfield, causing a major traffic jam and general chaos as convoys ground to a halt. It was finally towed to the end of the runway to a safe position and the Army convoys continued.

While all this feverish activity was taking place, with everyone who could be spared lending a hand, a Hurricane of 28 Squadron and a Spitfire of 81 Squadron, returning from ops, obviously aware of the scene below, attempted to land on the edge of the strip, the Hurricane first followed by the Spitfire. Unfortunately, either because of its slower speed or impeded by soft ground, the Hurricane slowed down rapidly causing the Spitfire to overrun into the Hurricane's tail, slicing it almost to the rear of the cockpit. The Spitfire then cartwheeled and skidded to a halt upside down in the centre of the runway. Though badly bruised, the pilot was alive and, apart from the aircraft, the only casualty was an airman who lost the tip of a finger by trapping it in one of the elevators while the plane was being lifted.

Rather appropriately, the Spitfire markings were F-LY, but it never did again.

The Hurricane pilot, who was unhurt, managed to extricate himself and had a few choice words to say as to the lineage of all Spitfire pilots. His aircraft, quite naturally, was a complete write-off.

In the midst of all the activity, there suddenly appeared an Army officer in a Jeep. He was plainly agitated and wanted the strip cleared immediately as a plane carrying Gen. Wingate wanted to land, but no one took any notice of an unknown Army bod. Not until the airfield controller came on the scene was the order complied with and the strip was cleared for the fourth time that day. The wreckage of the two aircraft was hauled to the verges, to be cleared the following morning.

After circling around for a while, Wingate's aircraft, an American B-25H, the type fitted with 75mm. cannon, eventually touched down and taxied to the manifest hut, guided by a couple of blokes. When all the passengers had got out, Gen. Wingate, complete with his familiar 'Bombay Bowler', surveyed the scene of devastation and commented to Geordie Hopper and Jock Brown, who had marshalled the plane in, 'You're doing a good job, keep up the good work.' He then left the airfield in a Jeep with the same Army officer who had ordered the strip cleared and accompanied by two of the aircrew.

No doubt because it was Wingate's personal plane, the aircraft was placed under armed guard. That was the end of it as far as 132 RSU was concerned and everyone went about the usual duties. That same evening, after a late meal, about 1900 hours, it was decided to remove the hazards from the edge of the runway, ready for flying activity the next day and the expectation of further prangs. It was extremely slow work and pitch dark, the only illumination being from the Coles crane and a couple of trucks.

Suddenly, out of the darkness appeared the same Army officer who had ordered the strip to be cleared that afternoon. He wanted it cleared again to allow Wingate to take off. The request was received with disbelief: a B-25 taking off at night from an unlit strip? Nevertheless, it was true. There was no alternative but to haul the crashed aircraft again on to the verges amidst a great deal of cussing and grumbling at the duplicated work.

About an hour later, Gen. Wingate turned up, accompanied by the pilot and navigator. In the meantime, the guard on the aircraft, a young airman who had recently joined the unit, was challenging anyone who approached for the password. Unknown to him at the time, he challenged Wingate himself. Only on the intervention of the pilot did he let a very irate general pass. The guard was given a roasting for not having recognized Wingate, though he was of course quite within his right as a guard. In all fairness, Wingate might well have been a familiar figure amongst his own troops, but it was only his reputation that many of the RAF personnel were familiar with and very few had seen him in the flesh.

The runway at Imphal had no flare path. The only illumination available was a 'panic' light. This was a reflector light operated by a small generator from a hut at the end of the runway. It had not long been installed and up to that time had never been used.

After the strip had been cleared and made safe, Chiefie Grey, a couple of chaps and the MT drivers were dispatched to the end of the runway to organize the lights, the idea being to use the reflector light to indicate the end of the runway and position the two trucks opposite each other with their headlight beams shining across the runway as a guide to the width. By this time, it was evident that a violent storm was brewing over the surrounding hills. Brilliant flashes of lightning were plainly visible outlining the contours of the mountains surrounding the strip, followed by the distant rumbling of thunder.

Meanwhile, it was apparent to the men waiting around for final instructions as to what was going to happen, that there was some sort of argument taking place in the control hut. Voices were raised, though it was impossible to say whose they were. As the only occupants were Wingate and his ADC, a couple of other officers, including the one who had had the strip cleared, an RAF officer and two of the American crew, it was obvious that some sort of dissent had arisen among them.

The two civilian war correspondents, Stuart Emeny of the *News Chronicle*, who is alleged to have coined the now famous phrase 'The Forgotten Army', and Stanley Wills of the *Daily Herald*, who had been there since they arrived in the afternoon, were waiting outside with the rest of the crew and were chatting quite amiably to everyone as a decision was awaited. Bert Brown was talking to one of the crew standing outside and he addressed him as Sergeant, to which he replied, 'I'm known as Sadie.' (Top Sergeant Frank Sadowski.) They exchanged small talk and he recalls saying it was not the best of nights for flying, especially with the weather conditions as they were in and around the hills. He agreed, but with typical Yank casualness and a shrug of his shoulders, just said, 'If Wingate wants to go, we don't have much option.'

After they had all come out of control, the pilot paused for a moment to talk to his crew who were waiting outside. He seemed to give them a meaningful look and shook his head despairingly before climbing aboard, followed by the co-pilot, Wingate, still wearing his 'Bombay Bowler', his ADC, the rest of the crew and his two civilian passengers. Bert counted nine altogether and thought it must be a bit of a tight squeeze and not very comfortable.

Len Kebbell confirmed again, through the cockpit window, to the rather dour faced pilot, what the take-off drill would be. He could see that the lights at the end of the strip were on. He said, 'OK, good luck' and started the engines. Len thought to himself, 'You're the one who's going to need the luck.' After a few minutes run-up, he signalled he was ready and gave a typical Yank salute. Geordie and Jock were in position at the wing-tips, ready with torches to guide the aircraft down the runway. Geordie Hopper recalls that it was 'as dark as a bag except for the lightning flashes over the hills'. With Geordie on one wing-tip and Jock on the other, they marshalled him out, almost running by the time they got to the take-off point. He turned on his landing lights and swung round to begin his run.

Ten minutes later he was airborne and they watched him until his lights disappeared from view. He seemed to be heading straight for the threatening storm. The lights were shut down, the trucks collected and everyone went back to the billets. It was about 9 p.m. It had been a very long day and they were all shattered. The main topic of conversation on the way back to the billet was, quite naturally, the dicey circumstances of the take-off when daylight was only a few hours away. Later on, one of the blokes on the reflector light, it was probably Chiefie, told Geordie, 'I thought one of the engines sounded a bit rough.'

No one was really surprised when they heard the following day that the aircraft had crashed somewhere west of Imphal. Most of them thought at the time that this would be another salvage trek up into the hills for the unit.

From this point on, every account from so-called 'official' sources reveals discrepancies. Not one single report bears out another. The nearest is perhaps Maj.-Gen. Claude Rome's account of the pilot's concern at Broadway as to the aircraft's serviceability, and that of the ground crew's comments regarding the 'rough' engine at Imphal.

Christopher Sykes, in his book *Orde Wingate*, Chapter 23 'The End', in describing the events of the afternoon and evening of 24 March, has written: 'On the 23rd March 1944, Air Marshal Sir John Baldwin wrote to Wingate on the subject of the removal of the Chindit Advance Headquarters from Imphal to Sylhet. He considered that it placed the Chindit staff too far from his own or any other air headquarters... On the 24th March, learning that Wingate was due to fly into Imphal, and knowing he was an irregular correspondent, he decided to meet him and get an answer personally and flew in from Comilla in a Lockheed Hudson... He landed at Imphal shortly before Wingate arrived from Aberdeen.' (It was in fact Broadway.) This is where the conflict of accounts really begins.

The Air Marshal could not possibly have landed at Imphal before Wingate at the time stated. The strip was completely blocked and had to be cleared specifically for Wingate's aircraft to land. He may of course have landed at Kangla and driven to 221 Group to meet Wingate. His Hudson aircraft was certainly not parked either at the control hut or anywhere else on the strip.

The impending arrival of the Commander of the 3rd Tactical Air Force must have been known in advance and would have prompted a warning for everyone to be on their toes, as was always the case when any high ranking officer flew in. It was not, for some reason, the case in this instance.

The account then goes on to say: 'It was about 5 o'clock in the afternoon when they, the Air Marshal and General Wingate went to alert the crews of the two aircraft... Sir John, proposing that the Mitchell, being the faster of the two aircraft, take off first.' The B-25 took off swiftly, followed by the Lockheed.

The last Sir John saw of the Mitchell was flying over the Bishenpur Hills. 'In the main the weather was fine and isolated storms could easily have been avoided.' This is yet another discrepancy and is borne out by subsequent events.

The records and accounts of these events following the crash really beggar description, for even the official USAAF crash investigation conducted by Brig. Ray Clark between 1 and 9 April reveal some startling anomalies and conflicting statements which seemed to have been either overlooked by the investigating officers or, at worst, ignored as being of little consequence to the final outcome. Not least of which is the statement of Col. Cochran indicating that he had spoken to Wingate at 1600 hours by radio telephone and he had informed him that he was going to see VINCENT on his way back — not Sir John Baldwin!

Although Air/Cdre Vincent's account is vague and a trifle contradictory, it points some way to confirming that the take-off was in the dark and not as implied by Sir John Baldwin in the afternoon. But just how the air commodore saw him take off without going out to the airfield, is anyone's guess.

The weather conditions at the time also vary from account to account. In *The Air Battle of Imphal* by Norman Franks, it is quoted that the RAF would not fly from Aberdeen (it was in fact Broadway) because of inclement weather, 'so he hitched a ride back in a B-25 to Imphal'. The weather conditions may well have been correct at the time at Broadway but at Imphal it was fine and sunny that afternoon. The 'hitching' was far from the fact, the B-25 had been allocated to him from the start by Col. Philip Cochran of the 1st Air Commando Group, 10th US Air Force based at Hailakandi, on the instructions of President Roosevelt.

F/O Maurice Kay, who was the Flying Control Officer in the Ops Room of 221 Group HQ at Imphal that night, recalls the 'friendly' plot on the Operational Table which was identified as Wingate's aircraft moving west, and he watched until it disappeared from the screen. There were no other aircraft movements that night.

Eyewitness accounts at the time of take-off state that 'a violent storm was brewing over the surrounding hills. Brilliant flashes of lightning were plainly visible outlining the contours of the mountains.' Another was economical with his description and merely said, 'It was dark as a bag except for the lightning flashes over the hills.' The stormy conditions are also supported by the probability that the aircraft was observed by P/O Joe Simpson of 194 Squadron flying to Silchar in his Dakota. He is quoted in *The Air Battle of Imphal* as seeing a Mitchell spiralling down through the clouds with the storm about it, though there is no verification that it was Wingate's aircraft. There were, after all, a great many Mitchells in that theatre of operations.

A further inconsistency on three counts is the location of the wreckage. Sqn/Ldr Norris, on reconnaissance a hundred miles south-west of Imphal over the Lushia Hills on 25 March, observed wreckage of an aircraft, whilst a report by one of Col. Cochran's pilots puts it near the village of Pabram in the hills west of Imphal, north of Sylhet and near the summit of a 7,000 feet high ridge. Field Marshal Slim, however, in *Defeat into Victory* says that 'the aircraft was found at the foot of the largest hill, but does not appear to have brushed it, as there were no tell-tale marks at the top'. This would imply that someone had actually climbed to the summit to check though nothing in the search report indicates that this actually happened.

Maj.-Gen. Tulloch, in his book *Wingate in Peace and War*, describes how he dispatched Capt. Frank Barns, accompanied by the Rev. Christopher Perowne, Chaplain to Headquarters Special Force at Sylhet, to search for the aircraft: 'After an exciting journey, Barns reached the wreckage and identification was confirmed.' However, the description of the state of the wreckage given at the official inquiry and Capt. Barns' report to 3rd Indian Division HQ, and that of Sgt Samp's report, vary to such an extent that one wonders if the various descriptions are of the same aircraft.

Lt.-Col. Smith, the OC of the Bomber Command Section of the 1st Air Commando Group, made an aerial recce to try to confirm the reported sighting of the crashed aircraft but unable to be sure, returned and set up a sweep with two light aircraft in an attempt to positively identify the wreckage. In the meantime, the Army patrol had gone out to the reported scene of the accident.

Sgt Samp, one of the light aircraft pilots who had searched the area the previous day, with Sgt Walters of D Squadron, 1st Air Commando, were dispatched from Hailakandi in a US L5 to the scene of the crash to try to establish contact with the patrol. Unfortunately, they crash landed not fifty yards from the wreckage and Sgt Walters broke his leg in the accident. After making his companion comfortable and following a rest, he went to the crash site. He stated that 'the Indians (Nagas) had uncovered the nose ... the prop was showing ... the cannon and machine-guns were visible ... landing gear and tyre still attached ... wing lying outside hole'. Capt. Barns, on the other hand, says, 'wings could not be found'. There was no mention of cannons, machine-guns or landing gear being visible.

Again, with the description of the remains, Sgt Samp, who had arrived first, stated that he saw various limbs and 'the bodies were covered up' before he left. Capt. Barns, who arrived later, is quoted as saying, 'we asked the natives to cover them up'. According to Tulloch's book, identification was not easy and the padre could only conduct a short service as it was not possible to conduct a proper burial. Yet at no time, either at the inquiry or in his report, did Barns mention a burial service or indeed that he was accompanied by a padre in the first place!

In Sykes' book, the same padre, Col. Christopher Perowne, set out three months later on 6 July, to bury the remains. He conducted a modified service because of the different denominations and set up a cross and a bronze plaque made in the workshops at Sylhet and engraved with the names of the deceased. It goes without saying that if the bodies were not buried when first discovered on 26 March, then there would certainly be nothing left to bury in July, though it might just have been a token burial with a few surviving bones.

The identification of the remains is also at some odds. In Sykes' book identification was almost impossible though Gen. Tulloch is a little more explicit: 'Not only was Wingate's helmet found near the wreckage, but also a revolver belonging to the ADC, George Borrow, bent into a complete semi-circle. While not far away were some papers belonging to Wingate and a bloodstained notebook.' This then begs the question, what was the positive and reliable proof? The helmet? Was the pistol brought back and the serial number checked? Or did the papers and notebook bear Wingate's signature? This is very doubtful.

The most indifferent attention has been given to the identification of the five American crew and the two civilian passengers. No dog-tags were recovered and only one American hand gun yet all the crew had holster pistols when they took off. The prime concern was the identification of Wingate.

Even more of a mystery is just how the patrol and Sgt Samp missed each other, especially as it had been arranged for Samp to pick up a message from the patrol who would have been waiting for the L5 under the circumstances and would have surely heard the aircraft before it crashed. Also one would have assumed that the locals at Thilon, where Capt. Barns rested for four hours, and knowing his reason for being there, surely would have indicated to him that another aircraft had crashed in the vicinity near to the wreckage of the B-25.

Various causes of the crash have been put forward. Sir John Baldwin gives the most convenient and simplest of explanations. Dead men tell no tales and cannot defend themselves, so put it down as pilot error, a terrible stigma to place on any pilot, especially considering the unknown circumstances and lack of positive evidence.

A lightning strike is a distinct possibility. Other aircraft had suffered the same phenomenon in the region. This could well have put the electrics out of action and have accounted for the lack of radio signal. But whether it could have knocked out both the pilot and the co-pilot is open to question.

Sir John Baldwin, it seems, has a change of heart, for now, according to Michael Calvert in his book *Chindits, Long Range Penetration*, Sir John Baldwin's account is probably the best evidence for he (Sir John) thinks that the likely cause of the crash was that the pilot may have left out the trailing aerial from the aircraft in flight and that static which would have gathered, would have been sufficient to knock him out, when he switched on to talk to Sylhet and that the co-pilot could not have crawled through the tunnel in time to have gained control. This again is not based on fact. The co-pilot was in his usual seat when the aircraft took off from Imphal.

Air turbulence or an incorrect altimeter setting can also be discounted if the aircraft was already in flames when it crashed.

Sabotage can almost certainly be ruled out, although Jap infiltrators had been reported around Imphal at the time and it would have been a simple matter, could they have got near enough, to have placed an explosive charge on the aircraft. As it was, the aircraft had an armed guard from the minute it arrived until the time it took off, plus the fact that the passengers and crew were still in the vicinity the whole time. It leaves two other highly improbable possibilities: it was shot down or involved in a mid-air collision, the only other incidents which might have caused the fire in the air witnessed by the villagers.

Though only conjecture, the most likely cause was engine failure. B-25s were powered by Wright Cyclone engines which were not only prone to oiling up but it had been long known on rare occasions for the drive shaft to the oil pump to sheer. The consequences of this would be for the engine to eventually seize up, causing a tendency for the propeller to disintegrate. It needs very little imagination to picture the devastation as it sliced through the cockpit, probably killing the co-pilot instantly and whoever was in the upper turret as it tore unhindered through the fuselage. Escaping fuel would have caught fire and probably exploded, damaging the starboard wing and putting the aircraft into an uncontrollable spin.

It would give some credence to Capt. Benjamin's account at the inquiry of witnessing an explosion in mid-air and again that of the villagers who saw the aircraft coming down on fire, followed by an explosion from the remaining fuel tanks as the stricken aircraft hit the ground, heat from the blaze igniting the cannon and machine-gun ammunition.

The questions at the inquiry relating to the effect the crash and fire might have had on the fragmentation bombs which the aircraft was purported to be carrying are surprising. Assuming that the opinions expressed at the inquiry by Lt. Taylor, the armaments officer, and the reported state of the wreckage when found, have some substance, three questions come to mind.

Firstly, why were no fragmentation bombs found along with other unexploded ammunition? Secondly, was there really time to open the bomb doors and jettison them before crashing? At least one of the invertors supplying power might well have been out of action and would have necessitated hand cranking the doors open. Not an easy task in an overcrowded aircraft let alone one that was probably out of control. Thirdly and even more to the point, if it was only in a transport mode from Hailakandi, why would it have been bombed up in the first place?

Maj.-Gen. Claude Rome gives a graphic account in *Wingate in Peace and War* of the incidents prior to the B-25's taking off from Broadway, though it is a pity he waited twenty-three years before disclosing his views:

> When Wingate was at Broadway one of my staff told me that the pilots of his aircraft (the B-25) wanted to see me. They told me that they were not happy about the aircraft's serviceability. An engine was not developing its proper power.
>
> They asked me to persuade Wingate to wait for a relief aircraft, which they would call for. They were obviously rather in awe of Wingate and pretty worried men.

After the conference I took Wingate for a short walk round Broadway. He was obviously worried and preoccupied and rather grumpy. I told him what his pilot had told me.

He was inclined to pooh-pooh the matter. He had a talk to the pilots ... I was standing apart. It was quickly apparent, however, that they would take off. I went over to see him off.

As the chocks were pulled away, I caught the eye of the pilot on the near side of the cockpit. I smiled at him and gave the 'thumbs-up' signal. I remember him very clearly, his giving me a wave but no smile, and he made a grimace at me, pulling down the corners of his mouth.

The aircraft fairly staggered off the runway, using every inch of it, and climbed very slowly. I thought it was flying one wing low.

You will appreciate that by then I had seen several hundred aircraft take off from Broadway and had enough experience to realise that this take-off was far from normal.

I was NOT, therefore, totally surprised to hear of the disaster. I thought that the inevitable had occurred. It was not until much later, after our return from Mogaung, that I heard that the aircraft had, in fact, landed and taken off again before the disaster.

This put an entirely new complexion on the matter and opened up all sorts of possibilities in what to me, at the time, appeared a 'closed case', and I was glad I hadn't broadcast what had happened at Broadway... One thing is certain, that at Broadway, the pilots were worried as to the aircraft's 100% serviceability and that, to the laymen the take-off was a disturbing sight.

One of the very few really vivid memories I have of our operations in Burma is that take-off and the sequel.

This, although discounted as evidence by Tulloch for some reason, confirms not only the eyewitness accounts of an unhappy pilot but the opinion of qualified engine fitters at Imphal that night that the 'engine sounded rough', remarks that ordinary airmen had no reason to make without just cause.

Although no flight plans have come to light, if one can believe the evidence available, Wingate left Hailakandi in early morning to fly to Broadway in his B-25, a distance of some 260 miles and about one hour and twenty minutes' flight time. There he transferred to a light aircraft, probably an L5, and flew to see Brig. Calvert at White City, about forty miles away. Leaving White City he flew over to Aberdeen, another twenty-five miles and talked to Lt.-Col. Green, commanding the Black Watch. From here he returned once more to Broadway, a further sixty miles, to change back to his B-25 waiting to return him to Imphal, a distance of 175 miles. All in all he had flown some 560 miles.

The B-25 would have been airborne for approximately 435 miles before arriving at Imphal. Although these aircraft carry sufficient fuel for six hours (970 gallons), given the overloaded condition of the aircraft in its cannon firing mode, with two extra passengers on the outward trip, plus the additional two war correspondents on its return from Broadway, along with the questionable serviceability of the aircraft, fuel consumption would have increased considerably. At a guess, the fuel would be running pretty low by the time of the crash and the resulting explosion and fire on impact was not as great as it might have been.

Meanwhile, following Capt. Benjamin's reports to Hailakandi of an explosion and a realization that Wingate was overdue, the wheels had been set in motion to investigate the possibility of an air crash. Junior Commander Vivienne Bartels, a WAC, who was the PA to Gen. Slim at Comilla, recalls: 'I was called back to duty from a dance in the Mess, around 10 p.m. There was quite a flap on, following a signal that Wingate was reported missing on his way back to his HQ at Lalaghat, and feared to have crashed in the mountains. I was to stand by and notify all units. Just after midnight, following signals to various commanders, we were stood down, as a search party had been organized and was to go out at first light. Two days later we were informed that his aircraft had been found, and that General Wingate and all the crew had perished.'

It is relatively easy, some forty-seven years later to speculate what might or might not have caused the crash and whether the argument in the manifest tent had any bearing on it and so on. But up to now, the overwhelming evidence would seem to suggest that it was engine failure as they approached Thilon. Further evidence came to light which would also seem to support the probability of a mid-air explosion.

In an article written by a Maj. P. K. Sur in the official Assam Rifles' Journal, the *Custodian*, he recounts how a patrol of the Assam Rifles was sent out in 1989 to the village of Thilon, close to where the crash occurred, to probe the mystery of the air crash. He actually located two of the eyewitnesses to the mishap, one aged a hundred years, the other eighty years, who recalled quite graphically the events of that night when they saw a ball of fire falling from the sky.

The picture of an aircraft coming down out of control before hitting the ground does coincide with the evidence of Sgt Samp and the native eyewitnesses at Thilon at the time, and indeed the state of the aircraft when it was found. Furthermore, the patrol was told that during cultivation a year later, the villagers found some silver coins scattered in the fields nearly three-quarters of a mile away from the site! This would seem to suggest that these coins could only have been scattered such a distance as debris from the air, before the impact!

One of the engines and the cannon were recovered by the patrol and are now mounted on an inscribed plinth in front of the Assam Rifles' Officers' Club in Shillong.

Nothing was found of the teak cross or the bronze plague which were erected at the site by the Rev. Col. Perowne.

In conclusion, these are most of the details known to date, some erroneous and misleading, others without question and factual. Why there should be such a mystery surrounding the events leading up to the crash and the variance in important details is obscure. Much has been made of the need for secrecy in order to fool the Japanese but this supposition can be scotched as his obituary appeared in the British national newspapers only a week after the crash.

Whether there was a political or military cover-up has not been possible to establish. The crash may well have presented a fortuitous opportunity for a strategy that has remained hidden in some dusty archive, waiting for some future student of Wingate to uncover.

Nevertheless, it is rather strange, in view of the importance of the crash and the passengers, that the authorities should choose to send a patrol of only three officers and never thought it necessary to send a qualified crash inspector and an experienced RAF salvage unit, either from 132 RSU based at Imphal who saw the aircraft in and out, or 124 RSU at Masimpur, both of whom were within about fifty miles of the scene. Without a doubt, both would have established conclusive evidence of identification and the probable cause of the crash.

Equally odd is that there was no inquiry as to the aircraft's serviceability at the point of departure other than the questions put to Air/Cdre Vincent and Sqn/Ldr Larson, neither of whom was on the strip, the latter relying solely on a second-hand report from the duty pilot who was also never called upon to give any first-hand evidence regarding the take-off or whether there was any discord in the control tent.

The preceding account, highlighting the inconsistencies and glaring discrepancies in the 'official' explanations of the tragic accident are not intended in any way to besmirch or discredit Gen. Wingate, nor give support to those who opposed his somewhat eccentric behaviour. It is only intended to give some credence to ordinary airmen who were doing their job, who were there at the time and whose opinions have never been sought or deemed of any importance. But most of all, it is hoped that the evidence, although there are still a great many unanswered questions which may never be resolved, might go some way to removing the unjustified stigma of pilot error from 1/Lt Bryan Floyd Hodges of the 1st Air Commando, USAAF.

The words contained in Wingate's last signal to Winston Churchill were 'Let the truth be told.'

Records show that the remains were exhumed in 1947 and taken to the cemetery at Imphal where they remained for almost two years before being transferred to a mausoleum in Manila then finally interred in one casket in the Arlington Military Cemetery in Washington on 10 November 1950 under the World War II Dead Programme. As the remains could not be positively identified, only a Government issued group headstone was provided at Section 12, Grave 288, until a new upright grave marker was dedicated in 1975, inscribed with the names:

Borrow, G. H., Capt. MC
Emeny, Stewart, War Correspondent
Hickey, James Walton, T/Sgt, AC-USA

Hodges, Brian Floyd, 1/Lt, AC-USA
McInnich, Vernon A., S/Sgt, AC-USA
Sadowski, Frank, T/Sgt, AC-USA
Wanderer, Stephen Albert, 2/Lt, AAF-USA
Wills, Stanley, War Correspondent
Wingate, Orde Charles, Major General, DSO

Chapter 11

No. 134 Repair and Salvage Unit

In October 1943, a party of 'store bashers', who had arrived in Bombay aboard the P. & O. liner *Mooltan* (The Hellship of the Indian run) were posted in to Barrackpore, twelve miles north of Calcutta. The current rumour was that they were to set up a supply depot in the forward area.

The site near Barrackpore was a disused racetrack and they were accommodated in the derelict tote office with no facilities other than a stand-pipe for water and pole and hole toilets. There were no amenities of any kind although a small lake near by afforded a welcome respite from the heat. That is, until someone discovered that it was also the home of water snakes. Though they were assured by the locals that they were harmless, no one had sufficient courage to prove it.

After about a fortnight of enforced idleness in which no stores or equipment arrived, the original idea of a supply depot was abandoned and the personnel were dispersed, some to join salvage units or squadrons at Asansol and Jessore, others to join a Repair and Salvage Section being formed in Calcutta to replace No. 1 FRD (Fighter) which was on the move to Singabil, 200 miles north-east of Calcutta.

As the numbers of personnel in Calcutta began to increase, someone somewhere must have decided that the status of Section was not really in keeping with what was then the hub of activity at AHQ and Group. In consequence, with effect from 31 October the unit was to be known as 134 Repair and Salvage Unit, with a strength of 180 men.

The accommodation at the Armenian College, which 134 RSU was to take over from 1 FRD (101 and 125) now that they had moved, was, compared to the general domestic standards of the majority of RSUs, luxurious. It was a three-storey building which had been a school prior to the war and before that it had been a private residence with the distinction of being the birthplace of William Makepeace Thackeray. The room on the ground floor in which the event took place had a commemorative plaque on the wall.

Separated from the main building by a courtyard were two other buildings which housed the cookhouse, an assembly room, a canteen, an indoor swimming pool and sick quarters. The latter, No. 7 Kyd Street, was one of the prophylactic rooms in Calcutta for those who had exposed themselves to the delights of the flesh in the various establishments which abounded in the city, while further along the street at 62A was the accommodation of the AHQ.

Though the food was mediocre and monotonous, the unit did have three meals a day. The dispersals and workshops on the *maidan* were only about ten minutes' walk away. The great advantage, of course, was access to the wide variety of off-duty diversions within a short distance of the billets: cinemas, restaurants, shops, everything that one might expect of a thriving city. Not least of these facilities was the Ronaldshay Hut in Outram Road, probably the best known of all service canteens. It was run on a voluntary basis by the European ladies of the city. It was non-profit-making so prices were extremely low.

An added advantage as far as 134 RSU was concerned, was that it was only about a hundred yards from the dispersals, near enough to pop in for an iced lime juice costing two annas or an egg banjo whenever the desire was felt. Its only shortcoming was that a large colony of baboons lived in the trees which lined the road. Though their antics were amusing while they stayed in the branches, any pedestrians carrying a package were soon surrounded by a menacing crowd of screeching monkeys trying to relieve them of their possessions. Similarly, any MT driver who parked under the trees while visiting the canteen stood a very good chance of having his vehicle ransacked. Should they be frustrated in their search for desirable items, drivers would often return to find the canvas covers of their vehicles torn to shreds.

Up to now the main preoccupation had been work, food and sleep and sorties into the delights of Calcutta, though these latter excursions are a subject for a book of their own. With a proper unit title and position in the scheme of things, the CO, known as Old King Cole, decided that now was as good a time as any to have regular bull parades. Within a week, 103 men including most of the NCOs had applied for postings. No one minded working hard for long hours in the interests of the war effort but Blanco, Brasso and Bull were not viewed as contributory factors to winning the war. Within a few days, the AOC arrived to hold an inquiry into why so many men had applied for posting at the same time. The outcome was rapid and conclusive; the CO was replaced by Sqn/Ldr Rowbottom who rescinded the bull parades and work returned to a more normal routine.

The tranquil lifestyle was rudely shattered when Calcutta was again bombed by a force of Japanese aircraft. Although it was a comparatively small raid, it killed about 500 civilians, a number of ships in the docks were damaged and various warehouses were set on fire. As before, thousands fled the city in panic. Subsequent air raid alarms, although often false, had the same effect. With the shortage of labour to unload essential supplies in Kidderpore Docks, Service personnel were brought in to assist. No doubt the Japs saw this as a cheap and safe way of reducing morale and disrupting the war effort. Piles of putrefying rubbish and even bodies accumulated because of the shortage of labour. Many of the jute mills around Kankinara found themselves having to pay a bonus of eight annas to every worker who returned immediately to work after the all-clear.

In early April 1944, the threat to Calcutta had receded. The bitter fighting in Burma seemed thousands of miles away. Being almost in the heart of the city, Red Road and the *maidan* airstrips were always a hive of activity, reminiscent of Air Day, with crowds watching single-engine aircraft of every desription taking off and landing at regular intervals, not always without mishap as they bounced in on the narrow road.

Anyone having a drink in Firpo's or sitting in the Curzon Gardens had a grandstand view as the aircraft dropped in on the approach down Old Court House Street which ran in front of the restaurant, though sometimes an aircraft flashing past the window seemed rather too close for comfort. One pilot, having misjudged his landing, opened up to go round again, an action which wasn't well received by the tote authorities, for in so doing he disrupted a meeting on the racecourse and threw the betting form to the wind.

The daily routine was disrupted when AHQ issued an order that all RAF personnel in South-East Asia Command not in the forward areas were to be trained in jungle warfare. Small parties of airmen were sent to the small Army camp at Barazar, about twenty miles from Calcutta. The dilapidated bashas, almost engulfed by the jungle and ankle deep in decaying leaves, only contained some charpoys which had seen better days and a couple of hurricane lamps and no cooking facilities. Course personnel had to fend for themselves as best they could with the rations they had been issued with before arriving. Reveille at first light was heralded with bursts of live ammunition through the roof of the basha by sadistic instructors who took a delight in trying to scare the pants off the 'Brylcreem Boys'. The course lasted a week and no one shed any tears when it ended, though it had given them an insight into the less savoury conditions they might be called upon to sample.

Since its inception, Red Road and the grass strip which ran at right angles across the *maidan* had only been used for single-engine aircraft such as Mohawks, Spitfires, Harvards and Tiger Moths. One day, to everyone's surprise and consternation, an American Dakota came into view over the top of the Great Eastern Hotel, wheels down and with the obvious intention of landing on Red Road. Almost immediately, a red Very light was fired to warn the pilot not to attempt to land on the narrow road. Opening up to full power, the Dakota pulled away and circled once more for another approach. Again he was warned off, again he circled. On the third approach, he dropped in on the road, making a perfect landing before taxiing to one of the dispersals.

It was a foolhardy escapade. What he could not have known was of the existence of a stone balustrade which lined the roadway. Fortunately, unlike Hurricanes which had to steer a straight line to avoid this hazard, the Dakota mainplanes were high enough to pass over them. No sooner had he taxied to a halt than the cargo door opened, the steps were lowered and a motor scooter was lifted out, to be mounted by two Americans who roared away down the strip through the control gate and disappeared into the city before anyone could stop them.

On being questioned about the reckless landing, the pilot said he had mistaken it for Dum-Dum and thought that the Very light had been to warn off other aircraft in the vicinity while he landed. It was a lame excuse, but it was accepted. He was then asked just how he thought he would take off again. On the face of it, it looked very much as if the aircraft would have to be dismantled and taken by road to Dum-Dum, a prospect which pleased neither the pilot nor the salvage crew who would have to undertake the task.

After a great deal of discussion, it was decided, because of the prevailing winds blowing across the Hooghly River, to allow him to take off from the grass runway. Even then it was a calculated risk and would need not only a great deal of skill but a greater element of luck, not a performance for the faint-hearted, especially with trees lining the runway. With the ambulance, crash truck and fire tender standing by and everyone turning out to witness what was going to be either a disaster or a miracle, the Dakota opened up to full power, the pilot released the brakes and it began its run towards the river. Before it was three-quarters of the way down the runway it was airborne, its undercarriage retracting almost as quickly as a scrambling fighter aircraft. Clearing the trees by a few feet, it climbed steadily before turning towards Dum-Dum and disappearing from view. With a sigh of relief everyone went back to work, glad not to have been witness to what could have been a major crash.

There are some orders from above, especially Movement Orders, which seem to defy all logic and one wonders just what is exactly in the minds of the 'dream schemers' who invent these movements. Whether the complexity of the orders are designed to impress superiors or to keep hordes of clerks busy is only a supposition. Nevertheless, they occurred with regular monotony to RSUs in the Far East.

The order to end all orders was the one detailing 134 RSU to move from its base in the Armenian College to the air base at Bobbili near Vizagapatam. This move was described by Phil Hopkins, a storekeeper of 134 RSU, who took part in this epic tale of incompetence.

Everyone realized that when the war in Europe came to an end the full weight of the Allied forces was obviously going to be concentrated against Japan and that their days at Calcutta were numbered. So it was no real surprise when they were given orders to move from the Armenian College to Baigachi, about thirty miles north of Calcutta. After a short stay, at the end of June they were told that their final destination would be the air base of Bobbili in the state of Andhra Pradesh, about 500 miles to the south-west on the Bay of Bengal, presumably for the forthcoming operations against Japan.

The most direct, and obvious, route would have been along the East Coast Road but the route they eventually took was anything but direct. On the first day they covered 170 miles to Asansol where they spent the night. The following day they drove 112 miles to Bahri. The staging post at Dehri was the aim on the third day but they covered 175 miles and were ahead of schedule so F/O Bird, who was i/c, decided to press on to Benares where we could have a look around.

The next stop was Allahabad, eighty-five miles further along the Grand Trunk Road, a misnomer if ever there was one. After a look around, they set off for Cawnpore, 122 miles to the north-west. Following a night spent on a stone floor, they headed south-west towards Jhansi, 139 miles away, and another hard floor to sleep on.

The following morning they left at about 0730 hours and arrived eight hours and 195 miles further on at Biota, only to find that nobody had bothered to mention that this staging post had been closed down months before. There was no alternative but to press on to Mhow, 125 miles further on. Again, there were no charpoys to sleep on but by this time no one really cared.

Late the following afternoon, they arrived at Dhuli having covered 145 miles. The floors were a sea of mud and, with no charpoys yet again, they had no alternative but to sleep in the wagons. At Nasik, the next stop, the gravel floor made a change from stone and mud. Spirits began to perk up as they left Nasik bound for Bombay, down Hill Road. Somehow or other they missed the staging post and Dicky Bird scrounged accommodation, with the luxury of string charpoys, at 305 MU.

Being on the opposite side of the continent, it was hard to believe they were bound for Bobbili and rumours abounded. Not only was Bombay the 'Gateway to India' but also the exit and the more optimistic thought that the unit was in fact bound for Blighty. How easily are dreams shattered! When they again took to the road, it was towards Poona, 113 miles to the south-east.

On reaching Kirkee, the staging post on the outskirts of Poona, they knew immediately that the horrible conditions encountered so far were not peculiar to that part of India. There was mud, inches deep, everywhere but they were allocated charpoys which were shared, unfortunately, with thousands of bugs. To add to the misery, it rained incessantly and no rations were available until midday so breakfast and tiffin were rolled into one. Immediately afterwards they left for Nagar, seventy miles south-east.

Frayed tempers did not improve when someone misread the instructions and instead of going to Sholapur they went much further south to Shorapur, only to find there was no camp anywhere near. Shahpur, away to the north-east, seemed a likely place but, arriving at 2100 hours, there was nothing which even looked like a staging post. When the mistake was finally realized, it was too late to turn back.

They had driven 170 miles, it was pitch dark, there was nowhere to sleep and they were hungry. With the drivers' approval they pressed on and by a stroke of luck found an empty house. Although it was derelict, there were some furniture remains which they used to make a fire and the cooks set to and produced a meal.

The following morning they drove to Secunderbad, a pukka military establishment with showers and real beds, luxuries they hadn't seen for some time. After twenty-one days and nights on the road they looked decidedly worse for wear but after a couple of days of civilized living they felt a little more human and set off for Vizagapatam, 370 miles away. There were no other staging posts so they drove until dark hoping to find somewhere suitable to spend the night. They were fortunate enough to come across a *dak*, one of many dotted about India and built primarily as a rest house for weary travellers. It was derelict and had been occupied by various animals, but mainly goats judging by the smell.

Previously they had encountered incessant rain but on the next leg of the trip it was dry and arid with high winds which stirred up dust that filtered into everything. By the time they arrived their hair and clothes were caked with dust.

The camp, again, was a grim one, infested with clouds of flies. They were allocated tents but at least were provided with charpoys. Fortunately they were only there a couple of days and on 21 July set out for Bobbili, seventy-five miles away over roads as bad as those they had encountered previously. Four hours later, they arrived at what could loosely be described as an RAF camp. It was set in semi-scrubland in the middle of nowhere with the usual bashas for accommodation and an airfield used by rocket-firing Typhoons.

It had taken twenty-four days and nights to travel 2,500 miles, five times the distance of the direct route. Though this was probably one of the longest time-wasting road trips undertaken by any RSU, many RSUs were to suffer the same state of almost perpetual transit. The number of man-hours lost, the cost in fuel, wear and tear of vehicles in some of these silly exercises is incalculable, nor can one suppose that anyone was accountable for the mismanagement of these moves.

As the purpose of this epic journey to Bobbili was to prepare for forthcoming operations against Japan, preparations got under way almost at once, packing equipment, labelling everything as well as issuing everyone with combat greens. It was all speculation as to where the unit would be sent; there was no clue in the packing and consignment notes.

It was not until AVM Keith Park arrived on 28 July and addressed the parade that they were given and inkling as to the likely destination. It was to be the invasion of Malaya. Though not known at the time, it was part of a large-scale operation codenamed Zipper, in which the Commandos would seize an airstrip on the mainland, followed twenty-four hours later by RSUs to provide a repair base for fighter aircraft.

After the relatively action free lifestyle of Calcutta, the prospects were not received with a great deal of enthusiasm. Their fears were dispelled when on 6 August the atom bomb was dropped on Hiroshima, followed by another on Nagasaki three days later. By 15 August Japan had surrendered. The unit was stood down for three days, though the opportunity for celebration was somewhat limited in view of the surroundings.

The question on everyone's mind was, would the unit now be going home? It didn't seem to occur to anyone that the territories which had been overrun by the Japanese would now have to be reoccupied; aircraft would still need servicing or salvaging. All the speculation was short-lived when it was announced that the unit would be going to Hong Kong. Crates and equipment were re-marked for the new destination, loaded on to trucks at a railway siding at Donkinavalasa ready for transporting to Madras for loading aboard the *Fort Buffalo*.

As with other units sailing from India, except for service kit, men and personal possessions had to travel separately, an order that invariably resulted in men finding that their treasured possessions had been looted *en route*.

On 7 September, the unit personnel entrained for Madras, 480 miles to the south, two days travelling in third-class coaches with wooden bench seats and infested with cockroaches. Even with the war over, conditions for troops showed no signs of improvement. Arriving at Madras, they discovered that the boat had not arrived and the unit was destined to spend a few days in the familiar substandard transit camp, again staffed by personnel who couldn't care less about the welfare of troops passing through.

The unit finally embarked on the *Highland Monarch*, a Royal Mail ship of 14,500 tons. Four days later they dropped anchor forty-five miles up the Irrawady River towards Rangoon and remained there for three days. During this stop-over hundreds of Indian, Malay and Chinese displaced persons were ferried aboard to be taken back to Singapore. Five days after leaving Rangoon the *Highland Monarch* dropped anchor in Singapore. Those to be repatriated were ferried ashore by Royal Navy craft.

Well over half the passengers had now gone and the unit had considerably more room to relax in for the final leg of 1,800 miles. While crossing the China Sea, a strange order was issued: the tin hats would no longer be required. Whether they could be put away or thrown away no one bothered to find out and without further ado the men lined the rails and ceremoniously skimmed them across the open sea, much to the consternation of the more dedicated store bashers who couldn't bear to see the abandonment of Service equipment unless it had been properly processed.

The ship finally berthed at Kowloon Docks on 29 September. The unit was billeted in a house called Ho Man Tin. It was large with a courtyard and each room could accommodate about ten men. There were no beds until someone found a store of Japanese beds, nothing like charpoys, just wooden frames with boards nailed across them and no softer than the floor but at least it kept one up out of the draught and away from the attentions of any nocturnal creatures.

The airfield at Kai-Tak was unserviceable and littered with the remains of wrecked Japanese aircraft which the unit had to remove so that the airfield could be rebuilt by the Airfield Maintenance Units. This time coolie labour was not required as the work was undertaken by Japanese prisoners of war under Army escort.

Five months later, orders were received to destroy all documents and records of the unit's stay in Kowloon. All the months of compiling records had been wasted. This action, of course, automatically removed any discrepancies and deficiencies and 'fiddles' were rife, particularly with regard to petrol. An occasion arose when it was found that 500 gallons of fuel were unaccounted for. The shortfall was resolved over a few weeks by removing half a gallon from every four and a half gallon jerry can before issue to the drivers who were in a take it or leave it situation so just signed. No one really cared. It became a day to day existence, the main preoccupation being the thought of getting home as quickly as possible.

With very little technical work, other than occasionally being called out to service the Spitfires of 132 Squadron, the unit had little to do to occupy its time and was mainly employed on guard duties against the systematic looting which made the 'loose wallahs' of India seem like amateurs. Lawlessness was rampant and bribery a way of life with men being constantly approached with offers of cash for items in short supply. One storekeeper was approached quite blatantly by a Chinese merchant with a detailed price list of what he was willing to pay for blankets, shirts, towels, petrol and even vehicles.

Some enterprising locals even found a way of replacing the sails on their junks by simply cutting the ropes on the canvas tilts of unattended MT vehicles, leaving the tilt in position so as not to arouse suspicion then as the vehicle drove away, they would simply hang on to the canvas. The driver would only discover his loss when he arrived at his destination.

On 27 April 1946 the unit was disbanded. No. 134 RSU, with its records destroyed, no longer existed and merely became yet another statistic of the Burma campaign. Those who were time-ex or Class B, returned home; the remainder were integrated into RAF Kai-Tak.

Chapter 12

No. 136 Repair and Salvage Unit

No. 136 RSU was established at Jessore in November 1943, from No. 3 Repair and Salvage Section which had been formed by India Command in Delhi as a paper unit only but had never actually got off the ground.

The CO was Sqn/Ldr E. C. Hucklebridge, formerly the CO of 129 RSU, and other than those who had been left at Cuttack to form 123 RSU, all the personnel who remained at Jessore were absorbed into 136 RSU. A new Station Commander, Gp/Capt Wingate, had taken over from Gp/Capt Wallace. The accommodation and facilities on the domestic site at Santola had been vastly improved, the airfield had been strengthened and was in regular use by heavy aircraft. Because of this increase in traffic, the MT workshops, offices and stores, set up by the previous occupants, had to be moved into one of the disused hangarettes as they were too near the new taxi tracks.

By the end of November, the unit became fully stretched. Not only were they dealing with Wellingtons of 99 and 215 Squadrons at Jessore with the occasional Liberator and Dakota thrown in, but now had to service the airstrip at Baigachi and the Hurricanes of 146 and 176 Squadrons plus an influx of Spitfires of 152 Squadron, recently arrived from Italy.

Salvage and servicing crews were having to make a round trip of some 100 miles with kit and equipment, and with transport in short supply it began to create problems until it was decided that a permanent detachment on site would be a more practical proposition.

The unit's area of salvage activity lay between the Hooghly River and the Ganges and included the Sunderbans. It was an area of some 4,000 square miles interlaced with innumerable rivers and tributaries which presented many problems during the monsoon season. The inevitable flooding of the surrounding areas made it extremely difficult for motor transport. A suggestion by the CO to Group that the unit would be better served with an issue of a couple of amphibious vehicles fell on deaf ears.

The aircraft, with few exceptions, seemed to plump for the comparatively soft landing of water or flooded paddy fields in which to crash land. One in particular, a Wimpy of 99 Squadron (HE650), had chosen to land in four feet of water in a paddy field. The salvage crew and vehicles could only get to within two miles of the aircraft and completed the rest of the journey in hired country boats. When they finally arrived, they were confronted by an irate mob, including the owner of the paddy field who demanded compensation for the damage caused. Naturally his demands were ignored and it was suggested that he get in touch with the District Magistrate at Khulna for the appropriate application forms.

After a couple of days, the engines, rear turret, tailplane, fin and elevators had been removed and floated on to dry ground with the aid of petrol drums. Unfortunately, the salvage had to be abandoned when a sudden torrential rain storm caused the water to rise rapidly and engulfed the aircraft completely. It was to be almost a year before the aircraft fuselage could be moved, though by this time the aircraft had been vandalized by the locals and was of little value other than metal scrap.

On another occasion when a Spitfire crash landed south of Khulna at Baitaghati, the locals had helped themselves to whatever was removable, including camera, wireless and ammunition, before the salvage crew got there. During some preliminary investigations, one of the locals gave a vague wave of his arms in the general direction of the horizon to indicate to Sgt McGarty where the items may be located. After consultation with Flt/Lt Rummell, OC RAF Khulna, and the District Magistrate, they sought the aid of Col. Sherwood of the Baluchi Regiment who instigated a thorough search until all the missing equipment was recovered.

On 12 August 1944, the unit received a casualty signal which stretched the imagination almost to disbelief. Seven Spitfires of 615 Squadron, returning to Baigachi, had crashed during a rain storm, all within ten miles of Tala Police Station and twenty-odd miles south of Jessore. A large party was dispatched immediately but when they arrived, they found to their amazement that every single one was a Cat. EO and they were either buried or burned out.

By this time, the unit's expertise was needed on a regular basis for the salvage and repair of Liberators of 159 Squadron operating from Dhubalia and 99 Squadron which was just converting to Liberators at Jessore. These aircraft were often found to be beyond mechanical repair following a particularly heavy landing. Any damage to the undercarriage invariably resulted in the plate carrying the trunnion block of the drag strut being torn away from the centre section. This major defect was brought to the attention of the unit for the first time with a Liberator of 159 Squadron (BZ982) which struck a bund on landing at Dhubalia, followed by a similar incident some time later with an aircraft of 99 Squadron (EW271).

Although the USAAF technical representatives were called in to help and advise, they could come up with no positive solution to the problem, though the consensus of opinion at the time seemed to suggest that the trouble was caused by too high a landing speed. It would appear that there was a tendency for the landing wheels to start rotating in the opposite direction when the undercarriage was lowered and this increased the inertia effect considerably.

One Liberator of 231 Squadron (KG925), returning from ops was reported to have crash landed somewhere near Fazadipur. The actual location was rather vague so the unit test pilot, Flt/Lt Whitman, accompanied by WO Young, flew in the unit Tiger Moth to locate its exact position and to reconnoitre the best possible route for the salvage vehicles. It was found finally at Talma, miles away from the reported sightings and although only some fifty miles from Jessore, would entail crossing two rivers, the Madhumati and the Madaganga, with all the hassle of loading and unloading at the various steamer crossings. It was therefore decided to send the salvage crew by rail the long way round to Ranaghat and Goalundo before striking out by road for the crash site.

It was found on arrival that the aircraft was not only burnt out but had set alight to a village, killing three villagers in the process. Although the rest of the crew had survived, Sgt McGlusky had been killed. He was buried with full military honours in the European Cemetery at Faridpur, the funeral service being conducted by the Rev. L. Barman, an Australian missionary stationed at Faridpur, and with a firing party provided by the civil police.

Meanwhile, at Baigachi, 155 and 67 Squadrons, in their recently acquired Spitfire VIIIs, were crashing left, right and centre and additional personnel had to be sent to reinforce the unit's detachment.

By March 1945, many of the fighter squadrons had moved further down into Burma and the unit's main occupation was the servicing of twin-engine aircraft used in supply dropping or long distance bombing raids. 136 RSU now seemed to operate under the guise of a Maintenance Unit and under the control of 231 Group. Warwicks of 292 ASR Squadron now appeared on the scene for servicing and major inspections, and to stretch the unit's expertise even further, Sea Otters of the same squadron came in for hull repairs or changes.

In June 1945, the CO, Sqn/Ldr Hucklebridge, was repatriated as tour-expired. Unlike the regular turnover of COs of other units, he had been in continuous command of 136 RSU for two and a half years, since its formation as 129 RSU in October 1942. His place was taken by Flt/Lt Ricketts.

With the occupation of Malaya and the surrender of the Japanese, most of the Salvage Units had moved out of Bengal and Burma and 136 RSU found itself at the beck and call of all and sundry, having to pick up the work that had been left behind in the upsurge of squadrons vacating the various airfields. Many of these aircraft were found to be half-completed, many of the log books were missing and the necessasry ground equipment unattainable, having been taken by the vacating units. It seemed a ludicrous situation that by the stroke of a pen, the commitments of one RSU could be handed over to another without leaving adequate provision and with no extra tradesmen.

Although 228 Group had been formed in Calcutta with the express purpose of dealing with all the admin problems of the RAF units remaining in Bengal and Assam, the ensuing chaos in increased paperwork did little to ease the problems besetting the unit. In fact, they worsened. On one hand they were getting new technical and servicing policies from 231 Group and additional admin policies from 228 though no extra personnel were posted in to deal with the mountains of paper.

An example of the less than co-operative attitude towards the problems besetting 136 RSU was when the wing commander of 357 Dakota Squadron, based at Jessore requested the loan of the unit's Jeep for a ten-day detachment. As this was the only Jeep on the unit and the only vehicle suitable for visiting crash sites, the CO was reluctant to comply with this request, much to the annoyance of the wing commander who said he would request 231 Group to instruct the CO to lend him the vehicle. Sqn/Ldr Ricketts replied that if Group would also release the unit from any necessity for the immediate inspection of a crash, he would happily oblige.

On another occasion the CO had a similar run-in with the same wing commander who this time wanted to borrow a Dakota, which was on the unit's charge, to fly personnel to 357's new location at Mingladon. The CO would not authorize this without sanction from Wg/Cdr Smethan-Jones of HQ RAF Burma. Obviously the wing commander had an ear in high places, for later that day, a signal came from Group requesting that Sqn/Ldr Ricketts afford every possible assistance to the wing commander.

In August 1945 the unit gave a sigh of relief when it was informed that it would soon be moving from Jessore. Expectations were short-lived when a further signal rescinded the order and informed the unit it would remain at Jessore under the direct control of 226 Maintenance Group.

Other units had been striking off charge and destroying aircraft which were deemed to take too long to repair but 136 RSU was informed that under no circumstances were any aircraft to be made Cat. ES if at all repairable or due to lack of spares. Why these double standards were applied is difficult to imagine, especially with a unit which was not only depleted of personnel but with additional commitments at other airfields vacated by other units.

Although the war was virtually over, the unit's activities and frustrations had become greater than at the height of hostilities and morale had sunk pretty low with the additional burdens placed upon it. None of the technical problems encountered were to have such an effect as when the Station Commander decreed that CO's parades would be reinstated, as in his view Air Force discipline and smartness had dropped to an unacceptable level during the war. Though a gradual enforced smartness did occur, it was far from enthusiastic, especially with reluctant airmen who were close to being civilians once more.

Up to now the unit had serviced or salvaged every make of aircraft on the Indian scene, from fragile Tiger Moths to twin-engine bombers and transports, so it was no real surprise when a Halifax of the Empire Navigation School (NA279) flew in to Jessore for an emergency double engine change. Its high priority meant that normal work had to be dropped in order to deal with it.

The final blow to the workload came when a message from Sqn/Ldr Naylor, the SADO at Alipore, stated that the station had to be cleared of all commitments immediately and that it was imperative that the RAF vacate Alipore by no later than 6 December. This was an impossible task if all the commitments and demands already on the unit's books were to be met.

Thinking that some error had been made, the CO immediately contacted HQ 228 Group who confirmed the instructions regarding Alipore but had no knowledge of the unit's involvement and could only confirm that the civil authorities were anxious to take over the airfield. In consequence, another signal was sent to 226 Group and repeated to BAFSEA, requesting some definite instruction and pointing out that the workload at Jessore and Baigachi alone would require a minimum of at least two months to clear.

The arguments as to the practicalities involved in clearing the strip were not accepted and a large detachment had to be sent to deal with the remaining aircraft. Some, after servicing, were flown to the MUs at Lahore and Allahabad, others to Salbani to 138 RSU acting as a holding unit, some were struck off charge, dismantled and conveyed to 75 Air Stores Park at Kankinara.

It was a vicious circle, for back at Baigachi and Jessore there was no relief for the rest of the unit. Aircraft were still coming in to be serviced and those which required major overhauls simply had to be stacked. Alipore was finally cleared, after a great deal of concerted effort. The ground equipment, cranes and MT vehicles were disposed of to Kanchrapara and the detachment returned to Jessore. Sqn/Ldr Ricketts relinquished command on posting to No. 3 OAS at Barrackpore for a Junior Commanders' Course, his place being taken by Flt/Lt Svenson, the unit test pilot.

A week later, on 18 December, the unit was advised to prepare for disbandment and that all sections should be ready for further instructions in the disposal of all equipment and aircraft. It was the best Christmas present the unit had had in its three years of existence. Work began immediately with a will, packing and labelling equipment for disposal. For once, aircraft took a back seat and very few men cared what happened to them. As far as the personnel were concerned, they had done their fair share, they had made their contribution to the war effort by servicing or salvaging almost 2,000 aircraft of one sort or another since their formation in November 1943.

The unit was finally disbanded at Jessore on 1 January 1946.

Chapter 13

No. 5 Repair and Salvage Section/ No. 138 Repair and Salvage Unit

With the formation of 118 Maintenance Wing in November 1943, No. 5 Repair and Salvage Section came into being on the authority of an AHQ India Formation Order dated 29 September 1943. It was a ready-made unit, formed from the disbanded 121 Repair and Salvage Unit with a technical and domestic site on the Semputa Road close to a small Indian village on the north bank of the River Cauvery, near Trichinopoly in southern India.

It had an establishment of five officers and warrant officers, twenty-three SNCOs, 221 BORs and forty-seven enrolled followers under the command of F/O P. W. Harrison with F/O A. E. Budgett, transferred from 121 RSU, as the Adjutant.

Like 139 RSU, which had been formed at the same time, its lines of communication were extensive and stretched as far as Bombay, 900 miles to the north-west. One one occasion they were stretched even more when a detachment from Poona was sent a further 900 miles to salvage a Spitfire (JF893) which had crash landed at Shikapur on the borders of Baluchistan.

By the middle of October, a further 200 airmen had arrived from the UK, bringing the unit strength to well over 400. The original establishment was 251. The domestic site became considerably overcrowded and intolerable so arrangements were hastily made to move out and take over the Regimental Headquarters of an Indian Army unit which had been vacated before the war. The reason for the Army's withdrawal was that the people, mostly Tamils, were docile and unwarlike and strategically there was no need for a garrison.

Although these buildings were completely unfurnished, by dint of scrounging from 336 MU and the Army, sufficient charpoys, tables and chairs were obtained to make them reasonably habitable. In comparison to many RSUs which had been formed in the north-east, whose accommodation was either in tents or straw bashas, 138 RSU's domestic site, with the benefit of brick and tile buildings, was luxurious.

The technical site at Golden Rock was part of the Southern India Railway workshops. One of the buildings was a large five-storey structure fitted with racks and was used as the main store, while additional buildings were converted to a POL, dope and paint store. There was even the luxury of a covered MT park.

The unit had no medical facilities other than a small sick-bay run by medical orderlies, until a Medical Officer, Flt/Lt O. B. Appleyard (122524) was posted in ex UK. Anything serious was transferred to the Garrison Military Hospital at St Thomas's Mount in Madras.

At that time, only large established stations and garrisons had their own padres and organized church parades, the authorities no doubt assuming, as they did with lots of things when it came to the welfare of RSUs, that spiritual welfare was of secondary importance to that of picking up aircraft and that any such matters could be adequately dealt with by the CO. 138 RSU were fortunate in this respect, for within a stone's throw of the unit at Woriur, there was a Methodist mission, superintended by the Rev. Arthur Bott who became very much involved with the unit in more ways than one.

His mission was in the grounds of the Officers' Mess of the old British East India Company, known colloquially as 'John Company', vacated when Trichinopoly ceased to be a garrison town. There was a high school, a boarding school and a small hospital. The church in the cantonment had been converted from the old arsenal. With walls six feet thick and a solid roof of concrete, it was probably the coolest place in the city where for nine months of the year the climate was hot and the remaining three months even hotter.

His first encounter with 138 RSU was one Sunday evening when he was lamenting the loss of his young Indian organist who had departed to join the Army. Standing at the door of his church, he spotted two rather unkempt bodies approaching, looking rather incongruous in very long shorts, known as Bombay Bloomers, topped off with regulation Bombay Bowlers. In desperation, and with nothing to lose, he asked one of them if by any chance he played the organ. 'No, I can't,' he replied, 'but he does,' pointing to his companion.

It transpired that 'he' was John Edmunds who in civilian life was the organist and choir master of a Baptist church in South Wales and, like many Welshmen, he also possessed a wonderful singing voice. It could be called providence, for it was a chance in a million that they turned up just at that moment.

Following the service, he invited them to dinner and from this chance meeting there developed regular gatherings in his bungalow, sometimes amounting to almost 200 men crammed into his dining-room and lounge. With an 'open house', his wife Sylvia, apart from having her own young family to care for, now took on the additional role of hostess, catering manager and head cook and bottle washer, but, more importantly, she was able to lend a sympathetic ear to many of the lads now thrown in at the deep end, in a strange and unfamiliar land and who could confide in her some of the hopes and fears in being 6,000 miles from home.

At that time, the Rev. Bott was a regular broadcaster on All India Radio and he and John Edmunds formed an RAF choir, with John as conductor, and broadcast a programme of carols on Christmas Eve 1943.

As more and more troops poured into India to prepare for the offensive against the Japanese, so too did all sorts of talent, though a Nativity play put on in one of the Hindu colleges, without the aid of a stage wardrobe and with 'angels' in hob-nailed Army boots must have been interpreted by the locals as a peculiar form of British pantomime.

A band had also been formed by the men of the Yorks. and Lancs. Regiment. Their CO, being something of an eccentric, had insisted that his Regiment would not sail to India without its own band. They were training around Ulster, prior to coming to India and he dispatched a party of men in a 10-ton truck to scour the countryside for instruments, with a directive that they were not to come back until the exercise had been successfully accomplished. With the enterprise and initiative for which the British Tommy is renowned, they succeeded in their mission.

With Trichinopoly once again taking on the role of a garrison town, this band used to play regularly on the large *maidan* near the junction station and although the natives took some time to attune to western music they always applauded with enthusiasm. It was said that when the band played, the elephants in southern India ceased to trumpet and took on the cry of the hyena.

The Rev. Arthur Bott had now become the garrison chaplain, serving not only the needs of his own 'troops' but also that of the RAF and the Army. However, in his capacity as treasurer of the YMCA in southern India, he was able to apply to the Governor of Madras's war fund for assistance to provide facilities for the troops in the shape of canteens, recreation rooms and even a cinema.

With the settling down of the unit into a more orderly routine, a unit magazine *Pukka Gen for Salvage Men* made its first appearance. A concert party had been organized. The unit carpenters built a stage in one of the buildings used as a canteen and the first show, called 'Silver and Blue' was staged before a mixed and somewhat vociferous audience.

In the early days, the airmen were regarded with a little suspicion but they quickly became on good terms with the local population. As part of the acceptance, parties of airmen used to visit the Pudukottah Palace for tea and buns at the invitation of the Rajah. This was a small Indian state within the Madras Presidency and although the term Rajah implied importance, the title was little more than a courtesy one. He carried no great power or legislative function and was, in fact, little more than a pensioner of the British Raj. Accompanied by a pantomime bodyguard, he would greet his guests very opulently in ornate silk clothes and bejewelled turban, but wearing down-at-heel ankle boots.

The airfield, north-west of the city, was a dirt strip which had been graded for use by the Lysanders of 4 RIAF and commanded by Flt/Lt Singh, a Sikh who was subsequently decorated at Imphal with the DFC by Lord Louis Mountbatten, when he commanded 1 RIAF.

Anxious to improve relationships even further, arrangements had been made between Training and Maintenance Command and representatives of the National War Front, for students of St Joseph's School, which was a Roman

Catholic school for Indian and Anglo-Indian boys in Trichinopoly, to visit the unit each Saturday for instruction and possible flying experience, with a view to subsequent training as pilots in the Royal Indian Air Force.

The original Formation Order also provided for a detachment to be based in the Poona area, 800 miles to the north-west, to cover activities in the Bombay area in conjunction with 305 MU and No. 1 Civilian Repair Organization based there. While final details of the detachment and the equipment requirements were being worked out, a casualty signal came through informing them that two Hurricanes of 20 Squadron had force landed at Sandamur, near Kalyan, east of Bombay.

It was decided that WO Ruffell, DCM and eleven airmen would proceed as an advance party by road with three 3-ton Chevrolet winch vehicles and kill two birds with one stone by first dealing with the two Hurricanes before returning to stay at Poona as an advanced detachment. Though it would have been much quicker to have sent the convoy by rail, it was decided they should travel by road, the idea being that in so doing they could carry out a survey of the type of road conditions the unit was liable to encounter in any future salvage operations on the western side of India.

When they arrived at the scene of the crash twelve days later, they were confronted with two aircraft which had belly landed, their undercarriages having failed to function or having collapsed on landing. It created something of a dilemma. No one had informed the unit of the state of the aircraft, other than that it was a forced landing, so they had no crane, sheer legs or artic for transport.

It looked very much as if the salvage would have to be abandoned until equipment could be obtained to lift the aircraft. Having spent twelve days getting there, they decided to have a shot at raising the aircraft by digging a trench beneath each one to allow the undercarriage to be lowered and locked down so that they could be towed to firm ground.

After a couple of days of hard graft, both aircraft were finally raised and towed out up the tapered ramp of the trench. Having achieved their objective, the next problem was what to do with the aircraft. It was decided that they would use the vehicles to tow them by road back to Kalyan. The mainplanes were dismantled and loaded into one of the vehicles and after making sure that the undercarriages were secure, they began the slow journey back. It was no mean feat, with a lash-up taking the place of a pukka tow-bar and the swaying cavalcade of aircraft caused some curious stares from the locals as they wended their way back through villages and rough winding roads on the 136 mile, three-day journey to Kalyan.

On 7 November, F/O Harrison, who had been Acting CO, was posted to Maintenance Wing, although staying on the unit as a supernumerary. His place was taken by Flt/Lt B. J. Chadwick, a Tech E from 6 RSS at Arkonham and a Tasmanian sheep farmer who had joined the RAF at the outbreak of the war. He was promoted a month later to Squadron Leader.

By the middle of December, the last of the 200 airmen who had been posted in had been dispersed to other units and detachments. The unit now had permanent detachments spread far and wide at Secunderbad, Bangalore, Poona, Hakimpet and Santa Cruz, near Bombay. The allocation of aircraft through these five detachments had now increased considerably, while the HQ at Trichinopoly had an additional role in dealing with any aircraft of the Fleet Air Arm, based at Ranasio in Ceylon, which came to grief.

This association with the Fleet Air Arm and the naval authorities was to prove invaluable when the unit found itself having to deal with a number of crashes near the coastline in southern India and required the assistance of boats in their recovery. One aircraft in particular, a Mosquito of 45 Squadron, had crash landed in the sea in the approaches to Cuddalore. Its wooden construction had enabled it to float long enough for a naval tug to get a line aboard in order to allow the unit salvage crew to remove some of the components. The task had to be abandoned when a sudden storm blew up and the mooring line came adrift. The now waterlogged fuselage sank beneath the surface.

Not being equipped for underwater salvage, it was left to the port authorities with a floating crane and the assistance of the Navy divers to recover the wreck which was now a hazard to shipping by obstructing the navigation channels to the harbour. It was, of course, a complete write-off.

Although the allotment of transport had been in accordance with the unit establishment, the additional demands had put a severe strain on what was now a limited and scarce resource. Detachments were having to borrow transport from whoever was willing to oblige. It was with some surprise that following a letter to Group pointing out these deficiencies, the unit was suddenly allocated as much transport as was required, including six artics and workshop trailers for every detachment, plus six bicycles. No doubt the latter were for the Orderly Room wallahs to carry urgent messages between sections.

But the unexpected bonus had to be repaid in other ways when forty airmen were posted away from the unit to 101 Air Stores Park which had just been formed at Cawnpore.

For some inexplicable reason, there is a gap in the unit records after 26 December 1944, following the report of a sports meeting held in the grounds of Trichinopoly Prison by kind permission of the Governor, Col. Hitchin, with the prizes, worth fifty rupees, being presented by his wife. It can only be assumed that the unit had now moved from Trichinopoly and its servicing commitments were taken over by 336 MU or 2 CMU who were to remain there. The next entry is dated 25 July 1945, with new unit headquarters at Charra, about sixty miles east of Ranchi, on a site which was described as 'mosquito-ridden and had to be drained and sprayed with oil to make it habitable and bearable'.

Again, the records seem to have been compiled rather irregularly, sometimes with gaps of two months.

On 10 September 46051 Sqn/Ldr H. A. Gordon assumed command from Sqn/Ldr Chadwick who had been posted to Group.

In October 1945 the unit was ordered to Salbani in Bengal, to a site formerly occupied by 135 RSU since 1943 but who were now moving to Singapore. All the personnel were flown to the new location by Dakotas of the Airborne Salvage Section but the ground equipment and MT had to travel the 1,200 miles by road.

Tremendous changes had taken place in the disposition of some thirty squadrons and supporting units, including RSUs, following the decision that SEAC's Headquarters and those of ALFSEA and ACSEA should be established in Singapore.

The role of 138 RSU now changed to that of a holding and servicing unit, being allotted all the outstanding aircraft of not only 135 RSU but also those of 136 RSU which was also shortly to be disbanded at Jessore. Many of these aircraft were dispersed at detachments at Alipore, Dum-Dum, Agartala and Barrackpore, and along with their own commitments still outstanding in various locations, were stretching the resources of the unit to the limit.

To try to ease the situation, a decision was made that as far as was humanly possible, all these servicing and repair commitments would be centralized at either Salbani or Baigachi and that all detachments would eventually be withdrawn to deal with the wide variety of aircraft which the unit now found itself saddled with. To add further to the confusion, it was now anticipated that two squadrons of Lancasters and possibly some Stirlings were soon to be flown in from the UK to Salbani. This was the first occasion that these aircraft had been on the scene in India.

Very few of the personnel had any knowledge of servicing four-engine aircraft of this type and certainly no experience of salvaging. There were no spares or heavy lifting equipment available until two Bay City cranes and heavy-duty tractor units were hastily made available from Digri, followed by a demonstration servicing party flown in especially to help with the initial problems.

Many of the unit's personnel by this time were due for repatriation. Although their departure was offset by replacements from the UK, the inexperience of the replacements did little to ease the urgency of the demands placed upon the unit.

With the centralizing and reduction of the areas of responsibility, aircraft which had the misfortune to crash in or around the now abandoned airfields were simply struck off charge, no attempt being made to salvage the once needed and valuable spares or return engines and airframes to MUs. To avoid these aircraft falling into the hands of any unscrupulous Indian scrap dealers, still with an eye on making a few rupees from the departing forces, the aircraft were simply set on fire, reducing them to a tangled heap of unusable scrap.

There were occasions, however, especially in the rather more remote areas, when the jungle telegraph forestalled the unit's intentions and aircraft were found to have been either spirited away without trace or stripped of their components. Just how this was accomplished without adequate tools and equipment will remain one of the mysteries of the East.

By the end of June 1946, the Lancasters had withdrawn from Salbani and no aircraft remained on the unit's books. The very last aircraft to be dispatched was a Spitfire XIV (MD364) to 8 RIAF. On 7 July 1946, as one of the last remaining units in India, 138 RSU was disbanded. Some of the personnel were repatriated, some posted to Singapore and others absorbed into 329 MU in Calcutta. The final F540 being signed by WO A. L. Pritchard on behalf of the CO, blew no trumpet nor drew any thanks for achievements during its three years of existence.

Chapter 14

No. 6 Repair and Salvage Section/ No. 139 Repair and Salvage Unit

Towards the last quarter of 1943, RAF India Command, based in Delhi, had formed twenty-two Repair and Salvage Units throughout India and Ceylon. At the same time they had also established a further eight units known simply as Repair and Salvage Sections and numbered 1 to 8. Their purpose and actual function is rather obscure, though it would seem, judging by their locations, that they were offshoots of various Maintenance Units and Air Stores Parks which had also been set up throughout India.

The only exceptions were Nos. 5 and 6 RSS. They had actually been formed on the disbandment of 121 RSU based at Arkonham, near Madras and 127 RSU stationed at Vivunya in Ceylon. The function of the six remaining sections, however, was short-lived, for with the formation of SEAC in November 1943 and the integration of the Allied Air Forces in December of the same year, all were absorbed into other units under the control of 226 (Maintenance) Group at Delhi.

No. 6 RSS now took over all the commitments, personnel and equipment of 127 RSU which had been in operation at Arkonham since October 1942. Arkonham was a small Indian town and railway junction, west of Madras and, as with other units close to railway workshops, used these facilities as part of their technical site.

Their area of activity was enormous, far greater than any other RSU in existence at the time and encompassed the larger part of central and southern India, with lines of communication extending as far south as Trichinopoly, north-west to Poona, 900 miles away in the north-east.

The unit's commitments had increased considerably by the middle of 1944, not only as far as salvage operations were concerned, but in the servicing of Hurricanes of 60, 113 and 135 Squadrons at St Thomas's Mount and Cholavarum, as well as the Catalinas of 191 and 240 Squadrons based at Redhills Lake, a deep, land-locked freshwater lake near Madras. In addition, the unit was called upon to maintain a permanent detachment at both Ranchi and Cuttack, even though 143 RSU, conveniently based at Bishnupur, had similar detachments at the same locations.

By January 1944, the title of Section seemed hardly appropriate for a unit with 300 officers and men, so 226 Group recategorized the unit as 139 Repair and Salvage Unit. This change of title, although improving its status, at least on paper, did not resolve the problems besetting the unit. In fact, it worsened them to some extent. Following the change of title, the CO, Sqn/Ldr C. G. Bircham, was informed that the unit would now also be responsible for the maintenance of all stationary diesel engines in the geographical area of 225 (Coastal) Group, Bangalore. This additional responsibility would be achieved by taking over No. 2 Mobile Diesel Repair Unit, based in Madras, which would now be known as No. 139 (MDRU).

As most squadrons and stations had diesel generators, it was inevitable that detachments required for servicing these engines and the detachments for aircraft servicing requirements would create not only technical but administrative problems, as indeed they did. The long lines of communication and the similarity of the unit prefixes resulted in mail going astray and spares being delivered to the wrong place at the wrong time.

Although the unit was in existence for almost two years, very little of its activities are shown in the unit's Operational Records except for the first few months which give an almost daily record of the happenings in the unit. Most of it is inconsequential and of little interest, except of course for the records of crashes. Not unusually, very little is known of the personnel except for a few officers being named on posting, either in or out. The reason for the dearth of information may well have been because the compiling officer took to heart comments in a letter from Wg/Cdr Clare at HQ 188 (M) Wing which states: 'It is noted that the Operations Record as submitted by your unit, particularly that of February, contains many entries which are merely a record of very minor events such as the dispatch of a truck loaded with spares, or the receipt of an aircraft casualty signal. It is requested that such entries are omitted on any future returns.'

From then on, the record comprised mainly one-line entries detailing the make of aircraft, its number and the site of the crash, though two seem to have been deemed noteworthy enough to merit a reasonable description and comment.

The first was of a party called out to assist another salvage crew from 121 RSU, based at Vivunya in Ceylon, in recovering a Vultee Vengeance (AN845) which had crash landed at Cholavarum, not far from Madras, whilst on a ferry flight to 110 Squadron. During the salvage, a sudden and unexpected typhoon swept the area creating extensive floods. Although the aircraft had been loaded on to an artic, it had to be rapidly abandoned as the flood waters engulfed the district, making any movement by road impossible. The salvage crew had to seek shelter in the safety of Government House in Madras until the floods subsided a week later.

These same floods devastated areas of southern India. Entire communities were marooned, thousands of palm trees were uprooted and the year's crop of coconuts destroyed. The unit at Arkonham also found themselves cut off and unable to collect supplies from the ration depot at Trivellor. Fortunately, thanks to having assisted the Army depot at Raniept with transport and technical assistance whenever needed in the past, they reciprocated by agreeing to supply the unit with rations until such time as the road to Madras was reopened.

The anomalies of this salvage operation not only highlighted the ambiguity of the situation confronted by 139 RSU, with its long lines of communication but also indicated a complete disregard for economy of movement of men and equipment by those who allocated the salvage in the first place. Whereas 121 RSU had to travel some 500 miles from their base in Ceylon, transshipping all their vehicles across the Mannar Straits to Danishkodai on the southern tip of India before commencing their long haul to Cholavarum, 139 RSU was only a matter of a couple of hours away from the crash site.

Following a second cyclone, four Catalinas of 240 Squadron broke away from their moorings in Redhills Lake in Madras. Three were submerged completely and the fourth was driven ashore by the high winds, sustaining some superficial damage but was made serviceable again after some minor repairs, and refloated. The others, dragged ashore by winch vehicles, had been damaged beyond repair, though the engines were removed and sent by rail to 322 MU at Cawnpore for stripping and servicing.

Reducing what remained to disposable scrap with axes and hacksaws was a laborious job even though no finesse was required and consideration was given to the possibility of blowing them up. Following consultation with an Army bomb disposal unit in Madras, experiments with small quantities of gelignite were carried out under their guidance. In less than two days the aircraft fuselages were a heap of metal scrap. With the success of the experiment, arrangements were made for an official allocation of gelignite, primer cord and detonators to be held at the Army base in Madras for use when and if required. An NCO armourer and two airmen were sent for training in handling explosives for any future eventuality.

The long lines of communication were still causing the unit a great many problems, particularly with the allocation of aircraft at Ranchi and Cuttack and their servicing or salvaging categorization. On viewing the aircraft, the detachments would find that the damage or repair needs were well within the scope of the squadron, though the casualty signal sent from a particular squadron to Maintenance Group would exaggerate the problem and indicate it as a task which needed to be carried out by an RSU.

Concerned that an unfair advantage was being taken of the unit by the frequency of these incidents the CO found it necessary to send a blunt letter to Group drawing attention to the matter:

> I would draw your attention to the instructions concerning the categorization of damaged aircraft which are contained in India Command Maintenance Instruction No. 1.
>
> These instructions are frequently not being adhered to by holding units

and other formations. These instructions state clearly that the final arbitration of the category of damage will be in the hands of crash inspectors of the appropriate Maintenance Wing.

Yet in the past months, several aircraft have been allotted to this unit without the opportunity of an examination by the unit crash inspector being accorded, in spite of the fact that our inspector has, in all cases, been present on the same airfield.

In consequence, work which is well within the capacity of the units concerned has been transferred to 139 RSU.

In one instance, it is known that a certain squadron's maintenance section was closed down completely while this unit undertook a straightforward and simple engine change on one of their aircraft, so called beyond the squadron capacity...

Although there is no record of the reply from Group, judging by the number of times the unit was called out to effect simple maintenance, it seemed as if the CO's frustrations were ignored.

Whether his outspoken comments were the cause is a matter of conjecture, but shortly afterwards, Sqn/Ldr Bircham was posted and the problems of the unit were inherited by Flt/Lt R. T. Cole, the unit Tech E, now appointed CO. When he also found that nothing had changed and the unit was still being used as a general convenience at Ranchi and Cuttack, he too made his sentiments quite clear in a letter to Group:

Relevant extracts of correspondence exchanged between this unit and HQ 226 Group are quoted to illustrate the typical situations encountered by this unit. The picture can be seen in the correct perspective when it is realized that the area covered by this unit still extends south to Trichinopoly and north to Calcutta and still amounts to 1,200 miles.

From an operational aspect, the subject is covered by HQ 188 Maintenance Wing letter dated 28 April.

This letter clearly presents the picture at Ranchi and Cuttack for which detachments, or no establishments of any kind, exist.

There is a further aspect concerning the morale and general welfare of the airmen that are on the strength of these detachments.

The scope of the position is not yet clearly understood, otherwise action would long ago have been taken to rectify the lamentable state of affairs which now exists. The very term detachment is a complete anomaly and really clouds the issue, since it suggests an intimate and close liaison with this unit's HQ, which in view of the distances involved and the acute shortage of supervising personnel is quite impossible to maintain,

These men are out in the blue and they feel there is no one who is interested enough to properly look after them. They are dependent on strange units for their physical needs and at Cuttack especially, are merely chattels of the station.

Because of the lack of resources, it has not been possible to set up a full-blown detachment and we have only been able to reinforce the Squadron Maintenance Flight.

Although these men at Ranchi and Cuttack are under my command, I have never had the opportunity of seeing them, nor does it seem likely that I shall do so for some time to come.

Furthermore, their chances of promotion are being jeoparized by the continued absence of an establishment and in this connection, I desire to cite the case of Cpl Sargison.

Action to promote this airman to Sgt was taken by this unit on 15 March. At that time this unit had suddenly taken on its strength nearly 200 men, all of them a thousand miles away and for whom there was no establishment. The whole thing was a paper transaction, but there was no paper to go with it.

Cpl Sargison's promotion was withheld, pending the issue of a new establishment, which two months later has yet to be issued. This airman is now about to be repatriated and the outstanding services which he has rendered this unit will pass unrecognized.

It is requested that these matters be given your most earnest attention.

The reply from Group was short and swift:

This Headquarters is well aware of the unsatisfactory position of 139 RSU detachments at Ranchi and Cuttack, and has, since 20 January 1945, been pressing for the formation of a new RSU to undertake repair, salvage and 2nd line maintenance in the area now undertaken by the Repair and Salvage Section of No. 308 MU and its detachments at Ranchi and Cuttack.

HQ Base Air Forces SEA have now agreed to form this RSU. As soon as it is formed, those detachments will be absorbed into it.

Although the reply implied that something was being done, it came as an unbelievable surprise to the CO that Group still regarded the detachments as a Repair and Salvage Section attached to an MU, when in actual fact the RSS had been disbanded fourteen months before, in order to form 139 RSU.

Obviously original signals had become crossed somewhere or Formation Orders had gone astray which, to some extent though not excusable, would account for the singular lack of response to appeals for help from the unit in the past year. As far as the admin wallahs in Delhi were concerned, these detachments had never been on the strength of 139 RSU in the first place, though of course these arguments could be thrown out quite easily given the number of aircraft which had been allocated to 139 RSU at Ranchi and Cuttack and confirmed by the previously exchanged correspondence.

Nevertheless, apart from the so-called intention of forming another unit, its effect on Cpl Sargison's promotion, unless he was promoted while with 139 RSU, would be to reduce his seniority by posting him as a corporal to a new unit. Again the CO wrote to Group pointing out the anomalies but apart from noting his comments, they merely reiterated the Group's future intentions which, in the event, never materialized, as no further Repair and Salvage Units were ever formed. Quite the reverse in fact, for many of the well-established units were on the point of being disbanded.

In July, Flt/Lt Cole was posted and his place taken over by Flt/Lt E. G. Abercromby, followed a month later by Sqn/Ldr F. J. Sandeford, a Tech E from 144 RSU at Risalpur (356 MU).

No further records exist of this unit's activities and a year later, on 4 July 1946, the unit was disbanded at Arkonham. Many of the personnel were repatriated. Those who were not time-expired joined the ever-increasing numbers at 390 MU at Seletar.

Chapter 15

No. 1 Civilian Maintenance Unit/ No. 304 Maintenance Unit

It was never the intention to add a history of the MUs, for between January 1942 and the end of 1945, there were some fifty Maintenance Units, six Civilian Maintenance Units and three Civilian Repair Organizations. The most well known of the latter was the Hindustan Aircraft Company at Bangalore. These units were spread throughout the length and breadth of India, though some eventually moved to Burma and Singapore.

Many of these MUs had specific tasks; some dealt with the major servicing and repair of twin-engine aircraft, some with fighters, others dealt with radial and in-line engines or gun turrets and one dealt specifically with vehicles. However, No. 1 CMU at Kanchrapara, thirty miles north of Calcutta, was so closely allied to the work of the Repair and Salvage Units, east and west of the Brahmaputra River that it was almost an integral part of the successful salvage and return of aircraft into service, particularly on the Burma Front.

The site it occupied was the main overhaul workshops of the Bengal Assam Railway Company and managed by a Mr Ivens. It employed about 3,000 out of the population of 30,000 who lived in the surrounding villages, including several hundreds of Chinese, all supervised by British or Anglo-Indians. These supervisors lived in luxurious bungalows set aside in a large compound and they even had their own coolie-powered canopied rail cars to convey the memsahibs to the station or church.

In March 1942, although the arrival of RAF personnel was expected, no thought seemed to have been given to their accommodation and they were housed in disused railway carriages which had seen better days and had been shunted into a nearby siding close to the workshops. Although only deemed a temporary measure, it was to be over a year before purpose built accommodation was provided.

The Airmen's Mess was a large marquee. Food was prepared in a deserted workshop close by and entailed a race across the intervening space between airmen and the ever-present kite hawks as they swooped to relieve them of their food. The sick-bay was in one of the classrooms of the local Railway School and with any outbreak of dysentery or malaria, which was endemic on the site, it soon filled to capacity and patients and charpoys overspilt into the school playground.

The area itself, although a very convenient centre for receiving aircraft by road, rail and river, was low lying and subject to flooding due to the proximity of the River Hooghly and the Bargar Khal which ran through the site. There were large areas of marshland and a lake about two and a half miles long by half a mile wide, covered in water hyacinth which continually floated down through the camp and was a breeding ground for mosquitoes. Eventually, a bamboo boom was built across the lake and gangs of coolies were continually employed in clearing the weed and spraying with DDT.

There were no recreational facilities as such, though the Rev. Firth, a Methodist minister, with limited resources, did his best to provide some amenities in his small church. The Bell Institute, a club for the railway supervisory staff, was strictly out of bounds and only accessible by limited invitation, whilst the Masonic Hall was definitely taboo. On rare occasions, some of the more fortunate would be invited to a meal with one of the staff families.

The RAF took over a number of the wagon repair shops and set up two production lines, one to overhaul Bristol Mercuries, the other for Merlins, followed by the building of a large hangar to carry out major servicing and repairs to aircraft. Sections were also organized to deal specifically with armaments and prop repairs.

A flexible fuel tank repair shop was set up in a disused, open-sided blacksmith's shop roofed with asbestos. Unfortunately, as the day wore on, the atmosphere became severely overheated and the high vapour hazard caused by the Formgar cement and ethyl acetate solvents used in the repairs, created a very toxic environment, causing all sorts of disorders to the airmen who supervised the work, although the Indians seemed immune to these chemical maladies.

The original concept of the unit was that hands-on work would be done by local labour, supervised by RAF tradesmen. It was hard going, for not only was there a language barrier but staff more used to 'hammer and chisel' repairs on railway wagons found difficulty with the finesse and accuracy required on aircraft or engines and occasionally caused more damage.

The dirt airstrip, under the control of P/O Janweja of the RIAF, was about a mile away from the camp and had been hacked out of the undergrowth. During the monsoons, it reverted to something resembling a paddy field, considerably curtailing any flying activities.

Now that the RAF had virtually taken over responsibility for Service aircraft, the unit was renumbered 304 MU (CRO) with Wg/Cdr J. F. Grey as CO. He was eventually posted to Group and his place was taken by Sqn/Ldr W. H. Terry on 2 February 1943.

With the Japanese threat to India escalating, the airfield was guarded by No. 1 Coastal Defence Battalion, commanded by Maj. G. C. Rose who one day gave an impressive demonstration of fire-power to members of the National Defence Council and frightened the local population out of their wits.

With the first air raid on Calcutta, in common with the population of the city, the vast majority of workers downed tools and fled through the open gates. The Indian guards at the entrance, wielding their iron bound lathis were powerless to stop them, as panic-stricken, they streamed towards the open countryside.

By the end of 1943, apart from their normal servicing and repair commitments, the unit had to set up a glider erection section. Though not known at the time, they were to eventually convey Wingate's forces into Burma.

The influx of aircraft for repairs and major servicing had increased dramatically, especially from Assam, and with its major role now firmly established, additional personnel began to arrive in order to cope with the extra workload.

With the unit strength now somewhere in the region of 900 officers and men, it was obvious that the substandard accommodation and domestic facilities left something to be desired and became a matter of concern from a medical standpoint. Although the health of the station had remained relatively good under the circumstances, there had been a few fatalities from malaria and one from smallpox following an outbreak of the disease in one of the nearby villages.

Finally, the PWD took its finger out and built a brand new camp, east of the workshops, divided into three sites, one with nineteen bashas to hold 450 men, complete with cookhouse, dining-hall and canteen, plus a cinema. A second, about a mile away, held 240 men along with a station sick quarters of twenty-five beds and a third held 190 men. The SNCOs were also provided with new quarters on the Ranighat Road, three miles away. Except for the NCOs' quarters, which had ceiling fans, all the billets were cooled by punkahs, hand operated by natives. An added luxury was that they all had electric light.

In common with all active airfields, Kanchrapara, or KPA as it was now known, also had its fair share of prangs. Many were dealt with by 60 RSU who shared the site until they eventually moved to Chittagong.

Arthur (Lofty) Jacklin, an F2E, recalls the salvage of an aircraft which not only involved a certain amount of initiative but indicates that even out in the bush one sometimes couldn't escape from Service bull. At that time, 60 RSU were short of fitters and Arthur was glad to be attached to them to help out as it made a change from the daily routine of workshop life and would, he thought, give some relief from bull.

The unit was called out to salvage a Hurricane which had crashed somewhere near Mangalkot in an area known as the Parganas. It had evidently had an engine failure through loss of coolant, which was not uncommon with Merlin engines.

They went by gharry to a landing stage at Naihati, a few miles down the road, on the River Hooghly. Waiting for them when they arrived was a pretty dilapidated motor launch with a barge in tow, complete with a crew who could loosely be described as captain and mate. All the gear and tool boxes were loaded into the barge and they set off along the Hooghly, before turning and heading north-west along a tributary of the river.

The first night was spent lying on the deck of the launch under a rather tattered canopy, with slacks tucked into mozzie boots and hands and faces liberally covered in anti-mosquito cream as a protection against the swarms of these pests which seemed to follow the boat. They hadn't a clue where they were going although the captain obviously did.

The following day, they pulled in alongside the bank, near a small village and were met by the local doctor who spoke English and was to direct them to the scene of the crash. He proved to be a really helpful character and organized some local labour to help with all the gear.

Arriving at the site, which wasn't very far from the village, the aircraft looked pretty sick. The port undercarriage had collapsed and it was tipped up on its nose, the starboard mainplane pointing towards the sky. There was no sign of the pilot who presumably was all right and had somehow returned to civilization. After a fry-up and some char, a tent was draped over the wing and everyone got their heads down for an early start the following morning.

Although the dismantling was a comparatively simple task, there were some problems removing the prop which had been twisted with the impact, but after a great deal of cussing, hammering and levering it was finally removed. They had no lifting gear and had to rely on local labour, at the going rate of one rupee a day, negotiated by the doctor who, no doubt, took a commission on the transaction.

Everything had to be manhandled from the site to the river bank with the aid of bamboo poles. With everything now assembled on the river bank, the next problem was to get it aboard the barge. There was no landing stage, so one was concocted from bamboo poles lashed together with rattan rope. Although it looked very flimsy, they were assured by the locals that it would be '*tik hai*'. All they could hope for was that they were right. At high water, the barge was manoeuvred into position for the loading. It was then a question of sheer brute force to slide the fuselage and engine on rollers on to the barge, followed by the mainplane.

As the bamboo began to flex in an alarming manner with the weight, Arthur recalls thinking, 'How the hell are we going to get it out of the river if it breaks?' In the event, the staging proved to be a lot stronger than was thought and the loading was completed without mishap.

An incident which occurred during this salvage was reminiscent of Stanley discovering Livingstone. The crew were in the middle of dismantling the aircraft when an officer suddenly appeared from nowhere to conduct a pay parade. It seemed so ludicrous as to be unbelievable and why should anyone want to bother? Most of the men had money when they left Kanchrapara and there was certainly nothing to spend it on so far out in the blue, except perhaps on a few eggs or a very scrawny chicken. There was definitely no night life to squander their cash on.

However, in spite of the circumstances and the surroundings, he wasn't prepared to just hand it out in a casual manner, it had to be a pukka pay parade. In order to carry out this rather stupid charade, he set himself up at one end of the barge with a tool box covered with a blanket to act as a desk, while everyone had to stand at the other end. When each man's name was called, he had to step smartly forward, salute, give his number, hand over pay book and receive whatever sum he was entitled to then return to the end of the barge until the pay parade was over.

The natives who were lining the bank, watching the proceedings with some interest, must have thought it was a pantomime peculiar to the British. At the time, Arthur thought, 'I know that King's Regulations lay down how things should be done in the Air Force, but this is bloody ridiculous.'

After the fiasco was over, he boarded the launch which had brought him all the way from Kanchrapara and the last that was seen of this stickler for the rules, was him heading back up the river. It had probably cost more to hire the launch to bring him than the total amount paid out.

Two days later, the aircraft was back at the landing stage at Naihati where it was unloaded on to an artic by the unit's Coles crane and delivered to the Air Frame Repair Shop.

One incident in particular which happened on the airfield and could be described as a static crash, occurred with a Blenheim of 113 Squadron awaiting an air test by F/O Gardner. As he approached the aircraft, one of the fitters, who was doing a final cockpit check, for some reason best known to himself, operated the undercarriage selection lever and the aircraft collapsed. Unfortunately, as it did so, the mainplane struck the pilot, knocking him for six. Following an inquiry into the incident, the airman was court-martialled under Section 39 (a)(i)(e) of the Air Force Act.

By 1944 the amenities had improved considerably; there were ample recreational facilities, the station cinema had shows six days a week, the Bell Institute had had a change of heart and there were now Saturday night dances. There was a soccer pitch and even a badminton court, with education classes and a music appreciation society for the less energetic. The BESA concert party made regular visits and there was even an open air boxing tournament between a USAAF team from Kharagpur. The result was USAAF 6, KPA 4.

The station even warranted a visit by Sir Harold G. Howitt, a member of the Air Council, accompanied by Air/Cdre Mason, closely followed by Rear Admiral Bedale, Commodore Shroeder and other naval brass-hats of the Fleet Air Arm, investigating the possibilities of using MUs' engine and repair facilities for FAA aircraft.

In June 1944 the site was expanded even further to accommodate No. 327 MU, formerly No. 2 Reserve Aircraft Pool at Dum-Dum, who would now share the increased load. But with the large increases in personnel, the number of illnesses from endemic diseases began to rise sharply and a decision was made in November 1944 to construct an entirely new domestic site as far away as possible from the Indian railway employees' compound which had been considered the cause of the high rate of sickness.

Rather surprisingly, considering its size and strategic importance, very little of the day to day activities are recorded for posterity and the unit, at least as far as its number was concerned, was eventually disbanded at Chittagong in March 1945.

There is no doubt, however, juding by the number of aircraft and engines which were sent by road, rail and river from RSUs all over India and Burma, not counting the spares sent out in return, that 1 CMU/304 MU made a tremendous contribution to the Burma campaign.

Chapter 16

The Transient Units

This chapter deals specifically with units which although documented, were little more than 'paper' units in a filing cabinet in some remote Orderly Room, miles away from the scene of the action.

By the end of 1943, the number of Repair and Salvage Units formed in India had increased dramatically, both real and imagined, but it is a strange coincidence that many of these 'ghost' units have usually been in the same location as either an MU or an Air Stores Park, formed on the same date. How a handful of men, with no equipment to speak of, possibly living in tents in some remote place can possibly be deemed an MU is difficult to imagine, let alone explain. It is as if the admin wallahs were hedging their bets, uncertain of the role these units were to play.

For some inexplicable reason, some units were formed then officially disbanded almost immediately, before frequently emerging for a brief period, only to disappear again. No. 101 RSU is a good example. Following their formation in July 1942 in Calcutta, according to their records, they ceased to exist in January of the following year. Yet in actual fact, apart from servicing aircraft on airfields in Assam and Mingladon under various guises, they went to Singapore for final disbandment in August 1945.

There are a number of units, numbered and labelled RSUs which had nothing to do with aircraft and were formed specifically for transport salvage. These units were only recognizable when they chose to use their suffixes of MTRU, MTLRD and MTSU. These signified Mobile Transport Repair Unit, Mobile Transport Light Repair Depot and Mobile Transport Salvage Unit. To confuse the issue even further, especially concerning locations, some of these transport units were attached to aircraft salvage units, sometimes adopting their particular number, at other times retaining their own formation number, but for some reason dropping their identifying suffix.

Nevertheless, although the ORBs of these short-lived units in some cases are very sparse, sometimes amounting to little more than a couple of pages detailing the brief activities, in every case there are at least some incidents worthy of note and which made yet another contribution to the overall picture and history of the salvage units during the Burma campaign.

Six of these rather lesser known units survived only a matter of months, three survived their first birthday while one, formed towards the latter part of the Burma campaign in 1944, managed to hang on till the end until it too was disbanded along with the majority of RSUs either in India or Singapore.

No. 130 Repair and Salvage Unit

Although having no inkling as to what role they would be taking or what unit they eventually would be joining, on 27 July 1942 sixty men embarked on the HMT *E15* (*The Majola* of the P. & O. Line) at Liverpool and arrived at Gourock the following day to join a mixed convoy.

After an uneventful journey, with a five-day halt at Freetown and a further two days at Cape Town, they arrived at Bombay on 21 September 1942 after fifty-four days at sea.

They were accommodated at the Worli Transit Camp for five weeks pending a decision as to where they should be posted. During their stay, as they were seen more or less as 'gash' airmen, twenty-six of them were detailed to be attached to 303 MU at Ambala. No officers had accompanied them as part of a regular unit so they had no option but to accept the nominal roll that appeared on DROs as being 'pukka gen'.

On 24 October 1942, the remainder of the personnel entrained at Victoria Terminus, bound for Agartala, arriving eight days later via Allahabad and Calcutta. Although the unit establishment had been officially formed on 22 October under the control of 224 Group and exercised through 169 Wing, there were still no officers posted in or attached and unit discipline was under the control of an equipment warrant officer of 92 ASP at Agartala and an NCO of the unit.

Although there was no technical work to speak of, the amount of paperwork made up for it and office accommodation was found, after some difficulty, by sharing the Orderly Room of the ASP.

Following a further two months of inactivity, the unit was finally instructed to move to Chittagong and was housed in a girls' high school. On 16 January 1943, the unit was combined with No. 60 RSU to form Repair and Salvage Unit (Forward Area).

As an RSU in its own right it had had a life span of slightly less than three months.

No. 123 Repair and Salvage Unit

There is very little on record regarding this unit from its formation at Lahore on 1 March 1942 until it was disbanded in December of the same year, and it would appear to be little more than a holding unit.

Of what little remains, it would seem that about 200 men of various trades, under the command of a Flt/Lt A. N. Dale, all ex UK, were posted in to RAF Station Lahore, a peacetime station commanded by Wg/Cdr S. R. Ubee, AFC, a former CO of 60 Squadron who was subsequently posted to China Bay, his place being taken by Wg/Cdr Burnside, DFC.

Although given the title of Repair and Salvage Unit, its primary policy at that time was to assist an advance party of 60 Squadron with the influx of rather elderly Blenheim IVs flown in from the Middle East to replace the Mark Is lost in action by 60 Squadron in the retreat from Burma. During the same period, 28 Squadron were replacing their Audaxes with Lysanders.

When 60 Squadron was finally re-formed and reorganized and moved on to its operational base at Asansol, followed by 28 Squadron to Ranchi for Army co-operation duties, very little remained for the unit personnel to occupy their time, other than servicing visiting aircraft. Obviously this duty could not profitably occupy the time of 200 airmen of various trades.

On 7 May 1942, 307 MU was formed at Lahore under the command of Sqn/Ldr H. Barker and the unit personnel were attached for duty to this new unit. Personnel were now occupied in unpacking spares and ground equipment and acting as an R & I Flight for visiting aircraft when required. Contemporary accounts would seem to suggest that this was not the most popular of duties on account of the amount of bull which accompanied the many VIP visits, none more so than when His Excellency the Governor of the Punjab arrived in connection with the reception of Lt.-Gen., HRH The Duke of Gloucester.

When the Duke did arrive, he was met by the Governor of the Punjab, the Premier of the Punjab, Gen. Hickman, Wg/Cdr J. G. Towle and a whole entourage flown in from Delhi. The British Raj was in its element and bull oozed from every quarter. His departure for Peshawar that same afternoon required the same pomp.

This continual turn-out of spit and polish and guard of honour duties was by now beginning to disenchant the airmen and they began to feel somewhat misemployed. It was with some relief that the unit was informed it would be moving to Calcutta in the near future to take up repair and salvage duties in that area. On 4 July 1942, the first convoy left Lahore by rail for Dum-Dum, leaving behind a detachment which was to follow on when the various aircraft allocations had been dealt with.

Within a day of arrival, their first task was to take over from 60 RSU the salvage of a Blenheim of 60 Squadron (Z7691) which had suffered a landing accident. It was dismantled and conveyed to No. 1 CMU at Kanchrapara. A few days later they had to salvage a Blenheim of 34 Squadron (Z7611) which had also suffered a landing accident at Dum-Dum.

On 27 August 1942, the unit had the onerous task of salvaging Blenheim Z7647 which had swung off the runway at Dum-Dum when its port engine failed and collided with a steam roller being used to extend the runway. The pilot, Wg/Cdr C. B. Wallis, DSO, the CO of 60 Squadron, was fatally injured and died later in hospital in Calcutta. P/O Page, his observer, was killed instantly. Lt Dorner, travelling as a passenger, suffered severe leg injuries while the other two occupants escaped with minor injuries.

Having just settled in and established a working routine, the unit was again instructed to move. This time it was to be by road to Pandaveswar, some sixty miles north-west of Dum-Dum. No account is given of the unit's activities at the new location though it is recorded that the unit moved again in November to Salbani, eighty miles due south.

Only two accounts of any salvage operations have come to light during their occupancy of Salbani.

One was when a detachment was sent to Chittagong to salvage a Blenheim of 34 Squadron (Z7421) which, following an engine cut-out, had hit some trees and crash landed at Chrandradona and was a complete write-off. The pilot, Sqn/Ldr P. L. Keeble, and the navigator were killed in the accident, though the air gunner survived.

The other was when a Wellington of 99 Squadron (HE106) based at Jessore, had crash landed on a sandbank in the middle of the river. The salvage crew had to cut an approach road with the help of local labour in order to get to the site.

Once again, it seemed a rather odd situation that the unit detachment should not only have to travel 250 miles by a round-about route by rail and river, bypassing not only 122 RSU at Asansol but 60 RSU at Kanchrapara, but should also have to salvage an aircraft in an area near a site at Jessore already occupied by 2 FRD. The agreement as to the area of responsibility for salvage, which had been agreed by 224 Group in September, between 122, 101 and 60 RSUs did not seem to apply in the case of 123 RSU and remains another of the many unexplained irregularities regarding the salvage and operational policies of RSUs which seemed to permeate their histories.

In the meantime, the detachment which had been left behind at Lahore when the unit first moved to Calcutta, seemed to have been conveniently ignored and found themselves at the beck and call of not only 307 MU but also that of 306 MU which had also been formed at Lahore (Flt/Lt A. W. Mosdell) and became employed in servicing the Hudsons of the newly formed 194 Squadron until they too left from Palam in February 1943.

By this time, their parent unit, 123 RSU, had been disbanded. Personnel at Pandaveswar were posted to 122 RSU while those still remaining at Lahore, with few exceptions, found themselves absorbed into 306 MU.

No. 129 Repair and Salvage Unit

Two flight sergeants, five sergeants, twenty-seven corporals, 230 airmen and F/O Vivian, a Tech E, but no commanding officer, arrived at Bombay and entrained for the RAF station at Cuttack, arriving at Charpatia on 11 October

1942. Sqn/Ldr Hucklebridge arrived from the UK two weeks later having spent some time in Delhi with Air/Cdre Carter ironing out the working policies of the unit.

On arrival at Cuttack, the unit found that it was attached to the station for accommodation and messing and under the control of the Assistant Adjutant of 175 Wing. Two buildings occupied by a detachment of Light AA on the edge of the airfield were allocated to the unit. The gunners who had been there for some time and were well settled in were not at all happy at being ordered to vacate the site within twenty-four hours.

As 129 had no ground equipment to speak of and very few tools, most of the personnel were detailed to help service the Hudsons of 62 Squadron, whilst a detachment was sent to Jessore to render assistance to the squadrons based there.

Again, the odd thing was that 122 RSU, based at Asansol 250 miles to the north, also had detachments at Cuttack and Jessore, an arrangement which was far from satisfactory and created many problems as far as the allocation of crashed aircraft were concerned and, of course, not very conducive to economy as far as man-hours and transportation were concerned.

Many servicing personnel will know the feeling of having spent hours and hours in the blistering heat, repairing an aircraft, only to see it crash on air test. One Hudson of 62 Squadron (FH243), with its repairs completed and ready to be flown to Kanchrapara, failed to take off and overran the runway, coming to rest on some rough ground. The undercarriage collapsed causing considerable damage to the underside of the fuselage as it slithered to a halt, twisting the airframe in the process. Following an inquiry as to the cause, it was returned to 129 as scrap salvage.

A similar incident of wasted effort also occurred with another of 62 Squadron's Hudsons (AE580) which force landed in the sea off Puri, sixty miles south of Cuttack. The aircraft stayed afloat sufficiently long for the salvage crew in a launch supplied by the Navy, to recover the wireless and some of the more easily removed equipment, before having to abandon it and watch it finally sink in fifty fathoms of water.

Although a watch was kept on the beach for a couple of days in case the strong tides swept it ashore, it proved a fruitless exercise and the salvage was aborted.

Following a visit by Wg/Cdr B. A. Chacksfield of 226 Group, it was revealed that the unit was to be disbanded. The Commanding Officer protested, pointing out the valuable work that the unit had carried out in the short time of its existence. After extensive discussions, it was agreed by Bengal Maintenance Wing to rescind the Disbandment Order but to transfer the unit to Jessore, leaving sufficient personnel behind to clear up any outstanding commitments remaining at Cuttack.

On 18 February, all the equipment was loaded without mishap on the Bengal Nagpur Railway, thanks to a very helpful crane driver who took it upon himself to make sure the trucks were in the right place at the right time, in spite of the stationmaster's protests that it wasn't a lowly crane driver's job to marshal railway trucks.

Unusually, the journey was without any incident or delay whatever and they arrived at Jessore on time in the early hours of the morning. The domestic site at Jessore caused some misgivings, especially when a high wind followed by torrential rain played havoc with all the bashas, leaving many of them uninhabitable and it seemed a good opportunity to look for an alternative site. There was another large condemned domestic site outside Jessore so it was decided to try to renovate it and make it serviceable.

It needed a great deal of investigation and discussion, for it was known that the civil authorities were very anxious to get the RAF out of the town and any information forthcoming was likely to be unreliable and exaggerated in their keenness to get rid of the RAF. After seeking the advice of Capt. Avery of the Indian Engineers, who was in charge of the airfield work sites, it was decided to go ahead with the renovation.

However, the Station Commander, Gp/Capt J. B. M. Wallace, was, in general, opposed to the scheme and the matter had to be dropped until a more opportune moment to proceed arose.

The unit was now fully occupied servicing Wellingtons of 99 and 215 Squadrons as well as the Hudsons of 62 Squadron which had now followed on from Cuttack.

By June 1943, a new domestic site was near completion at Santola, four miles from Jessore and one mile from the technical site. It had an Officers' and Sergeants' Mess and another building was divided into corporals' and airmen's recreation rooms, complete with dry canteen and a supper bar, with electric lights provided by a diesel generator. A full-size football pitch was also established and P/O Hobbs was appointed as Sports' Officer.

On 30 October 1943, a Formation Order was received at Jessore, stating that the detachment at Cuttack would now remain there and form the nucleus of a new unit to be known as 123 RSU. Somewhere along the line, someone must have had their wires crossed, unless they were to perform a miracle of resurrection, for this unit had been dead and buried ten months before when it was officially disbanded and all personnel had been absorbed into other units.

This was followed a week later by another signal to 129 RSU, almost a year since their arrival in India, stating that the whole of the unit would be disbanded and absorbed into the new 136 RSU currently assembling at Jessore.

No. 131 Repair and Salvage Unit

Although this unit survived for eighteen months, their records are very scant and little more than an occasional diary with gaps between, sometimes amounting to months from one entry to the next.

It commences at Chittagong on 1 January 1944 with the arrival of F/O

Kukulka (Polish Air Force) and F/O G. A. Roberts on engineering duties. They were followed later by F/O J. B. Fawcett as the unit MO and Sqn/Ldr Briggs who at one time had been the CO of 122 RSU at Asansol and who was subsequently mentioned in dispatches.

On 9 September 1944, the unit was visited by the Supremo who gave his usual pep talk and quotes about The Forgotten Army.

Judging by the various reports, they must have worked very closely with 126 RSU, also stationed at Chittagong, and had a string of detachments at Nidinia, Dhoapalong, Ramu, Dohazari and Chiringa.

However, an account of one salvage job reveals again the close relationship that many salvage units had with the RAF Regiment when, on 12 September 1944, WO Simms and three men were sent to St Martin's Island about ten miles off the mouth of the Naf River to salvage a Spitfire VIII of 273 Squadron (MD229) operating from Cox's Bazar.

Piloted by F/O 'Pip' Piper, it had belly landed on the beach at 1415 hours two days previously after returning, along with another Spitfire, from convoy patrol. A message had been received by 2942 Field Squadron of the RAF Regiment at Maungdaw only forty-five minutes after the crash. It gave an estimated location of five miles south-west of Maungdaw (Jaliapara Island) and requested that efforts be made to help rescue the pilot and destroy the aircraft's IFF.

The following account, extracted from a Regiment Situation Report of the incident, courtesy of Frank Lowers, indicates what was involved.

Following the signal for help, Capt. Irwin of the IWT was contacted and a launch was made available for the journey. The CO, Sqn/Ldr E. M. John, Flt/Lt Fawcett, the MO of 131 RSU, Sqn/Ldr Hay of 853 AMES, F/O Mitchell, Cpl Johnston and LACs Birchall and Andrews set off to Jaliapara Island to find the aircraft. After a fruitless search, they observed two Spitfires circling St Martin's Island, about ten miles south, obviously indicating the crash site.

Heading in that direction, they encountered a Royal Indian Navy vessel already standing off at the scene, with the crashed Spitfire clearly visible on the beach. They had launched a dinghy but owing to the strong current and the rocks, were unable to make the shore so Sqn/Ldr Hay decided to swim to the beach.

After the guarding party had got ashore, according to the incident report, the IFF was blown up, though this is disputed emphatically by Frank Lowers, one of the party of relief guards who landed a couple of days later and is substantiated by the fact that the IFF had had no charge fitted in the first place. In any case, having found the aircraft more or less intact, it seems odd that anyone would want to blow up a valuable piece of equipment.

After the arrival of WO Simms and the salvage crew, it was decided that there was no way in which the aircraft could be loaded on to a barge after dismantling from its present location. It would have to be manhandled to the opposite side of the island to a sandy beach where it could be loaded on to an invasion barge which had been floated ashore, then when the salvage was finally completed, could then be towed off.

By dint of hard work by the salvage crew and the Regiment chaps, along with some native labour keen to earn a few rupees, the aircraft was finally moved and loaded on to the barge. Unfortunately, the tow rope from the steamer which was to tow it back to Maungdaw came adrift and one of the Regiment men was detailed to take the rope out with the aid of a rather primitive canoe, manned by two natives. The fact that Frank Lowers, who had been detailed for the job, couldn't swim, didn't seem to have been taken into account.

On his return to the squadron at Cox's Bazar, F/O Piper was given a roasting for not having blown up the IFF. He had been informed on a number of occasions that they were fitted with charges and he had presumed that this would have detonated when he hit the beach but being in a slightly shocked state from the accident, it hadn't occurred to him that this had not happened. Had it been the case, he wouldn't have been able to radio to advise he was OK.

These charges, in the form of a cartridge fitted to the radio, were not designed to blow the radio to smithereens but merely to destroy only the coil so that nothing could be deciphered to reveal the frequencies, and in most cases were fired by an electrical circuit operated by the pilot.

The Merlin 66 engine, after overhaul, was eventually installed in another aircraft.

On 24 March 1945, the unit was moved to Akyab by the Dakotas of 85 RSU and apart from details of various accidents, nothing further is recorded until 28 November 1945 when the unit was officially disbanded by AHQ and was henceforth to be known simply as 132 RSU Detachment (Akyab).

No. 135 Repair and Salvage Unit

This unit was formed at Salbani in January 1943 under the command of a Sqn/Ldr Bond. It was to be semi-static with an operational function for repair and salvage work on aircraft within an approximate area, between the rivers Hahandi, in the south, and the Ganges in the north. It would considerably overlap the salvage areas of 122 RSU at Asansol and that of 134 in Calcutta. The nearest town of any note was Kharagpur, about twenty-eight miles away.

Within a couple of weeks of formation, the number 135 was deleted and the unit became known simply as No. 2 Repair and Salvage Section. As with other units, there seems to be no logical explanation for the reversion to a title which implies that it is only part of another unit. It may well have been a temporary formation, keeping the original number in abeyance pending a reassessment of either the success of the unit or the actual servicing needs. Whatever the reason, the title reverted to 135 RSU eleven months later on 1 December 1943 and it was commanded by Flt/Lt Bullen, a Tech E.

Again, although sited at Salbani for more than two years, its activities are rather obscure but from the very few aircraft and their locations logged in its ORB, it must be assumed that it functioned some of the time as an actual salvage unit.

Only one human incident seems to have been worthy of occupying more than a couple of lines in the ORB. On 18 October 1944, the CO, accompanied by the public relations photographer of AHQ Bengal, proceeded to Palamau to present on behalf of the RAF an engraved walking stick to ASM Nurul Huda, in addition, in the presence of His Excellency the Governor of Bihar who was on an official visit to Palamau, a large sum of money was handed over to the District Commissioner to enable cloth to be purchased for the men and women of the village of Kumundi.

It seems that on 11 June, a Harvard flown by an Indian pilot had force landed, because of a fuel shortage, on the bed of the River Auranga. Assistant Station Master Nurul Huda, an overseer, on his own initiative, had organized 150 villagers of Kumundi who by working all day, accomplished the task of raising the aircraft from the river bed and carried it bodily fifty yards to higher ground to a clearing made by another sixty villagers. But for this initiative, the aircraft would have been lost when the rains came.

On 8 August, Flt/Lt Bullen was posted to 132 RSU and his place taken by Sqn/Ldr Richardson.

Following a signal, the unit proceeded to No. 35 PTC in Calcutta in October 1945 and then to Singapore for disbandment along with other units destined for the same fate. Their duties were taken over by 138 RSU who had been flown in from Charra, near Ranchi, to take over the vacated site.

No. 137 Repair and Salvage Unit

Although taking over a ready-made unit at Dacca (4 RSS) in December 1943, complete with workshops and equipment, very little of the new unit's activities remain on record which is rather strange considering that it occupied a very important and strategic site for carrying on the transport of aircraft by river to Kanchrapara.

No evidence remains to indicate that it carried out the function of a repair and salvage unit and it seems to have been disbanded sometime in June 1944 and become part of No. 100 Air Stores Park at Dacca and Narayanganj, primarily as a dispatching unit for aircraft and spares under the command of Sqn/Ldr A. E. G. Cole who had taken over when Sqn/Ldr W. R. Middleton was posted to an AFTU.

Nos. 140, 141 and 144 Repair and Salvage Units

These were three of the units which had been hastily formed in October and November 1943, initially as Repair and Salvage Sections in preparation for the vast number of aircraft which were envisaged as the war in the Far East escalated.

No. 140 RSU, formed at Allahabad and commanded by Sqn/Ldr A. A. Bell, had, by January 1944, over 300 men out on various detachments at MUs in a servicing role rather than a salvage function. In May 1944, on instructions from 226 Group, it was decided that the unit would disband and move *en masse* to 322 MU at Chakeri near Cawnpore, leaving a party of seventy men and one WO to remain at Bamrauli. The CO was posted at the same time to take over the MU as the Wing Commander Engineering.

No. 141 RSU, formerly 8 RSS at Drigh Road, now based at Jodhpur and commanded by Sqn/Ldr Spry, was formally disbanded and became the nucleus of 355 MU on the same site, with a change from salvage policies to those of maintenance.

Similarly, No. 144 RSU, known previously as No. 3 FRD when it was formed in October 1943, based at Campbellpur on the North-West Frontier and commanded by Flt/Lt Sandeford, also became involved in the general shuffle of movement which occurred at a conference at Cawnpore in June 1944. It was attended by the COs of all three units. Group decided that the personnel of 140 RSU on attachment at Bhopal and Cawnpore would be posted to 141 RSU at Jodhpur. Those at the Air Landing School at Delhi would move to 144 RSU at Risalpur whilst the detachment at Allahabad would be posted to 135 RSU at Salbani.

All these movements would be accompanied by a corresponding adjustment of the various trades and re-allotment of establishment transport. By the following year, 144 RSU had also been absorbed into 322 MU at Cawnpore and was disbanded in December 1945, along with the MU, while 141 survived in its role as 355 MU until it too was disbanded in January 1946.

Transport Salvage Units

Although not concerned with the salvage of aircraft, it would be remiss not to give them a mention as an important part of the salvage scene. They had two things in common: their salvage categories were identical to those of aircraft units, write-offs, repairable on site, remove to an MU, etc. and of course many shared the same hardships, the same traumas and the constant upheavals as the aircraft salvage units as they moved into Burma.

Their life span, however, except for one unit, was relatively short, amounting to no more than about nine months and very little is known of their actual activities, so one can only assume that they carried out the policies implied by the titles.

Contemporary accounts suggest that except for No. 83 RSU which reformed as an MU and became the main repair depot in Calcutta where it could service heavy transport or cranes shipped to them in the same fashion as aircraft, many of the mobile MT salvage units were not a very practical proposition in the rapid advance through Burma. Most squadrons and even RSUs either relied on their own MT sections or called on the Army Recovery Depots for assistance with major breakdowns whenever the need arose.

No. 83 Repair and Salvage Unit

This unit came direct from the UK in December 1942 to Lahore and was placed at the disposal of 307 MU, pending authority from 226 Group, before moving to Calcutta to become part of 335 MU as an MTLRD and was disbanded in February 1945 at Tollygunge.

No. 146 Repair and Salvage Unit

Formerly known as No. 1 Motor Transport Salvage Unit, it was formed at Calcutta in February 1943 and commanded by P/O N. W. Evans, before moving to Chittagong and becoming a Motor Transport Repair Depot as part of the overall salvage strategy which had been organized by Sqn/Ldr Bennett of 60 RSU. They were quartered temporarily on a site in Love Lane until they moved to the vacated quarters of 224 Group.

Within weeks of arrival, they had detachments at Feni, Comilla and Agartala. It was at this latter station that they were to lose some of their transport in a Jap raid on the strip in April. Eventually they moved to 362 MU, a Motor Transport Repair Depot in Madras and were disbanded in August 1944.

No. 147 Repair and Salvage Unit

Formerly known as No. 2 Motor Transport Repair and Salvage Unit, it was formed in November 1943 at Kharagpur, about thirty miles from Salbani and disbanded there in August 1944.

No. 148 Repair and Salvage Unit

It was formerly No. 3 Motor Transport Light Repair Depot and formed in December 1943 at Silchar, with detachments at Sylhet, Imphal and Palel. It moved to Kalemyo, Schwebo and Meiktila and later became No. 18 Transport Salvage Unit at Rangoon, before moving to Hong Kong where it was disbanded in December 1945.

No. 149 Repair and Salvage Unit

It was formed as an MTLRD in January 1944 from a section of No. 146 RSU at Chittagong and commanded by Flt/Lt E. T. C. Shepherd, with its HQ at Mambur not far from Ramu. It had technical and domestic sites at Dohazari, Chittagong and was disbanded in September 1945.

No. 150 Repair and Salvage Unit

Formerly No. 5 Motor Transport Light Repair Depot, it was formed at Comilla in November 1943 and was disbanded in August 1944.

Chapter 17

No. 60 RAF Mobile Field Hospital

Though not coming under the heading of a technical salvage unit, a field hospital could be loosely described as a 'medical salvage unit'. The task, in somewhat primitive conditions, was salvaging airmen from the many ailments all were prone to and which few escaped before returning them 'serviceable' once again to their units. Most units had their own sick quarters staffed with their own MO and nursing orderlies. Usually it was no more than a couple of bashas, one equipped as a 'consulting room' and dispensary, the other with beds for the sick. It dealt with the more mundane ailments of sick parades or panic-station inoculations whenever an epidemic of smallpox, typhus or cholera hit the area. Anything more serious was usually referred to one of the many Army Military Hospitals which had been established throughout India and Burma.

The Royal Air Force units in the Imphal Valley were fortunate enough to have their own hospital. In 1943, No. 60 RAF Mobile Field Hospital was set up. It was built on a hillside not far from Kanglatongbi on the famous Dimapur Road which led to Imphal. It comprised a collection of huts made from woven rattan and bamboo plastered with mud and topped by straw roofs.

Fresh air, and flies, came through square holes that served as windows. Woven shutters, propped open with bamboo poles, were protection against the rains. Electricity for the more important functions of the hospital was provided by a portable generator. The only illumination in the wards was furnished by Tilley lamps which gave a brilliant light but attracted swarms of insects that sizzled as they flew against the hot glass, leaving piles of charred remains to be cleared away each morning.

Very little could be done in the daytime to ward off the swarms of flies which at times, depending on the weather, seemed to reach plague proportions. No spray seemed to be very effective. Even an exasperated attempt by one of the airmen to manufacture fly papers from jam and Bronco rolls, laid in strategic places, made little difference to their persistent attentions.

Occasionally, a stray pye-dog would nose its way into the ward scavenging for scraps, only to be chased out yelping under a hail of boots or anything else that the patients could lay their hands on.

There were four wards, a pathology lab, an 'ops room' and a laundry of sorts. The domestic quarters of the medical staff and the nurses were some way away further up the hillside and were strictly out of bounds. Water was obtained by bowser from a natural standpipe fiercely guarded by an ancient Manipuri armed with an equally ancient shotgun.

The wards were very basic at first, just rows of charpoys complete with mosquito nets slung on bamboo poles attached to the corners, plus a couple of chairs and a table. There were no lockers at first to hold the patients' kit, though one Sister, unkindly called 'Sherman' for obvious reasons, insisted that anything that didn't belong to the hospital was out of sight. Just where was never explained but most of it, of course, was merely stuffed under the bed. This habit was soon abandoned when it was found that snakes and other nocturnal horrors had a penchant for empty boots and open haversacks. One airman, whether anxious to please or scared of Sherman's wrath is uncertain, hung his small kit out of the window only to discover later that day that someone had taken a liking to the contents.

Sister Sherman had been in India for years and was one of the old-school, where sheets had to be folded just so, corners had to be square and the red lines on blankets had to be exactly in line. She believed that ward discipline was a distinct aid to recovery. She was probably right in a way — blokes were glad to escape from her clutches. However, in all fairness, in spite of her sergeant-major attitude and somewhat brusque manner, underneath it all she had a heart of gold and was a very caring person. Many a sick airman had cause to be grateful for her nursing.

The Senior Medical Officer was a Welshman, Sqn/Ldr Williams, or 'Willy' behind his back! Flt/Lt Dickens ('Dicky') and Flt/Lt Bernard ('Barney') made up the rest of the team.

Oral care was the responsibility of Flt/Lt Jefferson-Smith whose stock phrase to all his patients was, 'This will be uncomfortable for you, but quite interesting for me.' The rest of the staff were male orderlies. One in particular, who, when it came to inoculations, was thought by many to be a failed dart player, was aptly named Savage.

Prior to the Siege of Imphal, all female staff were flown out and returned some time in May when the 'flap' was over. One new Sister in particular, Anne Jones (where are they now?), was quite a willowy maid. This was emphasized when she stood in the doorway with the sun shining brightly behind her. It was some time before she twigged the interest that patients took in her arrival in the ward each morning and why airmen seemed to want to engage her in conversation on the doorstep.

There was little privacy in any of the wards; examinations and the administering of injections were always a source of curiosity and amusement to onlookers in the other beds. Then, mysteriously, large rolls of the material used in the manufacture of mosquito nets appeared and were promptly made into screens with frames constructed of the ever plentiful bamboo.

Large drums of bright yellow paint also appeared from somewhere. It was suspected that it was left over from the days when Mohawks of 5 and 155 Squadrons had to have their engine cowlings painted in order to distinguish them from the Jap Zeros, several having been shot up by Hurricanes by mistake. Bedside lockers were ex-ammunition boxes liberally daubed yellow, as was anything else that didn't move. It did, however, have a rather funny side-effect. Many of the patients, already looking pretty gaunt from the effects of amoebic dysentery and regular doses of anti-malaria mepacrine, looked even ghastlier in the reflection of the paint.

Spaces between the beds and through the wards were laid with Bithess, normally used in the construction of airstrips, which had obviously been scrounged in the same way as the paint and the material for the screens.

The majority of the patients were suffering either from dysentery in one form or another or one of the brands of malaria prevalent in the area and some had contracted scrub typhus. Unfortunately, some were more serious cases and had a combination of one or more of these maladies, and of course there were the victims of accidents.

Pathological treatments varied from castor oil, arsenical enemas, M. & B. tablets or a course of emetine injections, and sometimes a combination of one or more, depending on the MO, each of whom seemed to have his own particular remedy, and not forgetting the mandatory daily dose of mepacrine. Flt/Lt Barnard swore by Vegemite taken as a medicine, plus injections of vitamin B. Some of the remedies occasionally caused awkward and embarrassing side-effects. The emetine injections seemed to stiffen the muscles and slowed down any rapid exit to the toilets. As one airman remarked, 'It was like having St Vitus's dance and rheumatism at the same time.'

If any cure was designed to test mental stamina it was the retention enemas which had to be held for at least seven hours. Only those with the strongest of willpowers and determination usually survived the distance. To aggravate matters, at tiffin, when bread and jam and hot char was served, some of the more sadistic patients not on the same treatment would go to great pains to pour out char slowly, dribbling it into the mugs as a means of auto-suggestion. Towards the 'deadline' at five o'clock, eyes would be scanning watches as men sat on beds close to the ward exit. To rush would be catastrophic. There were no courtesies like 'after you, mate' in the anxiety to get rid of the 'medicine'. It was sometimes quite amusing, at least for those not on that treatment, to see airmen walking very slowly down the ward, with apparent dignity and gritted teeth to the exit, hoping against hope to make it in time and not have to report to Sherman for clean pyjamas.

In all fairness, however, most of these assorted cures seemed to work to some degree, though the majority suffering from this malady, which didn't distinguish between ranks, all knew of a prescription that was guaranteed to cure — an immediate medical board and a boat ticket to Blighty.

Those attending sick parade as out-patients, suffering the agonies of prickly heat or tinea, could usually tell who was on duty by the colour of the first airman who came out of the medical basha. He would be either bright blue with gentian violet, bright red with mercurochrome or shades of yellow to green with acriflavine. No one cared particularly what he looked like so long as it cured the discomfort. There was nowhere to go except work, and in any case, the locals thought we were mad anyway and quite used to seeing multi-coloured BORs.

Meals were regular if somewhat monotonous; boiled eggs for breakfast, tiffin was either cheese or tinned salmon which most certainly was not John West's and dinner would be McConachie's stew or 'beef' which had probably come from a Manipuri bullock tired of pulling a cart. At times many thought that the meat was a redundant Army mule. Occasionally one of the herd of goats that seemed to wander about the site would end up on the menu.

With every meal there was always char and bread and jam, always plum jam, supplied in large seven-pound tins, thick first thing in the morning, somewhat runny by teatime as the heat of the day increased. Oleo margarine, more suited to greasing axles, which, along with soya links, had been developed by the Americans, provided a substitute for butter. For special occasions, such as visits by senior officers, wild pineapples and thin custard would be provided. It was strange that in the land of rice, never once was there a good old-fashioned rice pudding on the menu.

A large bucket of cocoa always appeared around eight o'clock, with lights out at ten o'clock, to end a day which had begun at 0530 with temperature taking and the somewhat incongruous request, 'BO?' Under the circumstances it would have been more appropriate to have enquired, 'Bowels closed?'

One day the hospital was warned that the Viceroy, Lord Wavell and Air Chief Marshal Sir Richard Peirse, the AOC, would be visiting the hospital. Everyone began to run round like headless chickens trying to smarten the place up. Just how one could spruce up straw bashas was anyone's guess, other than make sure that the charpoys were in line to within a hair's breadth and kit was laid out reasonably tidily.

Sherman dished out new pyjamas which had been made by the ladies of the Indian Red Cross. They were bright blue, the most fantastic garments ever seen, hardly describable except to say that the waist size was equivalent to the leg length. Basically, it appeared as if they had taken two squares of material, stitched them together along each side, split them up the middle and sown them to form the legs, whilst the pyjama cords would have anchored a battleship. Some of the patients who had lost a great deal of weight could have paired up and got into one leg. They were a tonic in a sense because everyone momentarily forgot his troubles and burst into uncontrolled laughter.

The great day came. Those who were ambulant had to sit impassively at the bottom of their beds; bedridden patients lay stretched out almost to attention under new sheets. Of course, there was no smoking and definitely no card games. Sherman strode up and down defying anyone to step out of line.

Promptly at 4 p.m. the Viceroy and the AOC arrived with a retinue of Delhi wallahs, closely followed by reporters and cameramen who were to record the occasion. Stopping to talk to one of the airmen, Wavell asked him what was the matter. 'Dysentery,' replied the airman. 'Mmmh, bad luck,' and he moved on quickly as if it was contagious and not a suitable subject for discussion, before stopping further down the ward beside an airman holding a crutch and with one foot in plaster. Photographers gathered round and clicked away. The following week the headlines read: 'Viceroy stops for a friendly chat with a wounded airman at a hospital in the Front Line.' What the general public hadn't been told was that this same airman had in fact fallen into a slit trench and broken his ankle.

It was a stark contrast when returning to the UK and RAF Halton for a check-up in 1947: wide, cool wards, polished floors, no mozzie nets to worry about and plenty of amenities. The food was good; even bully beef that had been sliced and not poured out of a tin seemed to taste differently. There was the occasionally Sherman-type Sister, but then what hospital would be complete without one?

The only thing that hadn't changed was that damned Mark 1 sigmoidoscope...

Chapter 18

Of Rhymes and Reasons

Although censorship was a necessary evil, many airmen felt frustrated at not being able to convey their true feelings in letters home, especially as the censor might well have been one of the officers one worked with daily.

Similarly, criticism of authority by other ranks was forbidden under KRs and ACIs. Democracy was only a word in those days and could not be used as a defence. Orders were simply obeyed, no matter how farcical they appeared. In consequence, many of the orders issued by Authority, generally seen as distanced from harsh reality, seemed to have no relevance to particular circumstances and were usually received with silent criticism by airmen at the sharp end.

Unable to voice themselves publicly, many of the thoughts were usually put down in the form of basha rhymes or poetry as an opinion and record of a particular event. All covered a multitude of topics, some were in praise, some in protest. Others were personal feelings and portrayed thoughts of home and aspirations for the future, unable to be expressed in letters.

The following, written by the author, are not in any chronological order and cover a period of four years of the Burma campaign. The subject of the first one will be recognized by any serviceman, whether or not he was in the Far East.

The Shite Hawk

The Shite Hawk is a crafty bird, as it hovers in the sky.
Its beady eyes are searching for *konna* passing by.
On silent wings it plummets down; its speed does not abate,
Its talons pointing forwards, to nick things from your plate.
If it misses first time, it has another go,
And woe betide the airman who moves too bloody slow.

They wheel and swoop and loop the loop, cause panic all around,
Till some poor sod has tripped and spilled his grub upon the ground.
Though we try and catch them with bully on a string,

Those birds are just too crafty for such a simple thing.
Then when we think we've beaten that menace from the sky,
He swoops down fast and low again and craps right in your eye.

The Troop Train

The 'Harriers' from Singapore at Karachi all entrain.
No one wants to know us and we're on the move again.
We don't know where we're going; no one seems to care
So long as we are off the camp and out of someone's hair.

Into carriages like hen coops but good enough to carry troops.
No cushions or padding, merely slats on which to lay our bedding mats.
The toilet, just a slot like a keyhole in the floor,
With a bar each side to stop one's head from banging on the door.

Water is available from a stagnant tank
But a simple thing like a Bronco roll leaves an awkward blank.
The engine has seen better days, spitting steam from every quarter,
But worldly airmen in the know make char from rusty water.

At last we're off across the Sind to places yet unknown
And ponder on the circumstance in which we've now been thrown.
As we rumble on and night descends once more,
A plague of silent cockroaches emerges from 'neath the floor.

They scurry, silent as the night, over sleeping men
And irritate the sweating flesh, till daylight breaks again.
The bugs and mosquitoes, from through the broken grill,
Also appear in thousands, to have their bloody fill.

Twelve hours later, with rations spent,
A halt for food is heaven sent,
For there on the platform, the Catering Corps,
With bacon and eggs, have set up store.

It stimulates a concerted rush
To have some nosh, plus the chance to have a wash.
There's vendors flogging sticky cakes smothered in black flies,
With oranges all boiled, to make them double size.

'Baksheesh, sahib. Baksheesh, sahib,' all the beggars say.
Fat chance they've got from airmen on three rupees a day.

Now we are replete and climb aboard once more.
We've been informed the next stop is somewhere near Lahore.

The train halts in the evening, by a water tower
And scores of blokes descend to have a cooling shower.
Although we're miles from anywhere, beggars never miss a trick.
They all appear out of the gloom as if by some magic.

But what they get from all the blokes, standing in the nude
Is lots of fruity language, some of it quite rude.
As we clank on into the night pursued by all the smell,
We ponder on the poet who wrote of 'India's spell'.

Two days now, we've been on our way, and a thousand miles to go.
Why do all the troop trains have to go so bloody slow?
We stop at last; the Catering Corps again are on the station,
With McConachies and bread and jam, and half the Indian nation.

Again the beggars and vendors pestering for gain.
Blokes begin to wonder if they're travelling on the train.
We've now been told the next grub is four hundred miles away,
So they issued us packed rations to help us on our way.

They shunt us into sidings, to await a passing train.
What stopped the transit wallahs from sending us by plane?
At last we're on the Bengal Plain; we hit a wall of heat,
We breath hot air and dust, our lungs are near effete.

The train pulls in to Asansol, the Clapham of the East.
Five days of being cooped up and blokes are pretty creased.
Waiting at the station, to check as we detrain,
A little twerp of an RTO, pompous and inane.

'Get your kit and fall in line. Do it at the double.'
We look amazed, think to ourselves, 'This guy is seeking trouble.'
'Don't use that tone on my blokes, with your knees all lily white,'
Says Sergeant Dusty Miller to everyone's delight.

'We were in the Battle of Britain, chased from Singapore,
Been in Java and Sumatra, have you done any more?
So cut out all the bullshit, take your finger out,
Or I'll have your guts for garters, of that there is no doubt.'

With that the RTO back-peddled pretty fast;
'Glad to see you fellows have made it here at last.'
So into the trucks that were standing by, our journey's at an end.
A thousand miles in five days is hard to comprehend.

But when we get to the camp, there is nowhere to sleep;
The rotten sods have merely left some tents all in a heap.
Struggling with the canvas and ropes that seem perverse,
Blokes are pretty knackered as they heave and sweat and curse.

At last the chore is finished and night begins to fall,
When out of the gloom comes Chiefie who wants to take roll-call.
'You'll get no grub until it's done,' so the blokes concede
As they foolishly anticipate a slap-up welcome feed.

It was not to be; the cookhouse had knocked off.
They'd just left bully sandwiches for the starving mob to scoff.
So ends this tale of a journey from the Sind to the Bengal Plain,
Five days of utter misery, I hope never to do again!

Afflictions

Here in the East we have to contend
With pests and discomforts that ne'er seem to end.

There are mozzies whining round one's head
From early morning till it's time for bed.

Its black and white probe as sharp as a pin,
As it lifts up its rear and jabs it right in.

With ticks that cause typhus on every blade of grass
That transfer to clothing whenever you pass.

There's dhobi itch and tinea as well as guinea worm,
With other creepie crawlies that make a stomach squirm.

There are also snakes like cobras plus the dreaded krait.
Just one bite from either and life could terminate.

There's heatstroke and dysentery, cured by loads of dope,
Concluded by inspection with a shiny 'shufti-scope'.

Should we succumb to any ills, the cures are very few,
Such as gentian violet ointment that turns a body blue.

There's emetine, plus M. & B. topped up with castor oil,
With just a sterile razor blade to lance a giant boil.

To a BOR the only thing that makes it all seem fair,
The maladies hit everyone and the officers have their share.

In spite of this we soldier on and pray to the Almighty
For a travel chit to catch a boat to take us back to Blighty.

The Charpoy

The charpoy is a strange device,
Its legs in tins to stop the lice.
The hempen rope, forever lax,
Is not the place to press your slacks.
A wobbly frame to hang the net,
To tuck beneath, before sunset.
But even when Flitted and tucked in tight,
There's always one mozzie that bites in the night.

The Loathsome Leech

A loathsome pest is the jungle leech;
It attacks the parts that we can't reach.
It creeps through flies and tops of boots,
Buries its head up to the roots.
It sucks and sucks until its belly
Hangs limp and slimy like lumps of jelly.
And though this horrid, gruesome worm
Makes the stomach heave and squirm,
To pull it off is a fatal flaw;
The head breaks off to become a sore.
The only way, with gritted teeth,
A lighted fag is applied beneath.
It does need care, of course, as such,
If the little bastards are round your crutch.

The Erk

As an airframe fitter, I do some tricky work
Even though I'm still a lowly common erk.
The sweat is running down my thighs
And flies are clustered round my eyes.
Another discomfort I must add,
Is prickly heat that drives me mad.
But, in spite of ills, I'm always sent
To any kite that's just got bent.
Though I always grumble at my lot here in the 'blue',
I'm glad that I belong to this 'ere RSU.

Ode to the Road

At Manipur Road we all detrain
For a hairy ride to Imphal Plain.

Into a Chevy or Madrassi truck,
A smooth ride in either is a matter of luck.

Twisting and turning, climbing higher and higher,
Look down the khudside, one feels like a flyer.

Kohima first stop, some forty-six miles.
With luck you'll survive without getting piles.

At last there's a space to stop for some tea
And queue round the truck for a much needed pee.

Soon it's our turn to get up and go.
There's ninety more miles and the going is slow.

'Give over moaning,' curses Lofty, the driver.
'I've done this quite often and I'm a survivor.'

The reason's quite clear, if you glance down the khud;
The Nagas are clearing the results of a flood.

An endless procession, none seem to collide,
As baskets are filled and thrown over the side.

'Straight on for Tokio and the East' says the sign on the track.
The blokes are all knackered and can't wait to get back.

Five hours later, still in a daze,
The Plain emerges through shimmering haze.

We've made it at last and now back in camp,
All pretty sweaty, smelly and damp.

So it's into the basha for a wash and a kip,
Glad to survive that memorable trip.

Jungle Prang

The signal's in of another kite that hasn't made it back,
Somewhere south of Imphal and off the beaten track.
No gen about the pilot or if he is alive.
Perhaps the Nagas found him and helped him to survive.

The gharry has been loaded with rations and the gear
And off we set on a *khacha* road, directions not quite clear.
Arriving some hours later, where the track and jungle met,
Obviously it was going to be a case of toil and sweat.

The kite is found, a total wreck,
Buried deep beneath the deck.
Of the pilot there is no sign, not a single trace;
Assume he must have bailed out and walking back to base.

A brief brew-up beneath the shade,
As plans for salvage are discussed and made.
Of what is left is more than plain,
Little remains to use again.

There is not much that we can do, of that there is no doubt;
What bits that might be useful are very soon ripped out.
The job is now aborted, we've done our level best
And the mangled bits are left behind for the jungle to digest.

The Mohawk

The Mohawk is a Curtiss kite;
Flies by day but rarely night.
Looks like a Zero, flies like a bomb
But what a bind for working on.
Can't get the bits, spares are scarce.
All the bods just sweat and curse.

The engine mechs are full of moans.
'The Cyclone engine's a bag of bones.'
The cowlings are, one must admit,
Not the best to change and fit.
The instrument bashers forever shriek,
'Don't bugger the pitot head with overheat.'

The wireless bod says, 'I've had enough,
I can't get a signal, now the battery's duff.'
The airframe wallahs, with downcast hearts,
Try stopping leaks on undercarts,
While flapping around in solar hat,
The Chiefie's like a pregnant gnat.

But One Five Five we'll salvage no more;
They're collecting Spits from Alipore.
Still, whatever the name, no matter the kite,
There's bound to be something that isn't quite right!
For if it was perfect and things went OK,
What could we discuss as the kite flew away?

An RSU Day

None of the days ever seem quite sane,
Here in the mountains of Imphal Plain.
Wakey, wakey, now what's the score,
A general flap or the daily chore?
Is it 'two six',
There's a kite in a fix?

Is it a Spit or Hurricane?
Perhaps a Dakota in the monsoon drain?
Heave and grunt, shove and push,
The strip needs clearing with the usual rush.

Back at dispersal, the junk piles high,
Filled with kites which will never fly.

Undercarts twisted, mainplanes askew,
Nothing like the kites we knew.
0730 and time to eat,
Then back to work before the heat.
Engine changes or just DI?
With a bit of luck a few will fly.

Panic stations, another flap,
Someone's spotted a low flying Jap.
But is it a Mohawk? Hard to tell.
Take no chances, run like hell.
Into holes full of stinking *pani*,
Paddy wishes for Killarney.

Climbing wet out of the ditch,
It was a Jap, the son of a bitch.
On the strip, two kites a goner.
Get them salvaged in time for *konna*.
Back at dispersal the news is grim;
The Japs are slowly closing in.

All leave cancelled, what a bind.
All thoughts of 'Cal' are left behind.
Mail gharry in; letters for some,
Others unlucky, despondent and glum.
Off to the cookhouse, soya links and wet mash,
With prunes and thin custard plus anything gash.

Then back to the basha to read or to write
And battle with mozzies that swarm round the light.
What tomorrow will bring, one never can tell;
It might be quite cushy or just bloody hell.
So ends a day in the Burma campaign,
In the back and beyond called the Imphal Plain.

Jungle Pilot

I have a pal who's a pilot, an ordinary bloke like me,
But compared to me he looks quite old; I'm twenty-one, he's just twenty-three.
While I am safely on the ground, working without care,
He is over the Naga Hills, in storm and cloud filled air.
Peering through a rain lashed screen, above the towering height,
Alert for any enemy, spoiling for a fight.
Suddenly, from above, he sees with terrible chill,
Bursting through the cloud, a Zero hoping for a kill.
A short, sharp burst of fire, he's dealt a mortal blow,
And his stricken kite begins to spin, to the dark terrain below.
As he struggles vainly to try and gain control,
The silent jungle waits beneath to take its final toll.
Like some dark predator of the night,
Its arms reach out to enfold the kite.

But as he hits the deck, a prayer goes through his head.
'Dear Lord, preserve me, even though I'm dead.
Let not the jungle hide me, let my remains be found
And let my bones be buried in friendly, hallowed ground.'
His prayers for help were answered, he's managed to survive
With nothing more than bruises and glad to be alive.
With great relief from the jungle depth, he hears a friendly cry.
An Army patrol had spotted him, as he spiralled from the sky.
They had come to help him and get him back to base,
Back to civilization, away from this hostile place.
As he leaves, with a backward glance at his crumpled and mangled crate,
It passes through his mind, 'Was it prayer or merely Fate?'
So now you know why he looks old before his time is done,
Whilst I, unmarked by trauma, still look twenty-one.

The Wallahs

Everyone in India is known as 'Sahib' or 'Wallah',
From BORs to coolies living in their squalor.
There are 'khana-samas' and 'bobbagees' to prepare and cook a meal
And evil looking 'loose wallahs' who only want to steal.
There are 'dhurzi wallahs' who, for a chip or two in pay,
Will measure for a shirt or slacks and make them in a day.
There are 'nappi wallahs' to shave you while you're fast asleep,
And 'moochis' making *chapplis* reasonable and cheap.
There are wallahs selling char, everywhere you turn,

'Ek piala char, sahib,' from an ancient urn.
'Dhobi wallahs' bashing clothes at every stretch of water,
With 'soosti wallahs' doing their best to sell their youngest daughter.
When we want a paper, we yell for the 'coggagee'
Who also flogs rude pictures, given a suitable fee.
There are 'bhistis' for the *pani* and 'barafs' for the ice,
With 'dhud' and 'chini wallahs' trying to earn some price.
If we want a basha built, we call a 'misteri'
Who has the framework plastered by a wallah called 'mutti'.
There is one wallah, however, there's one on every station,
Who hoards rupees and annas and scorns most recreation.
He's known by all and sundry, by every BOR,
By the name of 'chatti wallah' and hoards his money in a jar.

More Thoughts of Home

As I lie here on my charpoy, bathed in rivulets of sweat,
Gazing idly at my gecko hunting mozzies round my net,
I wonder if the folks back home know what it's like out here,
Or can they read between the lines of journalists' veneer?

Pondering if in Blighty, six thousand miles away,
They've ever heard of Burma or the Road to Mandalay.
Out here I'm told of the Desert Rats and the fight for Alamein
And thousand bomber raids on Germany's terrain.

I hear rumours of the Yanks with nylons and Hershey bars
Getting fresh with English girls as they flash their big cigars.
I hear that Lady Astor's crusading against carnal sin,
Warning young ladies of the troops who have yellow skin.

'They are the syphilitic army of the East,' is her favourite quote.
A pity someone couldn't shove the words back down her throat.
I hear All India Radio daily dishing out soft soap,
But never any news that might give me some hope.

Then on comes Tokyo Rose, with her sweet talk bulletin,
'Surrender 14th Army, for the Japanese will win.'
The forces' paper SEAC tries hard to stimulate,
But the news at times is sketchy and often out of date.

So perhaps I am forgotten, maybe it is the case,
In a land where one could vanish without a single trace.

Lord Louis has now told us The Forgotten Army's not true,
With a simple explanation of our deeds out here in Burma, no one ever knew.

But as the night wears on, and I think of things I've missed,
I wish I had some Meakin's Gin in order to get pissed.
The solace from the bottle, alas it wouldn't last, for in the morning light,
The mozzies, flies and sweat and news would be as they were last night.

So the only thing that I can do is dream and take it day by day
And pray for a Movement Order to send me to Bombay.
And when at last I get there, I'll shed no tears, no lump in throat,
As I see India vanish from the arse-end of a boat.

The Siege

The Daks come flying in with help, like Galahad
But we're sure the pilots in them are really rather mad.
They fly in low, nigh nose to tail, the wheels scarce touch the ground,
While other kites are stacking and circling around.
Out of the open cargo doors, the 'kickers' shove supplies,
As gharries from the Service Corps wait for manna from the skies.
The drums and bales, they bounce around when the drop is in full spate.
Collecting them is dicey and could decapitate.
Sortie after sortie, supplying what we need,
Until the day arrives, we hope, when the Valley will be freed.
There's low level raids and kites veer away
As Zeros squirt the main runway.
The kites of 28 and 617 scramble to thwart the Sons of Heaven; into slit trenches, somewhere to hide.
They seem very shallow and ten feet wide.
Panic over, work as before;
Stand by as Daks resume their chore.
In spite of Japs and invasion rumour,
The blokes maintain their ribald sense of humour.
But it's not without cost, there is an account,
The evidence shows as the salvage piles mount.
So roll on the day when things become calm,
Free from the panic of an air raid alarm.

Panic Stations

The action here is getting rough, with alarms and squirts each day,
While 'jitter' patrols at night never seem to go away.
They've surrounded us with coils of wire and issued us with Stens,
And we have to sleep in Boxes near the aircraft pens.
On the wire they've hung some tins that are supposed to rattle
To warn the bods we must stand to and prepare ourselves for battle.

But the Japs are far too crafty to enter these zones.
To make it worse they've turned the scales and rattle tins of stones.
And as we blaze away at the enemy unseen,
We spot a lot of tracers where the prowlers had just been.
Those slimy Nips had fired at an angle to the side
And in response the Regiment with Bren guns had replied.

No one could see the enemy; all firing was at will.
It was in fact our own blokes on another hill.
On it went throughout the night, no one seemed to tire,
Till at last an NCO yelled, 'Hold your bloody fire.'
When daybreak came we looked around, nothing was in sight
And once again those slant-eyed sods had kept us up all night.

Will Anybody Care?

When we get back to Blighty when our job is done,
What will be left in Burma to show that we had won?
The airfields that were hacked from scrub and thick bamboo
Will be derelict and overgrown and vanished out of view.

The only memory left of the part they played to keep the Japs at bay
Are wrecks of some of the aircraft still mouldering away,
Obliterated for ever and cloaked from human eyes,
Inhabited again by birds and beasts and, of course, the flies.

Perhaps it will be discovered by a traveller from space
Who'll ponder on the conflict and perhaps the human race,
Who fought in desperation, in heat and pouring rain,
To defend a little bit of ground they called the Imphal Plain.

And will these deeds of airmen be added to Naga lore,
As they find the souvenirs above a *moraung* door?
But my guess is, when we get home, with a ticket to disband,

All that most will want to do, is forget this hostile land.

Escort Duty

'I want a volunteer', the CO looks at me, my knees begin to quiver,
'To take a kite to Cal by road and rail and river.'
'Not me again, I did it last. It's a bloody awful bind,
Shunted back and forth and sometimes left behind.'

'You're just the bloke I'm looking for. You know what it's about.
Draw some rations from the stores, get ready to move out.'
There's nothing I can do. My thoughts are quite profane.
Once more I am an escort to a clapped-out Hurricane.

Very soon we're on our way with the trailer load.
We get there eight hours later at a depot called Manipur Road.
Now starts the bloody hassle, offloading to the train,
As the kite is swung precariously on an ancient crane.

The kite's lashed down upon the truck, precisely in the middle,
Watching for a 'loose wallah' trying to pull a fiddle.
Kipping under tarpaulin, as it trundles through the night,
Waking every hour to check the load's all right.

Arriving at the ferry, surrounded by coolies,
The kite's transferred to a steamer, anchored at the quays.
A few hours' trip down the river, the loading starts anew,
For the final leg on the broad gauge, to the waiting CMU.

At last the journey's over, the paperwork is signed,
And thankful that the detail is now all left behind.
A few days off in Cal, compensation for the strain,
Hoping when I get back I'll not be asked again.

Leave

Now the Siege is over, we've shown the Japs who's best,
Leave has once more started to let us have some rest.
Not organized like Brownies in Darjeeling's hills,
But down to old Calcutta to sample city thrills.
Draw some cash from pay accounts with credits all accrued.
Lots of lovely rupees to spend on gorgeous food.

Warrants are available to go by road and rail.
Better though to go by air on a Dak that's taking mail.
Dum-Dum three hours later, the aircraft touches down,
A gharry or a taxi then takes us into town.
First stop is the APM in Park Street, to report our presence here,
Then round the corner to the Nip Inn for a glass of ice cold beer.
Some wander round to the 'Sally Ann', eight annas for the night,
These are usually 'chatti wallahs' renowned for being tight.
But as you get for what you pay,
A better choice is the Bristol at ten rupees a day.
They pander to one's every whim, each meal a big repast.
Why not enjoy the comfort? This leave could be the last.
Hand over crumpled KD, it's back within a flash,
Neatly starched and ironed to help one cut a dash.
The itinerary now, for the next ten days,
Is to eat and drink and generally laze.
To sit in the Globe or Regal, to see a film or two,
Drinking decent gin or whisky and not the native Zu.
We can go for a change to the Lighthouse or maybe the Elite
Before we go next door to Laidlaws for a typical English treat.
Not served in tin pialas but something really finer,
In cups and saucers, complete with spoons and made from best bone china.
One can wander up Chowringhee, wondering what to buy,
Or merely sit on the *maidan* watching girls go by.
Go by they do, for if you're an erk, you haven't got a chance.
The only way to touch one is by going to a dance.
They hold nightly jigs at Firpo's, Tuesdays the YMCA
And Saturday night for BORs at the Ronaldshay.
If one's feeling like some culture and quite prepared to stroll,
There's the Queen Victoria Monument or the infamous Black Hole.
Also the Indian Museum or the zoo at Alipore.
In one you'll find them stuffed, the other, as they were before.
For presents to send home, there's the Army and Navy Store
And Hall and Anderson's Emporium with commissionaires on the door.
But for those that want to haggle, there's the famous Hogg Market,
To chance your luck at what you see, is really what you get.
As darkness falls, the lights go on, make it just like day.
You'd never guess the Japs are just across the bay.
As we promenade through the city, looking at the sights,
One never ceases to wonder how the homeless spend their nights,
Covered in their dhotis, with pavements as their bed,
It's difficult to ascertain who's living and who's dead.
Some blokes, of course, are not content and search for bint delight,
That can't be found in Free School Street any day or night.

And then before they wander home, a visit to Kyd Street
To see if they've succumbed by being indiscreet.
But soon the leave is over; cash is running low.
Free char and wads at the 'Sally Ann' is the only place to go.
At least we lived like 'burra sahibs' and sampled their lifestyle,
Even though these pleasures were only for a while.
So it's off to Sealdah Station to catch a midnight train.
We are no longer civvies but BORs again.

The Movement Order

A signal's in that we are on the move, again to pastures new,
Aircraft and equipment to stay behind for another RSU.
Sitting in the basha, drinking char that tastes like stew,
We wonder about those wallahs back there in AHQ.
They move us here and there, with effect from such a date,
Absolutely clueless to the problems they create.
How they decide the reason to move us once again,
Is a puzzle that eludes us, for the answer is not plain.
They must have a map of Burma on which to play their games,
With lots of coloured pins and flags to stick in funny names.
And when at last they find one that looks a likely site,
It's probably not an airfield but a jungle satellite.
But because we are an RSU, used to living rough,
A scruffy village basha or a tent is good enough.
They think we are a different breed, living as we do,
And luxury is intended for a very selected few.
We have no marble bathrooms, no bearers for the chores,
Or carpets gracing bashas, just mud and cow muck floors.
There are no whirling fans or punkahs to keep the billet cool,
Nor port and fat cigars as an after dinner rule.
No snooker room or billiards to end a tedious day,
Just dog-eared cards to play some crib to pass the time away.
So wouldn't it be great to sample our lifestyle,
If Delhi wallahs volunteered to live here for a while.
Perhaps then they would appreciate the bloody awful chore,
Of having just settled in a site to be told to move once more.

Fantasy of Food

As I lie here on my charpoy in quiet solitude,
My tangled thoughts invariably turn once again to food.
I visualize crispy bacon and bread that's really fried,
With tomatoes and some sausages sizzling on the side.
With two fresh eggs with golden yolks I know are newly laid,
Followed by some toast and Hartley's marmalade.

I see a Yorkshire pud, all brown and thick and wide,
With Bisto gravy, roasted spuds and Brussels sprouts beside.
The slices of roast beef, all thick, not miniscule,
That does not need much chewing, unlike redundant mule.
Then there's apple pie and custard, with cloves to give it taste,
Set in shortcrust pastry that never goes to waste.

And in my dream it's summer, with strawberries and cream,
With fresh baked bread and butter with a golden gleam.
As my thoughts go on, a large fruit cake with cherries on the top,
Floats through the basha door but alas it does not stop.
It's followed by a pork pie that only Brits can make,
But I guess that too will vanish when I finally awake.

I smell the fresh ground coffee wafting through the air,
And keep my eyes tight shut, tasting food that isn't there.
But now I'm getting greedy, I don't want the vision to go,
For I've ordered a pint of bitter down at the Barley Mow.
The bar stands out quite clearly, in my animated dreams,
As does the buxom barmaid, beneath its oaken beams.

The illusion is now over, as the basha begins to stir,
And my stomach rumbles with the food that wasn't even there.
But given luck, my fantasy, at some future date
Will give me another menu to fill a phantom plate.
So until my dreams are realized in the home that is so far
It's bully beef and biscuits washed down with cookhouse char!

Oh For a Decent Twitter!

They say there's bluebirds over Dover and nightingales in Berkeley Square.
Elsewhere the song of blackbirds fill the summer air.
But there's nothing out here to remind us of the land we left behind,
For even the birds of the jungle are of a different kind.

We have long necked, scrawny vultures like harbingers of doom
And though not birds, the fruit bats when day turns into gloom.

There are shite hawks screeching in the sky,
Waiting to swoop at food passing by,
While the fever or deolali bird, with its high pitched call,
And endless piercing whistle drives us up the wall.
The carrion crows as black as night scavenge everywhere,
With mynah birds we try to catch and tame to teach them how to swear.

There are cuckoos that 'ooh' instead of 'cuck', an odd sound in reverse.
Then everything in this forsaken land is really quite perverse.
So whether it's the jungle or the hot plains of Bengal,
None of these feathered creatures impress us much at all.
But as for me, the only bird I want to hear, and I can hardly wait,
Is brunette, twenty-one, and stands just five foot eight!

Stamina

They've cut the road at Kohima, Tiddim and Tamu,
Leaving us all wishing we weren't an RSU.
Our rations have been cut but include an 'energy' pill.
What would we give to be in Cal to sample Firpo's grill?

We have Shikapara biscuits, so hard they'd pave a floor
And bully beef so soft, all you do is pour.
We have, of course, the soya link, invented by Henry Ford,
Which even the Yanks refuse to eat so they shipped them all abroad.

They've circled us with wire, like chickens in a run
And given each and everyone some ammo and a gun.
We've dug deep holes called Boxes; ours is called Sardine,
With little narrow trenches running in between.

There are no charpoys in them, on which to lay our head,
Just Army issue gas capes and the deck to call a bed.
When night-time falls we make our way, daubed with mozzie cream,
Cheesed off to the eyeballs, and ready to blaspheme.

When daylight comes we stagger out, feeling bleary eyed,
With a mouth like an unwashed jock strap and everything else beside.
We make our way to the Mess from the earthen damp boudoir
And breakfast once again on bully beef and char.

For tiffin the cook has told us, the grub will make us drool,
For he's going to make an Irish stew, out of redundant mule.
So we go about our duties and ponder on the fate
That caused a poor old Army mule to land up on a plate!

The Dakota

Where would the Army and the Air Force be
Without the Douglas DC3?
As a maid of all work, it's always there,
On spindly legs, with snooty nose up in the air.
The Pratt and Whitney engines, sometimes a difficult rating,
Need lots of skill on take-off and careful calculating.
With canvas seats to carry troops
Or bales of cargo secured by loops.

Rations, ammo, fodder or mules,
All a part of its flying schedules.
They pick up salvaged aircraft, bring in all the mail
And return to Agartala via a cloud filled trail.
They can carry 'neath the fuselage a vital spare mainplane
For another Dak or Spit or a shot-up Hurricane.
They fly unescorted sorties, trying to find a small DZ
And circle lower and lower to ensure the Japs aren't fed.

They zoom in low over Imphal Plain almost every day,
Hoping to avoid the others taking off the other way.
There's 31 from Agartala, 'The First in Indian Skies',
Who, along with 62, make sure we get supplies.
The 'Friendly Firm' of 194, along with 117,
Are but some of the Daks that fly the Burma heaven.
So although they haven't the glamour or the power of a fighter motor,
We'd certainly be in trouble without the old Dakota.

The Casualty

Down in the hot steaming jungle, in the hills that surrounded Tamu,
A party of airmen were hacking, doing their best to get through.
They'd gone to recover an aircraft, a Dakota that failed to get back,
For on its return from a sortie, it suffered a Zero attack.
Located some hours later, it was a crumpled and tangled array,
Its wings torn off like a butterfly, by a jungle that wouldn't give way.

The crew were still in their places, none remained alive.
The price they'd paid was heavy, helping others to survive.
They were buried with all dignity, with prayers for their spirits to soar,
Along a peaceful flight path, direct to Gabriel's door.
While here on earth a broken prop, as a headstone must suffice
As a testimony and memorial to the aircrew's sacrifice.
The wreck was set on fire to help to mystify
And prevent the Japs from gloating and shouting out '*banzai*'.
Returning to base empty-handed with dog-tags as evidence,
We wonder if this conflict really makes much sense.
So it goes on, as most days bring another SOS
And still the search continues for aircraft in distress.
But when this war is over, who will be aware?
Who will weep or even say a prayer
For all the kites not found, that failed to make the strip
And lie entombed for ever in the jungle's hostile grip?

The Mosquito

We've a Mozzie on the strip, not the malarial brand
But a Merlin powered wooden kite from de Havilland.
They've sent it here for tests, in the rain and scorching clime,
To check if all the joints, not riveted but glued, will stand the test of time.
The wooden frame and birch ply skin made riggers scratch their heads,
For lacking any riveting, was it hammer and nails instead?
It was viewed each day to check the ply
From hot and cold to wet and dry.
On one DI, in the starboard tail, the Chiefie saw some holes where ants had begun to chew.
They must have relished the balsa core and the taste of the glue!
For they'd munched and chewed voraciously through the outer skin,
Leaving piles of sawdust to show where they had bin.
It couldn't take the air; the kite was now u/s
And hordes of HQ wallahs came to view the mess.
There were no parts available as the plane was very new
And everyone just flapped around, wondering what to do.
So Taffy Gwynne the carpenter, who came from Aberdare,
Was detailed by the Chiefie to try and make a spare.
He had no spruce, no decent wood, just told to do the best he could.
So from an engine packing case that had a decent grain
He started on his task with chisel, saw and plane.
He lavished his attention, treating it with care,
Like a cabinet-maker with a broken Queen Anne chair.

Soon it was completed; he'd done his level best
And covered it with ply, sawn from an old tea chest.
When all was done and sanded down and covered with some dope,
The kite was ready for air test, with fingers crossed in hope.
The great day came and the pilot, after checking on the spar,
Put the Mozzie through its paces and flew to KPR.
So if you see this Mozzie on a squadron in the blue,
With 'Assam Tea' upon its tail, it came from 132.

The Broody Blues

As I contemplate my navel, like Buddha, in the Imphal sun,
I wonder what St Peter'll say if my time is come?
When I knock upon the hangar door and give him my last three,
Will he know I was an airman and issue me a key?
But if he says, 'What have you done? Why should I let you through?'
Would it be enough to tell him I'd served on 132?
And if this reference is not enough, where do I start my tale?
As he's supposed to be *au fait* with everyone's travail.

I could tell him I was an apprentice before I joined the mob,
Who generously awarded me a weekly wage amounting to ten bob.
I wonder if he's heard of Uxbridge, where I signed to serve the Throne,
My name exchanged for a number by which I would be known.
And sent me off to square bash on Driffield's windswept moor,
Where the PTIs were sadists and thought we were manure.
Perhaps they'd like to hear of my flight mechanic days at Weston-super-Mare,
Remustering later to instruments, as they thought I had a flair.

Or squadron days with 'Beaus' on No. 68, with Max Aitken as CO,
Until a Movement Order decided overseas I ought to go.
I could tell him of a rough trip *en route* to Singapore
And all the events that happened when the Japs got to Jahore.
Should I recall the days at 151 MU,
With all the experts saying the Japs cannot get through?
Would he want to know of Wirraways, Wildebeest and Albacores
And clapped-out Blenheims and Buffalos trying to even up the scores?

I could mention some of the Hurricanes that, alas, arrived too late,
And many that lay on the quay were destroyed still in their crate.
Or how they bombed Seletar, making it u/s,
With kites and most of the hangars a sorry looking mess.
Of being 'volunteered' as a 'Gregson Grenadier' to keep the Japs at bay,

An offer I declined or I wouldn't have got away.
Should I tell him of the *Kedah* as it slid through the gloom,
Allowing me and others aboard with a foot or two of room?

Then dodging through the Bandra Straits, avoiding Jap attack,
Praying every hour the ship would not turn back;
Landing in Batavia, six hundred miles away,
Thankful for the fortune that helped us get away.
And what about the *Orcades* that took us from Java's shore
And dumped us at Colombo to start another tour?
Or that stinking ship *Mendoza* that sailed the Arabian Sea,
Whose rats outnumbered the airmen, by a ratio of three?

Should I now remind him of the chaps who didn't make the quay,
Who languish still in prison camps, praying to be free?
And what about that journey in a bug infested train
From Karachi across to Asansol on the Bengal Plain?
Then 122 on the Grand Trunk Road, before moving to Jessore
And thence to the RSS at Dacca on the Brahmaputra shore.
Would he be impressed with the prangs or the gruesome sights I'd seen,
Searching through the Naga Hills where no one else had been?

Should I tell him of this Siege and how we have to cope
And it's only the efforts of 4 Corps that gives us any hope?
But as I make a mountain of a mole hill that's really small,
I wonder why I bother to think of these morbid thoughts at all.
For my spirit's now uplifted by mail that's just come through
And depressive thoughts exchanged for an optimistic view.
So hopefully now he'll have to wait for many more years to come
Before I report with my account of all the things I've done.

Appendix I

Maintenance Units
India and Burma

No. 301	Drigh Road. Formerly A/C Depot	Jan 42–Mar 47
No. 302	Allahabad, Manauri	Jan 42–Mar 47
No. 303	Ambala	Nov 41–Mar 45
No. 304	Asansol, Kanchrapara, Chittagong	Jan 42–Mar 45
No. 305	Bombay	Nov 42–Feb 47
No. 306	Lahore, Harbanapara	Oct 42–Mar 47
No. 307	Lahore	Mar 42–Mar 47
No. 308	Allahabad, Phaphaman	May 42–Feb 47
No. 309	Palam	May 44–Sep 47
No. 312	Cochin	Oct 42–Sep 47
No. 313	Kankinara	Oct 42–Jun 47
No. 314	Babugarn, Seletar	Oct 42–Dec 47
No. 315	Nappur	May 43–Apr 46
No. 316	Kasu, Begu, Mingladon	Dec 43–Feb 46
No. 317	Manipur	Jul 43–Feb 44
No. 318	Jubbulpore	Jan 44–Oct 47
No. 319	Peshawar, Jodhpur	Jul 42–Mar 45
No. 320	Drigh Road, Sind	Oct 42–Jul 47
No. 321	Calcutta	Jan 44–Dec 45
No. 322	Chakeri	May 43–Dec 45
No. 325	Drigh Road, Jamalpur	Dec 42–Feb 47
No. 326	Allahabad. Formerly No. 1 RAP, Asansol, Bishnupur, Agartala	Feb 43–Nov 45
No. 327	Dum-Dum, Red Road, Calcutta, Kanchrapara, Agartala, Cawnpore. Formerly No. 2 RAP	
No. 328	Bangalore. Formerly Mechanical Transport Storage Unit	Oct 42–Feb 47
No. 329	Calcutta	Jul 43–Oct 46
No. 330	Bombay	Apr 43–Oct 46
No. 331	Lahore	Feb 43–Jul 44

No. 332	Colombo, Ratmalana	Jun 43–Jun 45
No. 333	Comilla	Jul 43–Mar 45
No. 335	Calcutta, Tollygunge	Jul 43–Feb 45
No. 336	Ceylon, Trichinopoly	Aug 43–Feb 45
No. 337	Adavi	Jun 44–Jul 47
No. 338	Kurunegala	Dec 43–Dec 45
No. 340	Manipur Road, Lokajan	Nov 43–Feb 46
No. 341	Pulgaon	Jan 44–Nov 47
No. 342	Dimapur, Palel	Feb 44–Mar 45
No. 345	Chittagong	Jan 44–Mar 46
No. 346	Arkonham	Jul 45–Apr 46
No. 352	Dalbumgarh	
No. 355	Jodhpur, Salaween	Oct 44–Jan 47
No. 356	Risalpur	Jun 44–Dec 45
No. 361	Bihta. Formerly Glider Storage & Erection Unit	Jun 44–Apr 46
No. 362	Chittagong, Avadi, Madras	Aug 44–Sep 45
No. 363	Calcutta, Palel, Rangoon	Sep 44–Sep 45
No. 364	Comilla	Aug 44–Aug 45
No. 374	Korangi Creek	Aug 44–May 46
No. 376	Colombo	Jun 44–Apr 46
No. 377	Bally, Rangoon	Dec 44–Sep 45
No. 385	Panagar, Bengal	Aug 45–Jun 46
No. 386	Takoradi	Aug 45–Jul 46

Civilian Maintenance Units

No. 1	Kanchrapara
No. 2	Trichinopoly
No. 3	Bangalore
No. 4	Barrackpore
No. 5	Dum-Dum
No. 6	Poona
No. 7	Agra?

Civilian Repair Organizations

No. 1	Bombay	Jun 43–Oct 45
No. 3	New Delhi	Oct 43–Nov 45
No. 5	Madras	Apr 43–Mar 45
No. 6	Colombo	Jun 43–Apr 44

Appendix II

Squadrons

From the beginning of 1942 until the war in Burma reached its peak and final victory over the Japanese, there were sixty-five RAF squadrons and nine RIAF squadrons involved in the campaign and its aftermath in Malaya, Indonesia and the occupation of Japan, not including forty-seven squadrons of the USAAF and three of the RCAF. Thirty-four different types of aircraft and their variations were used in the conflict, all operating from one or more of the 300 permanent or fair-weather strips built at the time to reinforce the few which were already in existence.

It is doubtful if any one of the following squadrons which took part could lay claim to never having required the services of a Repair and Salvage Unit at some time or other, be it from the tiniest Comm Flight Auster to the giant B-29.

Royal Air Force Squadrons

No. 5	Mohawk, Hurricane, Thunderbolt
No. 8	Wellington, Liberator
No. 9	Lancaster
No. 11	Blenheim, Hurricane
No. 17	Hurricane, Spitfire
No. 20	Lysander, Hurricane
No. 22	Beaufort, Beaufighter
No. 27	Beaufighter, Mosquito
No. 28	Hurricane, Spitfire
No. 30	Hurricane, Thunderbolt
No. 31	Dakota
No. 34	Blenheim, Hurricane, Thunderbolt
No. 42	Beaufort, Blenheim, Hurricane, Thunderbolt
No. 45	Blenheim, Vengeance, Mosquito
No. 47	Beaufighter, Mosquito
No. 52	Dakota
No. 60	Blenheim, Hurricane, Thunderbolt

No. 62	Hudson, Dakota
No. 67	Buffalo, Hurricane, Spitfire
No. 79	Hurricane, Thunderbolt
No. 81	Spitfire, Thunderbolt
No. 82	Vengeance, Mosquito
No. 84	Vengeance, Mosquito
No. 89	Beaufighter, Mosquito
No. 96	Dakota
No. 99	Wellington, Liberator
No. 110	Vengeance, Mosquito
No. 113	Blenheim, Hurricane, Thunderbolt
No. 117	Hudson, Dakota
No. 123	Hurricane, Spitfire, Thunderbolt
No. 131	Spitfire, Thunderbolt
No. 134	Hurricane, Spitfire, Thunderbolt
No. 135	Hurricane, Thunderbolt
No. 136	Hurricane, Spitfire
No. 146	Mohawk, Buffalo, Hurricane, Thunderbolt
No. 152	Spitfire
No. 155	Mohawk, Spitfire
No. 159	Liberator
No. 160	Liberator
No. 176	Beaufighter, Hurricane, Mosquito
No. 177	Beaufighter
No. 191	Catalina
No. 194	Hudson, Dakota, Sentinel
No. 200	Liberator
No. 211	Beaufighter, Mosquito
No. 212	Catalina
No. 215	Wellington, Liberator, Dakota
No. 230	Sunderland
No. 240	Catalina, Sunderland
No. 258	Hurricane, Thunderbolt
No. 261	Hurricane, Thunderbolt
No. 267	Dakota
No. 273	Hurricane, Spitfire
No. 292	Walrus, Warwick, Sea Otter, Liberator
No. 353	Hudson, Dakota, Anson
No. 354	Liberator
No. 355	Liberator
No. 356	Liberator
No. 357	Hudson, Liberator, Dakota
No. 358	Liberator
No. 413	Catalina (Royal Canadian Air Force)

No. 435	Dakota (Royal Canadian Air Force)
No. 436	Dakota (Royal Canadian Air Force)
No. 607	Hurricane, Spitfire
No. 615	Hurricane, Spitfire, Thunderbolt
No. 656	Auster
No. 681	Spitfire, Hurricane, Mitchell, Mosquito
No. 684	Mosquito, Mitchell, Beaufighter

Royal Indian Air Force Squadrons

No. 1	Hurricane
No. 2	Hurricane
No. 3	Audax
No. 4	Audax
No. 6	Hurricane
No. 7	Vengeance
No. 8	Spitfire
No. 9	Hurricane
No. 10	Hurricane

Communications Flight aircraft used were Auster, Hadrian, Harvard, Tiger Moth, Fox Moth, Sentinel and the only Whitney Straight in India.

Appendix III

RSU Commanding Officers
1942 to 1946

Sqn/Ldr E. G. Abercromby	139
Sqn/Ldr F. N. B. Bennett	60, 126
Sqn/Ldr Bullen	132, 135
Sqn/Ldr C. G. Bircham	139
Sqn/Ldr R. D. Briggs	132, 143, 131
Sqn/Ldr Bond	135
Flt/Lt Bird	123
Sqn/Ldr Bishop	132
Flt/Lt H. C. Brown	3
Sqn/Ldr A. A. Bell	140
Sqn/Ldr R. F. J. Barber	2 FRD, 4 RSS, 124
Sqn/Ldr P. C. Crowell	101, 125, 142
Sqn/Ldr R. T. Cole	139
Sqn/Ldr A. E. G. Cole	134, 137
Sqn/Ldr A. M. Creedon	131
Sqn/Ldr B. J. Chadwick	138
Sqn/Ldr Davies	132
Flt/Lt A. N. Dale	123
Sqn/Ldr D. J. Ellory, MBE	121
Sqn/Ldr W. E. Grey	131
Sqn/Ldr H. A Gordon	138
Sqn/Ldr E. C. Hucklebridge	129, 136
Sqn/Ldr P. W. Harrison	138
Sqn/Ldr S. Kureishi	1 Airborne
Sqn/Ldr L. Kendrick	3
Sqn/Ldr H. M. Louch, MBE	126
Sqn/Ldr C. W. Lockhart	122, 101, 125
Sqn/Ldr W. R. Middleton	124, 137
Sqn/Ldr A. A. McLaren	124, 137
Sqn/Ldr de L. Markham	143
Sqn/Ldr Moody	101, 125, 142

Sqn/Ldr May	124
Sqn/Ldr H. J. Moon	3
Sqn/Ldr Pink	132
Sqn/Ldr Rowbottom	134
Flt/Lt H. Richmond	143
Sqn/Ldr Richardson	135
Sqn/Ldr R. Riley	3
Sqn/Ldr L. Raspison	126
Sqn/Ldr J. Ricketts	136
Sqn/Ldr F. J. Sandeford	139, 141
Flt/Lt Svenson	136
Sqn/Ldr Semple	124
Sqn/Ldr Spry	141
Flt/Lt R. Servos	1 Airborne
Sqn/Ldr E. T. Shepherd	149
Sqn/Ldr G. M. Tiffin	126, 143
Sqn/Ldr Touch, AFC	85
Sqn/Ldr G. W. Topping	1 Airborne, 82
Sqn/Ldr F. J. Winfield	126
Sqn/Ldr L. Welch	126
Sqn/Ldr J. F. Warren	121
Sqn/Ldr A. C. Ward, MBE	124
Flt/Lt Wood, DFC	85

With one or two exceptions, many of the Commanding Officers of Repair and Salvage Units rarely stayed with a unit for more than a year before being posted, either to AHQ or a totally unrelated unit. Some of them were former technical engineers, others had been test pilots. A few, perhaps because of their expertise, had at one time or another been the COs of more than one RSU.

Appendix IV

Most of the Dakotas of the US Combat Cargo Command which flew into Imphal during the Siege became instantly recognizable by the ornate artwork displayed on their fuselages, usually in the form of voluptuous maidens, now known by the name of 'Nose Art'.

The following are a few of those recorded at the time:

GERONIMO
RING CUTTER JANE
WINGS OVER THE WORLD
SNUFFY
SUSY Q
EASY MEAT
2 COME 11
SPEED
SNAKE
PROP WASH
GEORGIA PEACH
ELY
FAITHFUL FANNIE
JEWEL
OGDEN'S BABY
HOW COME?
DIRTIE GERTIE
OLD FAITHFUL
PIPE DREAM
HI-BABE
ZENNIE BELLE
OLE DAISY MAE
NELLIE DEAN
LADY FROM HADES 2
MISS CARRIAGE
CALAMITY JANE
PAPER DOLL
RACABOO HUNTER

HELLISH HELEN
I.AKER
EXTRA PRIORITY
RACABOO-KALO
THE RENEGADE
IN AND AROUND THE VALLEYS

Appendix V

Airfields used in the Burma Campaign

By the end of 1945, over 300 airstrips were in use, including about twenty seaplane landing areas. Twenty-five of these airfields were west of the Brahmaputra River in Bengal, with a further thirty north of the river bordering Assam. The remainder, some 250, stretched across the entire length and breadth of Assam and Burma.

Their standard varied, some were all-weather, capable of supporting transports and heavy bombers and constructed either of concrete or tarmacadam. Others were only fine-weather, surfaced with perforated steel planking or Bithess, a bituminized hessian laid directly on to the prepared ground. A great many, however, were simply dirt strips hastily graded out of the bush by bulldozers in very remote areas. Some even utilized paddy fields.

Some of these airfields are still in existence, having been modernized for civilian or military use. Others have fallen into disuse, whilst those which were only dirt strips have been reclaimed by nature and obliterated.

Almost without exception, every one of these airfields had at some time been used by the Repair and Salvage Units, either on detachment for a local salvage or on attachment for servicing squadron aircraft.

Aberdeen	Agartala
Aghgogra	Akyab
Alathaung	Alethangyaw
Alijan	Alipore
Allanmyo	Allagappa
Alon	Amherst
Amotu	Andrew Bay
Anisakan	Apauk W.
Aungban	Aungdaing 1 & 2
Ayo Bay	Baigachi
Balipara	Bansbaria
Barisal	Barrackpore
Bassein N.	Bassein
Bawli Bazar	Bilin

Bishnupur
Black and White
Broadway
Budalin
Cascade
Canadian Club
Chabua
Chandina
Chauk
Chaung N.
Chaunggwa
Chieng
Chiengmai
Chiringa
Chittagong
Chowringhee
Chunarughat
Comilla
Cooch Bihar
Cuttack
Danson Bay
Darang 1, 2 & 3
Dayindabo
Deganga
Dergaon
Dewar
Dhoapalong
Dhubalia
Dimapur
Dinjan
Dohazari
Dum-Dum
Dwelha
Ebon
Elephant Point
Fazipur
Feni
Fenton Point
Goakhpur
Golaghat
Guskhara
Gwa
Hailakandi
Hasimara
Hathazari
Hewo
Hsanswingyang
Hsenglian
Hwambi
Imphal
Indainggale
Indaw E.
Indaw W.
Jessore
John Haig
Johnnie Walker
Johrat
Junchari
Kadwe
Kalemyo
Kalewa
Kalyanpur
Kamaing
Kamsagar
Kanchrapara
Kangaung
Kangaw N.
Kangla
Kangpoki
Kangyaung
Kawlin N.
Katha
Kawlin W.
Kawlin E.
Kengtung E.
Kharagpur
Kin
Krishnagar
Kissebari
Kulaura
Kulaigauk Is.
Kumyuam
Kumbhirgram
Kutkai
Kurmitola
Kyaiktaw
Kwetnge
Kyaukkyi

Kyaikma	Kyaukpyu
Kyeintali	Kyaukse
Kynmagon	Lack Point
Lake Indawgyi	Lacksman
Lalaghat	Lalmei
Lalmanirhat	Lanka
Ledo	Letpadan
Lewe 1 & 2	Le-U
Lilibari	Loiwing
Magwe (Maida Vale)	Mambur
Manywet	Mardnaibunia
Mariani	Marabari Is.
Maubin	Maungdaw (Ritz)
Maunghnama	Mawbubyin
Maymyo	Mazin
Mehawingsawn	Meiktila
Mesarieng	Mesoht
Mingladon	Minhla
Minzu	Mogaung
Mohanhat	Mohanbari
Moklebari	Monkey Point
Monywa E.	Monywa W.
Monywa N.	Moulmein
Mudon	Myingum
Myingyan	Myitche
Myitinge	Myitkkyina N.
Myittha	Myotha
Myothit	Myoung
Naf River	Nagahuli
Namhkam	Namsang
Namtu	Narayanganj
Naungpuawang	Nazir
Nidinia	Nips
Nyaung	Nyaungbintha
Nyaungbinywa	Nyaunglebin
Nyaungyin	Onbauk
Ondal	Ondaw
Oktwin	Pa-an
Pabst	Pagan
Pagoda Point	Pakkoku
Palel	Panchmile
Pandaveswar	Parashuram
Patholipan	Pathakandi
Pauk	Paungdale

Payagyi
Pegu (Pilsener)
Piadoba
Piccadilly
Pinbaw (Blackpool)
Piribakshat
Port Owen
Prome (Park Lane)
Pyinmana 1 & 2
Pyu
Rampur
Ramree
Ramu 1, 2, 3 & 4
Rangoon
Red Road (Calcutta)
Rumkha
Rups
Sadaung
Sadiya
Sagaing
Sagyi
Salbani
Sapam
Schwebo
Scotts Club
Shadazup
Shamo 1 & 2
Shamsharnagar
Shibanj
Shingnwiyang
Shwegyin
Silchar
Singabil
Singu
Sinthe
Sooteraking
Sorbhog
Srimangal
Sylhet N.
Sylhet S.
Tabingaung
Tak
Taro
Taukkyan
Taungdwingyi
Taungtha
Tavoy
Tekna
Tennant
Toungoo
Teok
Tezgaon
Tezpur
Thabeikkyin
Thabutkon
Thayetmyo
Thazi
Thedaw
Thinbawgwe
Thinbonda
Tilin
Tingkawksakan
Tinsukia
Tulihul
Twante
Udarband
Vat 69
Wangjing
Warazup
Wettaik
White City
Willingdon Reach
Witok
Yazagio
Ye-U 1 & 2
Ywabo
Ywadon
Ywattaung N.
Ywattaung
Zayatkwin
Zibwuthaung
Zigon